"C. J. Hopkins is our moder described the strategies or predicted the perils of the emerging totalitarianism with such persistence and eloquence."
— **Robert F. Kennedy, Jr., Children's Health Defense**

"We'll look back on the Covid-19 period as one in which governments worldwide cynically stoked panic in search of draconian laws and speech controls. We made paranoia seem sane and asking, 'Why?' seem like insurrection. C. J. Hopkins was one of the only people in English willing to do the latter, and he did it with his trademark wit and bravado. He'll be remembered as a signature chronicler of the 'New Normal.'"
— **Matt Taibbi, TK News**

"C. J. Hopkins' essays over the past two years represent some of the most searing (and therefore satisfying) chronicles of life in — and against — the locked-down, masked-up, triple vaxxed madhouse of New Normal insanity. They remind us of the twisted mandates we were forced to endure, and offer a stark warning of what GloboCap has in store next."
— **Max Blumenthal, The Grayzone**

"Proverbs says 'guard your heart, for from it flows the wellsprings of life.' When my heart needs inspiration, I often head to the Consent Factory or into my C. J. Hopkins book collection. Hopkins' pathway through reality is within our intimate space. Grief comes with facing what tyranny causes us to do to ourselves and to each other. But there is power and redemption in mastering what Wordsworth called the 'thoughts that do often lie too deep for tears.' C. J. Hopkins' writings are essential intelligence for navigating these times, not to mention maintaining our sense of amusement and preserving a human culture. My advice? Don't leave home without him." — **Catherine Austin Fitts, The Solari Report**

THE RISE OF THE NEW NORMAL REICH

CONSENT FACTORY ESSAYS
VOL. III (2020-2021)

C. J. HOPKINS

CONSENT FACTORY PUBLISHING

This Consent Factory Publishing trade edition May 2022.

Consent Factory Publishing is a wholly-owned subsidiary of Consent Factory, Inc., a subsidiary of Amalgamated Content, Inc., distributors of quality literary content throughout the developed and developing worlds. For more information about Consent Factory Publishing, visit the Consent Factory's website: consentfactory.org.

Cover design by Anthony Freda.

Author's photo by Hans de Vries.

All other photos and images in this volume are in the public domain.

The essays in this volume were originally published by Consent Factory, and then republished by Off-Guardian, Dissident Voice, ZeroHedge, RT, Rubikon, Come Don Chisciotte, Ron Paul Institute for Peace and Prosperity, Mercola, Neue Debatte, Aube Digital, Mittdolcino, Le Monde, Estramuros, Rational Review, Signs of the Times, Tlaxcala, Le Grand Soir, Le Saker Francophone, Demokratischer Widerstand, Ken FM, The Automatic Earth, Anti-Empire, Global Research, 21st Century Wire, The Fire Online, Linke Zeitung, Réseau International, Steigan.no, Het News Dan Anders, Midt i fleisen, Nachdenkseiten, Heinrichplatz TV, Übersetzung aus dem Imperium, Insituto Rothbard, South Front, Contra Mundum, GeoPolítica, ColdType, The Duran, Burbuja, The Greanville Post, Entelekheia, Indignatie, The Libertarian Institute, Anarchist Federation, Western Rifle Shooters Association, and other outlets.

Printed in the United States of America

ISBN 978-3-9821464-2-3 (pb)

Contents

"'We are at war — a public health war, certainly but we are at war, against an invisible and elusive enemy,' Macron said, outlawing all journeys outside the home." — *Coronavirus: France imposes lockdown as EU calls for 30-day travel ban, The Guardian, March 16, 2020*

"From a technological perspective, the coronavirus pandemic is one massive testbed for surveillance capitalism … governments are rolling out surveillance measures, all in the effort to ensure that policies of mass behaviour modification are successful." — *Coronavirus Could Infect Privacy and Civil Liberties Forever, Forbes, March 23, 2020*

"As coronavirus lockdowns have been expanded globally, police across the world have been given licence to control behaviour in a way that would normally be extreme even for an authoritarian state." — *Teargas, beatings and bleach: the most extreme Covid-19 lockdown controls around the world, The Guardian, April 1, 2020*

"America's top coronavirus expert has warned Covid-19 is the new normal – and that the killer virus might never go away." — *Top coronavirus expert warns killer virus may be 'new normal' and never go away , Metro, April 7, 2020*

"'Imagine an America divided into two classes … it will be a frightening schism,' a World Health Organization special envoy on Covid-19 predicted. 'Those with antibodies will be able to travel and work, and the rest will be discriminated against.'" — *The Coronavirus in America: The Year Ahead, The New York Times, April 18, 2020*

Prologue

"The masses were not innocent dupes; at a certain point,
under a certain set of conditions, they wanted fascism."
— Gilles Deleuze and Félix Guattari, *Anti-Oedipus*

The New Normal Reich

On January 31, 2020, the corporate media began publishing photos of medical teams in hazmat suits collecting bodies lying dead in the streets of Wuhan, an industrial city in China.[1] According to the "news reports" accompanying the photos, these people had suddenly dropped dead where they lay, many with shopping bags still clutched in their hands, the victims of a novel coronavirus which would come to be known as Covid-19.

In the weeks that followed, the corporate and state media bombarded the masses with more photos of dead bodies, patients gasping for breath on ventilators, overwhelmed hospitals, refrigerated morgue trucks, mass graves, hospital ships, and so on. Scary-looking charts and graphs were disseminated. Horrifying personal accounts of people whose mother-in-laws' friends' accountants had died of multiple organ failure featured in respectable broadsheets. Global health authorities announced that, based on their computer models, this virus had a 3.4% death rate.[2] 160 million people were going to die!

This prediction was absolute nonsense, of course, and the "news reports" were lies and distortions, but that didn't matter, because the most powerful propaganda machine in the history of propaganda had just been unleashed on the unsuspecting public. During March and April of 2020, the masses were systematically terrorized and gaslighted on a daily basis, more or less around the clock, by government officials, corporate and state media, health authorities, the culture industry, the entire global-capitalist power apparatus ... all pumping out the same stark message, over and over, in perfect synch, like an enormous Goebbelsian keyboard instrument.

The message was unmistakeably clear. The message was, our lives, as we knew them, were over. Society was being radically restructured. *Reality* itself was being radically restructured. We were entering a brave new world ... a world the authorities called the "New Normal."

---

1 Agence France-Presse, "A man lies dead in the street: the image that captures the Wuhan coronavirus crisis," *The Guardian, January 31, 2020*

2 Lovelace Jr., Berkeley and Noah Higgins-Dunn, "WHO says coronavirus death rate is 3.4% globally, higher than previously thought," *CNBC, March 3, 2020*

We were undertaking this historic transition, this radical restructuring of human civilization, not in the wake of thermonuclear war, or a devastating meteor strike, or cataclysmic environmental collapse, but because of a respiratory virus.

With the mass hysteria in full swing, a global "state of emergency" was declared. Governments around the world suspended constitutional rights and placed their entire populations on "lockdown." To simulate an atmosphere of "deadly plague," everyone was ordered to wear medical-looking masks and follow an ever-expanding number of ridiculous "social-distancing" rules. Police, soldiers, and robotic dogs patrolled the streets, enforcing compliance. Protest was outlawed. Dissent was censored. Anyone questioning the official Covid narrative was demonized as a "conspiracy theorist," a "Covid denier," an "anti-Semite," or a "democracy-threatening far-right extremist" by government officials and the corporate and state media.

People started reporting their neighbors to the authorities for "being outdoors without permission," "leaving the house too many times," or "not wearing a medical-looking mask in public." Mobs of bug-eyed New Normal fanatics began surrounding, harassing, and sometimes attacking non-mask-wearing people in restaurants and shops, pepper-spraying maskless families at picnics, and otherwise behaving like fascist lunatics.

The rest, as they say, is history ... not official history, of course, but the history I have tried to document, at least in part, in this collection of essays, which were written and published as events unfolded, and which I hope will serve, if nothing else, as a record of the rollout of the "New Normal" as it happened.

Memories are short, and getting shorter every day. Many of us are already starting to forget how abruptly and easily Western "democracies" were transformed into pathologized-totalitarian police states in which those who questioned the official Covid narrative or refused to conform to the new official ideology were stigmatized, threatened, stripped of their rights, fired from their jobs, segregated from society, banned from traveling, denied medical treatment, censored, raided in their homes, churches, synagogues, and other places of worship, beaten and arrested by the police, imprisoned in "quarantine camps," and so on.

Many of us are also starting to forget how our colleagues, friends, and even family members transformed overnight into hate-drunk fanatics and started shrieking vicious insults at us if we dared to challenge the official "Science," or the claims of government and health authorities, or otherwise refused to switch our minds off, click heels, and mindlessly follow orders.

Now that the Shock-and-Awe phase is over (at least in most of the Western world), many of us are asking how this could have happened. How could our "democratic" societies suddenly morph into quasi-totalitarian, paranoid, biosecurity police states in which people who refused an unnecessary and potentially dangerous experimental "vaccine" were scapegoated, demonized, segregated, fined, and otherwise persecuted by their governments, the media, and the overwhelming majority of the masses? How could so many rational people — intelligent people, good-hearted people, many of whom consider themselves "liberals" or "progressives" — become fanatical totalitarians from one day to the next?

A number of psychological theories have attempted to explain this phenomenon, most recently "mass formation psychosis," but the root of the problem is not psychological. It is structural, political, and it is all too simple. The sad fact is, just as any individual, no matter how intelligent and psychologically healthy, can fall victim to a cult under the right set of conditions, any society can fall victim to totalitarianism. Totalitarianism is the horse ... mass psychosis is the cart. The latter follows the former, not the other way around. The question is not what is wrong with people; the question is what happened to the structure of society ... how, and why, did it go totalitarian?

The Milgram Experiment

Approximately two-thirds of any society — or smaller sample of human beings — will, if placed in the right set of circumstances, obey the orders of anyone "in authority," no matter how irrational, unethical, or harmful. As Harvard psychologist Stanley Milgram's classic obedience experiments demonstrated, it is all too easy for so-called "authorities" (or even those just dressed up as "authorities") to prod most people into behaving like monsters.

The subjects of Milgram's experiments were told that the experiments were designed to study the effects of punishment on learning ability. Subjects believed they would either be playing the role of "student" or "teacher" in the experiment. In fact, all subjects played the "teacher" role. The "student" was an actor, part of the experiment. The subjects were asked to apply what they believed were increasingly severe electric shocks to the "students" in response to incorrect answers. There were no shocks; it was all just theater. "Shock levels" ("15 to 450 volts") were labelled "slight shock," "moderate shock," "strong shock," "very strong shock," "intense shock," "extreme intensity shock," "Danger: Severe Shock," and "XXX." In response to the "shocks," the "students" would grunt at 75 volts, complain at 120 volts, ask to stop at 150 volts, and scream in agony at 285 volts. Thereafter, the "students" continued to scream, complained of heart pain, and refused to continue. At 330 volts the actor would fall silent. "Teachers" were told to treat silence as an incorrect answer and apply the next shock level. If at any point the "teacher" hesitated to inflict the shocks, the experimenter would pressure him with commands such as "the experiment requires that you continue." Some subjects refused to participate early on, which was the response Milgram had expected to be the norm, but they were were the minority (35%). Sixty-five percent (65%) of the subjects were willing to apply shocks to the maximum level. Subjects exhibited various types of discomfort as the experiment progressed. Some begged the "students" to answer more carefully. Other subjects laughed inappropriately. Some believed that they had killed the "students" once the actors had fallen silent. Still, they continued to obey, ultimately applying the maximum shock level. One man who wanted to stop the experiment, but was told that "the experiment must continue," kept applying the shocks, repeating to himself, "it's got to go on, it's got to go on."

Milgram explained the results of his experiments by theorizing that people in social settings exist in one of two states of consciousness, i.e., the "autonomous state" and the "agentic state." In the autonomous state, people direct their own actions, and take responsibility for the result of their actions. In the agentic state, people surrender their autonomy, allow others to direct their actions, and assign responsibility to the person giving the orders.

Milgram repeated his experiment many times, producing more or less the same result, but sometimes with minor variations, which appear to generally confirm his theory. For example, in the original experiment, the "authority" wore a lab coat (i.e., a symbol of his authority). In a variation, the "uniformed authority" was replaced by an "ordinary person" (wearing ordinary clothes) relatively early on in the experiment. The obedience level dropped from 65% to 20% in this variation. In another variation, the location was changed from Yale University to a "shabby-looking" office. Obedience dropped to 47.5%. In yet another variation, subjects were provided with "assistants" (i.e., collaborators) to press the electric-shock buttons for them. 92.5% of these subjects "shocked" their "victims" to the maximum level.[3]

The point is, it was the structure of the social situation, and not some aberrant psychological state, or fundamental moral flaw, that produced the results of Milgram's experiments.

Reluctant as some of us might be to acknowledge it, the majority of the masses in any society can be easily intimidated into mindlessly following orders and conforming to any new official ideology, regardless of how irrational or fascistic, if the "legitimate authorities" governing that society have the will and the power to act in coordination to implement the new ideology by force.

The German term for this "coordination" (or "synchronization") of every aspect of society in accordance with official ideology is *Gleichschaltung*. The term is associated with the Nazis and their efforts to establish "national unity" after Hitler became chancellor in 1933. Every element of German society was subject to "coordination," the government, the media, business, academia, scientific and health authorities, cultural and leisure activities, and so on. This "coordination" was not only imposed from above. Having perceived which way the wind was blowing, the masses carried out their own "self-coordination." (The German term for this is *Selbstgleichschaltung*.) Hitler was amazed at how quickly it all went.[4]

---

3 McLeod, S.A., "*The Milgram Shock Experiment,*" *Simply Psychology*, February 5, 2017

4 Fritzsche, Peter, *Life and Death in the Third Reich*, Harvard University Press, 2008 ("Even Hitler was surprised with the speed and ease of remaking Germany. He noted 'everything is going much faster than we ever dared to hope.'")

If this *Gleichschaltung* process sounds familiar ... well, it should, because we've been experiencing it again, except this time throughout the entire world rather than merely in a single country.

The New Normal

The roll-out of the New Normal ideology during 2020 and 2021 was an unprecedented historical event. Never before has any nation or empire had the power to impose a new official ideology on societies on a global scale. The only models we have to compare it to are fascist societies like Nazi Germany, Fascist Italy, or Francoist Spain, and the "cultural revolutions" in post-revolutionary societies like the USSR, Communist China, or post-revolutionary Iran or Cuba.

These attempts to radically restructure societies to conform to new official ideologies have never succeeded, not entirely, for they have always been haunted by the specter of other contradictory and competing ideologies, which is to say other competing "realities" ... because that is what an ideology is.

An ideology is only an "ideology" to those who are able to stand outside it and view it as a constructed system. To those inside it, it is simply reality. It is not constructed. It is not a system. It simply *is*. It's just "the way things are."

Other people's ideologies are "ideologies." Ours is objective, unquestionable Truth. If it is not objective Truth, if it is not reality, if it is perceptible as ideology, it is doomed.

And, thus, every ideology is an aspiring reality, and is at war with every other aspiring reality ... which is impossible, because there can only be one reality, and it cannot exist until the war is over, at which point the war will have never happened.

Such is the paradoxical morphology (or the fate) of every new ideology. Once born, it must encompass everything — and eliminate, or absorb, all competing ideologies — and then die, and be reborn as reality. In order to exist, it must cease to exist. It must cease to exist as ideology, and become imperceptible, axiomatic, unquestionable. It must become unquestionable, not because one is forbidden to question it (and will be punished for questioning it), but because it has become impossible to question it, because there is no longer anything there to question ... the question itself has become impossible, inconceivable, literally, as in it cannot be formulated, except by someone who is stark raving mad.

At which point the ideology will have become reality.

But first it must must encompass everything. It must erase, or absorb, all competing ideologies. Until then, it is just one "reality" competing for dominance among other "realities."

Which is why totalitarian systems and "cultural revolutions" have always failed. You can impose a new "reality" on one society by force, but your "reality" will never become reality until you can force it on the entire world, which has never been possible ... not until now.

We are, for the first time in human history, living in a de facto global society under a single predominate ideology, a predominate ideology that is fast becoming reality. Intramural conflicts notwithstanding, it is one big global-capitalist world. It has been since the early 1990s, when the last ideological adversary (and impediment) to global capitalism disappeared. This brave, new, global-capitalist world is still in its early evolutionary stages — thirty years is nothing in historical terms — but it is developing at breakneck speed, and it is doing so along predictable lines.

After the fall of the Soviet Union and the collapse of the credibility of communism as a viable competing ideology, the global-capitalist power network (or "GloboCap" as I like to call it) launched a global "clear-and-hold" operation, identifying and wiping out pockets of resistance, economically, militarily, and ideologically. It started in the former Soviet-bloc countries, the Middle East, and Africa in the early 1990s, and expanded throughout most of the rest of the world like an aggressive metastatic cancer during the 15-year-long "Global War on Terror."

As GloboCap was conducting this clear-and-hold op in far-flung places all around the world, it was also conducting it in the heart of the empire, not as dramatically, but just as effectively, gradually, and sometimes not so gradually, destabilizing, restructuring, and privatizing society.

Which is all global capitalism really knows how to do. GloboCap isn't a conspiracy of evil individuals with a megalomaniacal vision. It's a machine. A values-decoding machine. Its function, ideologically speaking, is to eradicate any and all social values that interfere with the flows of capital and replace them all with a single value (i.e., exchange value), rendering everything a commodity, and transforming society into a marketplace.

Of course, this machine is operated by people, many of whom *are* evil conspirators — there has never been a dearth of evil conspirators — but it is the structure and logic of the machine that is driving, not a clutch of globalist billionaires sitting around on one of Bill Gates' yachts, or in Klaus Schwab's castle, hatching schemes. You could shoot all these people in the head tomorrow, and they would be seamlessly replaced with other people performing more or less the identical functions, i.e., destabilizing, restructuring, and privatizing everything.

Anyway, that's what GloboCap was doing, identifying and wiping out pockets of resistance, and transforming the world into one big marketplace, when, suddenly, in the Summer of 2016, they finally noticed that they had a nasty "populist" rebellion on their hands.

As it turned out, a significant number of people didn't want to live in a big valueless marketplace where everything had been rendered an interchangeable commodity and nothing really meant anything at all. A lot of them were still rather attached to their values ... their traditional and/or religious values (like the traditional and/or religious values of those troublesome Muslims in the Middle East, but let's not delve into that analogy here), and their national values, and their national sovereignty, and other reactionary values like that.

So, they threw a monkey wrench into the Globocap works. The Brits abandoned the European Union, and the Americans elected Donald Trump president.

GloboCap did not take this well.

As I documented in previous volumes of these essays, the "Global War on Terror" was abruptly suspended and seamlessly replaced by the "War on Populism."

From 2016 to 2020, GloboCap taught the "populists" a lesson. The lesson, in a nutshell, was, "this is what happens when you fuck with GloboCap." For four long years, the GloboCap establishment demonized Trump as both a Russian operative and literally the Second Coming of Hitler. They demonized everyone who voted for him, or failed to vote for Hillary Clinton, or who dared to express a "populist" opinion, or who rebelled against GloboCap in any other way, as "racists," "anti-Semites," "domestic extremists," "neo-Nazis," and anything else they could think of.

They did this, not just in the USA, and not just to those on the political right, but to Jeremy Corbyn, the gilets jaunes, random people on social media, anyone not playing ball with GloboCap and parroting their official propaganda, regardless of their status and political affiliation. They did this relentlessly for four solid years.

It was basically an extended show of force, intended to remind us who is really in charge. It culminated in November 2020, when they removed President Russian-Agent Hitler from office (after terrorizing the country with "mostly peaceful" riots throughout the previous summer) and replaced him with a senile, finger-sucking stooge, just to rub the whole puppet show in our faces.

By then, the Shock-and-Awe phase of the New Normal roll-out was in full swing. Everyone was either "locked down" in their homes, tracking the daily "Covid death count" while they waited to receive their miracle "vaccines," or walking around with medical-looking masks terrified of a coronavirus that had been blown up into an "apocalyptic plague" that would melt all their organs the moment they contracted it, or cripple them for life, or whatever.

Nine months of non-stop official propaganda and de facto martial law had done the trick. The majority of the Western public had been terrorized, confused, and gaslighted into a state of shrieking mass hysteria, teeth-grinding paranoia, and rote obedience. They had had enough of Shock-and-Awe, and were ready to click heels and follow orders ... and to hunt down and persecute anyone who wasn't.

There wasn't any doubt about it at that point. GloboCap was done playing grab-ass. They weren't just putting down a "populist" rebellion. They were going totalitarian on us ... or as totalitarian as global capitalism can go. It can't go full-20th-Century totalitarian and start goose-stepping around in silly military uniforms hailing victory and singing globalist anthems, because (a) it has no ideology, or, rather, its ideology is "reality," and (b) it has to maintain the simulation of democracy, or at least a semblance thereof. So it is going pathologized-totalitarian on us.

I described it this way in one of the following essays:

> "The most significant difference between 20th-Century totalitarianism and this nascent, global totalitarianism is how New Normal totalitarianism 'pathologizes' its political nature, effectively rendering itself invisible, and thus immune to political opposition. Whereas 20th-Century totalitarianism wore its politics on its sleeve, New Normal totalitarianism presents itself as a non-ideological (i.e., supra-political) reaction to a global public health emergency. And, thus, its classic totalitarian features — e.g., the revocation of basic rights and freedoms, centralization of power, rule by decree, oppressive policing of the population, demonization and persecution of a scapegoated underclass, censorship, propaganda, etc. — are not hidden, because they are impossible to hide, but are recontextualized in a pathologized official narrative. The 'Untermenschen' become 'the Unvaccinated.' Swastika lapel pins become medical-looking masks. Aryan ID papers become 'vaccination passes.' Irrefutably senseless social restrictions and mandatory public-obedience rituals become 'lockdowns,' 'social distancing,' and so on. The world is united in a Goebbelsian total war, not against an external enemy (i.e., a racial or political enemy), but against an internal, pathological enemy."

This transition to a more totalitarian form of global capitalism was always inevitable. Once you occupy the entire territory of the planet, you have no remaining external enemies, so all that's left to do is "clear and hold," i.e., consolidate power and control over your territory.

Its "pathologized" character was also predictable. When you're a globally hegemonic ideological system, you are like the body of Spinoza's God ... a paranoid version of Spinoza's God, a ubiquitous body comprising everything that exists. There is nothing outside of you. There is no outside. The only threats that remain are internal.

Any threat to your omnipresent body is therefore a pathological threat ... a malignant insurgency within your own tissue, a cancer, a disease, an "abnormality" (as opposed to a political threat). And *any* form of deviance is a threat. Any part of your body that does not conform to the whole must be "cured" or surgically excised. Your ubiquitous body must remain pure. So you must constantly monitor and police your body — every organ and system of your body — for signs of impurity and pathological insurgency. You must do this in an obessive paranoid fashion, more or less around the clock.

This paranoid obsession with the purity of your body, and with establishing complete control over your body, every single organ and function of your body — your globally hegemonic ideological body, or whatever social body you comprise — is the primary directive of all forms of totalitarianism.

Totalitarianism *is* paranoia ... paranoia on a societal scale. And, ultimately, on a universal scale. It is a fever dream of becoming God, a terrified, obsessive version of God, a fascist, nihilistic simulation of God, desperately trying to establish order in a chaotic, rebellious, self-made cosmos ... a hostile, self-hallucinated cosmos.

We're still in the early stages of this pathologized, global-capitalist totalitarianism, but that is the fundamental nature of every form of totalitarianism — this paranoid obsession with complete control and total ideological uniformity — and this pathologized form is no exception.

I don't know exactly how it is going to evolve, how long it is going to continue, or how ugly it is going to get. It has already gotten rather ugly. Odds are, it will develop in fits and starts, with an intermittant series of "crises" — "pandemics," "ecological" and "financial" crises — interspersed with periods of relative calm to keep popular resistance from coming to a head, as it did at the end of 2021 with the protests in Canada, Western Europe, and Australia.

In any event, the Shock-and-Awe phase is over. The "restrictions" have been lifted, or are being lifted. The facts — i.e., the artificially inflated "Covid deaths" and "hospitalizations" statistics, the extent of the "vaccine" injuries and deaths, the irreparable damage done by the lockdowns, social-distancing, segregation of "the Unvaccinated," the polarization of society, etc., — are gradually being allowed to surface, and in some cases are even being acknowledged by the "legitimate authorities" and the corporate media ... now that it's too late to do anything about it.

The roll-out of the New Normal is a fait accompli, but the fight against this new global-capitalist form of totalitarianism is not over. On the contrary, it is just beginning. What I called "the Covidian Cult" is no more — the hypnotic spell has finally been broken — but the Covidian cultists are still in our midst ... or, rather, we are in *their* midst. They remain the vast majority of the masses, and they have been systematically gaslighted, terrorized, and conditioned to unquestioningly follow orders and parrot whatever official propaganda they are fed by GloboCap on any given day. They have been conditioned to believe absurdities and commit atrocities in the name of "solidarity." They have been programmed to hate whoever they are told ... the "anti-vaxxers," "the Unvaccinated," "the Russians," or whoever. They are the Wachowski Brothers' "Woman in the Red Dress." They are Orwell's "Outer Party Members." They are Hitler's "Good Germans." They are GloboCap's "New Normals." *They* will write the history of the Covid pandemic ... the official history of the Covid pandemic.

What follows is an unofficial history, not of the pandemic, but of what it ushered into being ... a history of the rise of the New Normal Reich. I'm sorry that it isn't as funny as my earlier collections of Consent Factory essays. I think I lost my sense of humor somewhere around the time my former friends and colleagues started shrieking that I should be "sent to a camp" for questioning "the Science," and the goon squads started checking people's "papers," and someone spray-painted "GAS THE UNVACCINATED" on the wall of a courtyard here in Germany.

As Kurt Vonnegut would say ... so it goes.

C.J. Hopkins
April 2022

2020

"The illusion of freedom will continue as long
as it's profitable to continue the illusion. At the
point where the illusion becomes too expensive
to maintain, they will just take down the scenery,
they will pull back the curtains, they will move the
tables and chairs out of the way and you will see
the brick wall at the back of the theater."
— Frank Zappa

The Great Chinese Bat Flu Panic of 2020

March 9, 2020

Pray for me, my friends, because I have the flu. No, not the Chinese Bat Flu, or Pangolin Flu, or Covid-19, or Coronavirus, or whatever it's called now, just the regular, annoying winter flu that goes around Berlin every year during flu season.

It's a particularly annoying flu this year. You get it, recover from it, and then you get it again. All you want to do is crawl into bed, or sit around watching garbage on Netflix. When you get it a second time, and sometimes a third time, it's kind of a low-grade version of itself, maybe because your immune system knows it, or something. I'm not really sure how that works. I'm not a professional virologist or anything.

Or, I don't know, maybe it is the Bat Flu. The more I read the corporate press, the more I'm beginning to suspect it is. My suspicion isn't based on facts. It's just a feeling, like the feelings people had that Saddam had secret WMDs, and that Trump was a Russian intelligence asset, and that the world was going to end in the year 2012.

OK, those feelings turned out to be wrong, but this one feels like an accurate feeling, and not like just the result of being relentlessly bombarded with hysterical headlines, pictures of people in hazmat suits, and obsessively researching ever-changing, wildly-varying statistics on the Internet, which … I really need to stop doing that.

According to my latest Internet research, the Bat Flu will either subside by late April or it will infect approximately 5 billion people (i.e., 60 percent of the world population).[1] If my little Windows calculator is correct, at a death rate of 3.4 percent,[2] that's 157 million dead people, and at a 4 percent death rate (which I just saw somewhere), we're talking 200 million dead people! If you consider that the 14th Century "Black Death" killed 100 to 200 million people, nearly a quarter of the world population (because there weren't as many people back then), and if you get hysterical and try to compare them (which I'm finding it increasingly difficult not to do), this Bat Flu plague could kill 2 billion people, or maybe 6 or 7 billion people, which is almost the entire human species … anything is possible, after all!

Plus, even if I just have the flu (i.e., the regular flu, not the Chinese Bat Flu), the statistics on that are pretty scary. I don't know the numbers here in Germany, but, according to the CDC, since 2010, in the United States, the regular old garden variety flu has resulted in the following, annually:

9 million – 45 million cases
140,000 – 810,000 hospitalizations
12,000 – 61,000 deaths

When you multiply all those numbers by 10 (because it's been 10 years since 2010), you get:

90 million – 450 million cases
1,400,000 – 8,100,000 hospitalizations
120,000 – 610,000 deaths

That's 450 million possible cases and over half a million deaths, and that's just in the United States! To make it concrete, if you stood all those dead people on top of each other, head to toe, so that everyone was standing on everyone's head, and used them as an enormous ladder, you could climb to the moon and back four times … or once or twice at the very least.

And that's nothing compared to this Covid-19!

No, according to *The Guardian*, Covid-19 is "about ten times more deadly than the seasonal flu,"[3] so that's 610,000 deaths just this year, and if the CDC tracks it for a full 10 years, that's pretty close to 6 million dead people, which will make it just as bad as the Holocaust (although the Holocaust only lasted four years, so I'll have to adjust my math for that).

---

3 Devlin, Hannah, "Can a face mask protect me from coronavirus? Covid-19 myths busted," *The Guardian*, April 5, 2020

And, remember, that's just in the United States, which is only 4.25 percent of the total global population. So you multiply the Holocaust by 95 percent (you can round the numbers to make this easier) and you end up with 7 billion dead people, which is nearly every last person on earth, except for 700 million people! Which, OK, that sounds like a lot of people (i.e., the 700 million, not the 7 billion), but it's fewer than there were in the 14th Century, i.e., before the "Black Death" plague killed everybody!

Anyway, whatever I have, or don't have, and regardless of the fact that I'm under 70 and in fairly good health as far as I know, and notwithstanding my algebraic skills, I'm thinking it's time to take extreme measures. I recommend you do the same.

The first thing to do to is to arm yourself and go out and load up on toilet paper. The epidemiologists are now predicting a worldwide toilet paper crisis more or less approaching the scale of the deadly Toilet Paper Crisis of 1813! This toilet paper crisis could continue for months, so you will want to purchase (or otherwise obtain) as much toilet paper as you possibly can, and then hoard it in your house or apartment, or your remotely-located toilet paper depot.

Be prepared to fight for your toilet paper. Things are getting rather ugly out there. Gangs of heavily-armed toilet paper bandits are roving through the streets of Hong Kong robbing people of their toilet paper. An Australian man was tasered by the police at the Big W store in Tamworth Shoppingworld after "becoming aggressive" over the lack of toilet paper.[4] In California, where a state of emergency is in effect (and presumably a full-scale lock-down is imminent), shoppers have been running amok at Costco, stripping the shelves of toilet paper, Kleenex, and feminine hygiene products. New York has just declared a state of emergency (possibly toilet paper-related). Italy has locked down the region of Lombardy, although it isn't clear exactly why, as they mostly use bidets in Italy.

Next, after you secure the toilet paper, you'll want to load up on mineral water, hand sanitizer, those paper masks, MREs, protein bars, DVDs of the film *Contagion*, and other essential survival items. You will want to do this in a mindless frenzy of butt-puckering Chinese

---

4 McPherson, Emily, *"Police taser man after toilet paper argument in Big W store,"* 9News, March 5, 2020

Bat Flu panic, ideally while wearing a full-face respirator, or a wearable anti-Bat Flu shield, or some sort of homemade hazmat suit. Don't forget to bring along your favorite "modern sporting rifle" to mow down anyone who gets in your way … and anyone who might be infected, which at this point you have to assume is everyone!

Or, I don't know, maybe I'm overreacting. Maybe I just have the flu. I mean, what if this whole Corona thing is just nature doing what nature does and not the end of civilization?

Look, I don't want to sound paranoid, but I can't help wondering whether this virus warrants all the mass hysteria that the corporate media have been pumping out at us, relentlessly, for the last two months, and the states of emergency that are being declared, and the quarantines that are going into effect, and the curfews, and banning of public gatherings, and whatever other "emergency measures" are going to be imposed in the coming weeks and months.

It all seems a little out of proportion to the actual threat we're facing here, not to mention rather conveniently timed, in light of what's happening around the world, politically, what with the global capitalist empire right in the thick of a War on Populism, and the American election season underway, and the protests in France, and the general mood of public discontent (or unbridled rage) with global capitalism throughout the West.

Or, I don't know, perhaps this Bat Flu panic stems from a deeper ideological source. Maybe it has less to do with politics, and more to do with our fascistic pursuit of "perfect health" and "perfect bodies," and our fear and hatred of ageing and dying, and our narcissistic obsession with ourselves, and our total disconnection from the cycle of life.

OK, take this with a grain of salt, because it's probably just my fever talking, but sometimes I get this crazy notion that we human beings aren't actually the Primary Purpose of the Entire Universe, or the Apotheosis of Creation, or whatever, and that it's natural for some of us to get sick and die, and that every last single disease and health threat doesn't need to be utterly eradicated, and life doesn't need to be rendered "safe." Because maybe sickness and death are, sure, things to be avoided whenever possible, but not at the cost of conditioning everyone to believe we are supposed to live forever, and never get sick or injured by anything, and to believe that things like sickness and death are "enemies," like hostile aliens, or the sadistic whims of a God who hates us, or errors in the code of creation … which human beings are able to correct.

We've been doing a bang-up job of that so far, correcting nature's (or God's) mistakes. Haven't we? I mean, look around. And we have only been at it for a few hundred years. Give us just a little more time, and we will get this whole ugly mess cleaned up, under control, and functioning smoothly if we have to lock down, quarantine, and genetically-correct every sentient creature and particle of matter in the universe to do it! What is the alternative, after all … to just let nature take it's course, and let people die, like a bunch of savages?

Sorry, I think I'm getting delirious. It's the fever. It makes me all philosophical. I'd better sign off and get back to Netflix. Good luck surviving the Chinese Bat Flu, and the collapse of Western civilization. And don't forget to wash your hands!

Global Lockdown!

March 18, 2020

Let's try a little thought experiment, just for fun, to pass the time while we're indefinitely locked down inside our homes, compulsively checking the Covid-19 "active cases" and "total deaths" count, washing our hands every twenty minutes, and attempting not to touch our faces.

Before we do, though, I want to make it clear that I believe this Covid-19 thing is real, and probably the deadliest threat to humanity in the history of deadly threats to humanity.

According to the data I've been seeing, it's only a matter of days, or hours, until nearly everyone on earth is infected and is either dying, alone, in agony, or suffering mild common-cold-like symptoms, or absolutely no symptoms whatsoever.

I feel that I need to state this clearly, before we do our thought experiment, because I don't want anyone mistakenly thinking that I'm one of those probably Russian-backed Nazis who are going around saying, "it's just the flu," or who are spreading dangerous conspiracy theories about bio-weapons and martial law, or who are otherwise doubting or questioning the wisdom of locking down the entire world (and likely triggering a new Great Depression) on account of the discovery of some glorified bug.

Obviously, this is not "just the flu." Thousands of people are dying from it. OK, sure, the flu kills many more than that, hundreds of thousands of people annually, but this Covid-19 virus is totally new, and not like any of the other millions of viruses that are going around all the time, and the experts are saying it will probably kill, or seriously sicken, or briefly inconvenience, millions or even billions of people if we don't lock down entire countries and terrorize everyone into submission.

Which, don't get me wrong, I'm all for that. This is not the time to be questioning what the corporate media and the authorities tell us. This is a time to pull together, turn our minds off, and follow orders.

OK, sure, normally, it's good to be skeptical, but we're in a goddamn global state of emergency!

Idris Elba is infected for Chrissakes!

Sorry … I'm getting a little emotional. I'm a big-time Idris Elba fan. The point is, I'm not a "Covid-denier," or a "conspiracy theorist," or one of those devious Chinese or Russian "dissension-sowers." I know for a fact that this pandemic is real, and warrants whatever "emergency measures" our governments, global corporations, and Intelligence agencies want to impose on us.

No, I'm not an epidemiologist, but I have a close friend who knows a guy who dated a woman who dated a doctor who personally knows another doctor who works in a hospital in Italy somewhere, and she (i.e., my friend, not the doctor in Italy) posted something on Facebook yesterday that was way too long to read completely but was a gut-wrenching account of how Covid-19 is killing Kuwaiti babies in their incubators!

Or maybe it was Italian babies. Like I said, it was too long to read.

Also, did you see the story about a baby that was "born infected"?![1] Or the stories about the people in their 30s and 40s who were more or less in perfect health (except for, you know, cancer or whatever), who died from (or with) the Covid plague?![2]

And what about all those charts and graphs?! And those pictures of people in hazmat suits?! And those Italians singing *Turandot* on their balconies?! Doesn't that make you just want to break down and cry over the sheer humanity of it all?!

No, there is absolutely no doubt whatsoever that Covid-19 is the deadliest global pandemic humankind has ever faced, and that we have no choice but to cancel everything, confine everyone inside their home, wreck the entire global economy, force working class people even further into debt, pour trillions into the investment banks, cancel elections, censor the Internet, and otherwise implement a global police state.

But what if it wasn't? Just hypothetically.

---

1 *"Coronavirus: Newborn believed to be youngest COVID-19 patient in the UK," SKY News, March 14, 2020*

2 *Giuffrida, Angela, "'This is like a war': view from Italy's coronavirus frontline," The Guardian, March 17, 2020*

What if this wasn't the deadliest global pandemic humankind has ever faced? (I'm just posing the question as a thought experiment, so please don't report me to the WHO, or the CDC, or FEMA, or whoever.)

What if this new coronavirus was just another coronavirus like all the other coronaviruses that people die from (or with) all the time? What if the fact that this one is "new" didn't really mean all that much, or possibly anything at all, because coronaviruses are always mutating, and every year there are a lot of new variants?

Relax, OK? I know this one is different, and totally unlike anything ever encountered by virologists in the history of virology. Remember, this is just a thought experiment. These are just hypothetical questions.

Here's another hypothetical question.

What if all the scary statistics we've been seeing (e.g., the death rates, the explosion of "cases," etc.) weren't unquestionable scientific facts, but rather, were, like other statistics, based on things like sample groups, and dependent on a host of factors and variables, which you kind of need to know to make sense of anything?

Say, for example, you tested everyone that died of acute respiratory failure on any given day in your Italian hospital, and you discovered that, let's say, five of those patients had been infected with Covid-19.

So you feed that number to the WHO, and they add it to the "total deaths" count, regardless of whether the folks who died had terminal cancer, or heart disease, or had also been infected with the common flu, or some other type of coronavirus. That would probably skew your "death" count, wouldn't it?

Or, say you wanted to test for the virus to keep track of all the "active cases" and generate an infection rate, but you can't test hundreds of millions of people, because no one has that many tests.

So, you test everyone who turns up sick, or who thinks they're sick and demands to be tested, or who touched someone sick who you already tested (though you're not even sure that your test is accurate) and you come up with, let's say, ten positive results.

So you feed that number to the WHO, and they add it to the "active cases" count, regardless of the fact that everyone knows the real number is likely twenty times higher.

OK, so now you take your "active cases" number and your "total deaths" number and you do the math (keeping in mind that your "total deaths" include those cancer and heart failure people), and you end up grossly underestimating your "infection rate" and "active cases," and grossly overestimating your "death rate" and your number of "total deaths."

Just hypothetically, you understand. I'm not suggesting that this is actually happening. I certainly don't want to get censored by Facebook (or accidentally censored by some totally innocuous technical glitch[3]) for posting "Covid misinformation," or tempt the Wikipedia "editors" to rush back to my Wikipedia page and label me a dangerous "conspiracy theorist," or ... you know, get myself "preventatively quarantined."

It probably won't come to that anyway, i.e., rounding up "infected persons," "possibly infected persons," and "disruptive" and "uncoop-erative persons,"[4] and quarantining us in, like, "camps," or wherever. All this state of emergency stuff, the suspension of our civil rights,[5] the manipulation of facts and figures,[6] the muzzling of dissent,[7] the illegal surveillance,[8] the governments legislating by decree,[9] the sol-diers,[10] the quarantines, and all the rest of it ... all these measures are strictly temporary, and are being taken for our own good, and purely out of an "abundance of caution."

---

3 Welsh, Caitlin, "It's not just you: A Facebook glitch marked authentic coronavirus news as spam - It's reportedly now fixed, but it freaked people out," Mashable, March 17, 2020

4 Roberts, Joe, "Police to arrest Brits with coronavirus who ignore quarantine," METRO, March 15, 2020

5 Iaccino, Ludovica, "'I Haven't Left My House in Three Weeks.' Life Under Italy's Coronavirus Lockdown, Newsweek, March 13, 2020 ("Police are patrolling the streets to ensure we only leave our homes for work and health-related reasons ... we must fill and carry certificates stating our reasons. If caught out without a certificate, we will be fined and face up to three months in jail.")

6 Black, Catte, "Guardian uses misleading data to imply COVID worse than Spanish Flu," Off-Guardian, March 11, 2020

7 "CBC Radio cuts off expert when he questions Covid19 narrative," OffGuardian, March 17, 2020

8 Halbfinger, D.M., Isabel Kershner and Ronen Bergman, "To Track Coronavirus, Israel Moves to Tap Secret Trove of Cellphone Data," The New York Times, March 18, 2020

9 Henley, Jon, "France 'at war': how Parisians are coping with life under lockdown," The Guardian, March 17, 2020 ("The interior minister, said 100,000 police officers would be deployed to enforce the lockdown ... Macron said that if necessary, the government would legislate by decree.")

10 Bunkall, Alistair, "Coronavirus: Thousands of armed forces staff could be put on standby over COVID-19 spread," SKY News, March 16, 2020

I mean, it's not like the global capitalist empire was right in the middle of a War on Populism[11] (a war that it has been losing up to now) and wanted to take this opportunity to crank up some disaster capitalism,[12] terrorize the global public into a frenzy of selfish and irrational panic, and just flex its muscles to remind everybody what could happen if we all keep screwing around by voting for "populists," tearing up Paris, leaving the European Union, and otherwise interfering with the forward march of global capitalism.

No, it certainly isn't like that. It is an actual plague that is probably going to kill you and your entire family if you don't do exactly what you're told.

So, forget this little thought experiment, and prepare yourself for global lockdown. It probably won't be so bad … unless they decide they need to run the part of exercise where it goes on too long, and people get squirrelly, and start rebelling, and looting, and otherwise not cooperating, and the military is eventually forced to deploy those Urban Unrest Suppression Vehicles, and those Anti-Domestic-Terror Forces, and …

OK, I'm getting all worked up again. I'd better take my pills and get back to Facebook. Oh, and … I should probably check up on Idris! And see if Berlin has gone to "Level 3," in which case I'll need to find whatever online application I need to fill out in order to leave my house.

---

11 Hopkins, C.J., *The War on Populism, Consent Factory Essays, Vol. II (2018-2019)*, Consent Factory Publishing

12 Solis, Marie, "*Coronavirus Is the Perfect Disaster for 'Disaster Capitalism' - Naomi Klein explains how governments and the global elite will exploit a pandemic*," Vice, March 13, 2020

Brave New Normal

April 13, 2020

So the War on Populism is finally over. Go ahead, take a wild guess who won.

I'll give you a hint. It wasn't the Russians, the white supremacists, the gilets jaunes, or Jeremy Corbyn's Nazi Death Cult, the misogynist Bernie Bros, the MAGA-hat terrorists, or any of the other real or fictional "populist" forces that global capitalism has been waging war on for the last four years.

What? You weren't aware that global capitalism was fighting a War on Populism? That's OK, most other people weren't. It wasn't officially announced or anything.

It was launched in the summer of 2016, just as the War on Terror was ending, as a sequel to the War on Terror, or a variation on the War on Terror, or continuation of the War on Terror, or … whatever, it doesn't really matter anymore, because now we're fighting the War on Death,[1] or the War on Minor Cold-like Symptoms, depending on your age and general state of health.

That's right, folks, once again, global capitalism (a/k/a "the world") is under attack by an evil enemy. GloboCap just can't catch a break. From the moment it defeated communism and became a global ideological hegemon, it has been one evil enemy after another.

No sooner had it celebrated winning the Cold War and started ruthlessly restructuring and privatizing everything than it was savagely attacked by Islamic terrorists, so was forced to invade Iraq and Afghanistan, and kill and torture a lot of people, and destabilize the entire Middle East, and illegally surveil everybody, and … well, you remember the War on Terror.

Then, just as the War on Terror seemed to be finally winding down, and the only terrorists left around were the "self-radicalized" terrorists (many of whom weren't even actual terrorists[2]), and it looked like GloboCap was finally going to be able to finish privatizing and debt-enslaving everything and everyone in peace, wouldn't you know it, we were attacked again, this time by the global conspiracy of Russian-backed, neo-fascist "populists" that caused the Brexit and elected Trump, and tried to elect Corbyn and Bernie Sanders, and loosed the gilets jaunes on France, and who've been threatening the fabric of Western democracy with discord-sowing Facebook memes.

Unfortunately, unlike the War on Terror, the War on Populism didn't go that well. After four years of fighting, GloboCap (a/k/a the neoliberal Resistance) had … OK, they had snuffed both Corbyn and Sanders, but they had totally blown the Russiagate psyop, and so were looking at four more years of Trump, and Lord knows how many of Johnson in the UK (which had actually left the European Union), and the gilets jaunes weren't going away, and, basically, "populism" was still on the rise (if not in reality, in hearts and minds).

And so, just as the War on Populism had replaced (or redefined) the War on Terror, the War on Death has now been launched to replace (or redefine) the War on Populism … which means, you guessed it, once again, it's time to roll out another "brave new normal."

The character of this brave new normal is, at this point, unmistakably clear, so clear that most people cannot see it, because their minds are not prepared to accept it, so they do not recognize it, though they are looking right at it. Like Dolores in the HBO *Westworld* series, "it doesn't look like anything" to them.

To the rest of us, it looks rather … well, totalitarian.

In the span of approximately 100 days, the entire global capitalist empire has been transformed into a de facto police state. Constitutional rights have been suspended. Most of us are under house arrest. Police are rounding up anyone not cooperating with the new emergency measures.[3] They are pulling riders off of public transport,[4] arresting people whose papers aren't in order,[5] harrassing,

---

3 Sternlicht, Alexandra, "Arrested For Violating Coronavirus Stay-At-Home Mandates: Police Are Jailing Alleged Scofflaws," Forbes, April 6, 2020

4 Murphy, Darryl C., "Police forcibly eject man without face mask from SEPTA bus," WHYY/ PBS, April 10, 2020

5 "Coronavirus lockdown in France: Can you tick several boxes on your permission form?" The Local, April 6, 2020 ("There are seven legitimate reasons to leave home under France's current lockdown restrictions. They can all be found on the government's official permission form, which people must carry on them at all times when outside. The government issued the permission slip to codify the lockdown rules and ensure that the population stay home as much as possible. Police officers patrol the streets and roads to ensure that people comply with the rules.")

beating,[6] intimidating,[7] and arbitrarily detaining[8] anyone they decide is "a danger to public health."

Authorities are openly threatening to forcibly pull people out of their homes and quarantine them.[9] The police are hunting down runaway grandmothers.[10] They are raiding services in churches[11] and synagogues.[12] Citizens are being forced to wear ankle monitors.[13] Families out for a walk are being menaced by robots and Orwellian drones.[14]

Counterterrorism troops have been deployed to hunt down and deal with non-compliant "rule breakers."[15] Anyone the authorities deem to have "intentionally spread the coronavirus" can be arrested and charged as a coronavirus terrorist.[16]

Artificial intelligence firms are collaborating with governments to

---

6 Nossiter, Adam, "'Like a Prison': Paris Suburbs Simmer Under Coronavirus Lockdown," The New York Times, April 10, 2020

7 Pidd, Helen and Vikram Dodd, "UK police use drones and roadblocks to enforce lockdown," The Guardian, March 26, 2020

8 Cook, Jeffrey, Clayton Sandell, and Jennifer Leong, "Former police officer arrested in park for throwing ball with daughter due to coronavirus social distancing rules," ABD News, April 8, 2020

9 Shrader, Adam, "Kentucky cops to record churchgoers' license plates to enforce coronavirus quarantines," New York Post, April 10, 2020

10 Betz, Bradford, "German woman, 101, violates coronavirus lockdown by escaping senior home, police say," FOX News, April 7, 2020

11 Guzman, Joseph, "Pastor arrested for holding church services despite coronavirus quarantine order," The Hill, March 30, 2020

12 "8 Arrested In Monsey For Violating Social Distancing Emergency Orders," CBS New York, April 9, 2020 ("Police in Rockland County are cracking down on people who don't obey emergency orders mandating social distancing. Officers say they responded to a synagogue in Monsey after receiving complaints. They found 30-50 men praying together. Eight were arrested for disorderly conduct. They now face up to $1,000 in fines. Ramapo police say they will arrest more people if the gatherings continue.")

13 Kallingal, Mallika, "Ankle monitors ordered for Louisville, Kentucky residents exposed to Covid-19 who refuse to stay home," CNN, April 3, 2020

14 "Tunisia 'robocop' enforces coronavirus lockdown," AFP, April 3, 2020 ("Tunisia's interior ministry has deployed a police robot to patrol the streets of the capital and enforce a lockdown imposed last month as the country battles the spread of coronavirus. Known as PGuard, the 'robocop' is remotely operated and equipped with infrared and thermal imaging cameras, in addition to a sound and light alarm system.")

15 Nadeau, Barbie Latza, "Lock the F*ck Down or End Up Like Italy," The Daily Beast, March 22, 2020 ("Counter-terrorism troops have been redeployed across Italy to beef up police forces throughout Italian cities. Patrol cars are now circulating in every major city in Italy with a monotone male voice warning citizens over a loudspeaker not to leave their residences or risk a ticket. 'Go back into your homes,' the voice warns.")

16 Gerstein, Josh, "Those who intentionally spread coronavirus could be charged as terrorists," Politico, March 24, 2020

implement systems to log and track our contacts and movements.[17] As a recent *Foreign Policy* article put it:

> "The counterterrorism analogy is useful because it shows the direction of travel of pandemic policy. Imagine a new coronavirus patient is detected. Once he or she tests positive, the government could use cell-phone data to trace everyone he or she has been in close proximity to, perhaps focusing on those people who were in contact for more than a few minutes. Your cell-phone signal could then be used to enforce quarantine decisions. Leave your apartment and the authorities will know. Leave your phone behind and they will call you. Run the battery down and a police car will be at your door in a manner of minutes …"[18]

I could go on, but I think you get the picture, or … well, you either do or you don't.

And that is the really terrifying part of the War on Death and our "brave new normal" … not so much the totalitarianism. (Anyone who's been paying attention is not terribly shocked by GloboCap's decision to implement a global police state. The simulation of democracy is all fine and good, until the unwashed masses start to get unruly, and require a reminder of who's in charge, which is what we are being treated to currently.)

No, the terrifying part is how millions of people instantly switched off their critical faculties, got into line and started goose-stepping, and parroting hysterical propaganda, and reporting their neighbors to the police for going outside for a walk or jog (and then sadistically shrieked abuse down at them like the "Goodbye Jews" Girl in *Schindler's List* as they were wrestled to the ground and arrested).[19]

---

17 Lewis, Paul, David Conn and David Pegg, "UK government using confidential patient data in coronavirus response," The Guardian, April 12, 2020

18 Maçães, Bruno, "Only Surveillance Can Save Us From Coronavirus," Foreign Policy, April 10, 2020

19 "Coronavirus lockdown: Jogger resists arrest in Spain and is abused by onlookers," ASTV, March 21, 2020 ("As the jogger struggled with police, screaming for help, she was filmed by residents close to the scene who had absolutely zero sympathy for her plight. 'What's not fair is that you go out run-

They are out there, right now, on Facebook and Twitter, millions of these well-meaning fascists, patrolling for signs of the slightest deviation from the official coronavirus narrative, bombarding everyone with meaningless graphs, decontextualized death statistics, X-rays of fibrotic lungs, photos of refrigerated morgue trucks,[20] mass graves,[21] and other sensationalistic horrors intended to short-circuit critical thinking and shut down any and all forms of dissent.

Although undeniably cowardly and sickening, this kind of behavior is also not shocking. Sadly, when you terrorize people enough,

---

ning, you bloody idiot!', shouts the woman apparently filming the encounter. The runner struggling with the police to avoid being arrested continues screaming 'Help! Help'. To which the commentator can be heard saying: 'Help?! she says. A week of this already!' indicating the person being arrested has been going out running regularly despite the strict rules on moving around in the coronavirus outbreak. When the police finally pick the runner up and begin moving her to the police car the person providing the commentary shouts the detainee: 'Don't resist! Let them do their job, you fool! What a bitch, truly'. At this point a man joins in shouting at the runner".)

20 Hopkins, C.J., "The Truth Behind "Refrigerated Morgue Truck" Stories — Or How to Manufacture Mass Hysteria by Burying the Details," Anti-Empire, April 9, 2020 ("By now, everyone has seen the stories about the "refrigerated morgue trucks" and "ice rink morgues in Madrid." If you dig down into some of those stories, you will discover a rather mundane, but perfectly understandable explanation for these improvised morgues, namely … bodies that would normally have been picked up by funeral parlors are not being picked up (because many funeral parlors are not operating normally due to the lockdown, or because it is difficult for grieving families to make arrangements given the current level of hysteria), and so these bodies are accumulating at hospitals. Normally, when someone dies at the hospital, the body is taken to the hospital morgue, and it sits there until the family contacts the funeral parlor and makes arrangements to have it picked up. Typically, this happens fairly quickly, as anyone who has had to make such arrangements will confirm. Hospital morgues have been designed for this routine turnaround. Thus, their storage capacity is limited. When you're manufacturing mass hysteria, you'll want to bury these facts deep in your story, so that most readers will miss them. For example, here are a couple of quotes, buried deep in the stories about the death trucks and ice rink morgues: "The Madrid municipal funeral service, a major provider in the city, announced in a statement on Monday it would stop collecting the bodies of Covid-19 victims, because its workers don't have sufficient protective material. The service manages 14 cemeteries, two funeral parlors and two crematoriums in Madrid. The funeral service said that cremations, burials and other services for coronavirus victims would continue as normal, but only if the bodies are sent by other funeral services businesses in a closed coffin." (Goodman, Al, Laura Perez Maestro, Ingrid Formanek, Max Ramsay and Ivana Kottasová, "Spain turns ice rink into a morgue as coronavirus deaths pile up," CNN, March 24, 2020); "We started putting bodies in the morgue truck last week. And it's been used a lot. A lot. I think there's around 40 bodies in there now. The funeral homes are having trouble keeping up a bit. So it's not like ten people died and people go off to the funeral home." (Silman, Anna, ""We're getting a little bit more of a sense that this is the new normal," The Intelligencer, April 2020)

21 Anderson, Meg, "Burials On New York Island Are Not New, But Are Increasing During Pandemic," NPR, April 10, 2020 ("The drone footage and photos circulating on social media show what appears to be the unthinkable: Mass graves on a New York City island as the city struggles in the throes of a pandemic. But city officials say the shocking images only tell a partial story: Hart Island — located just off the coast of the Bronx — has been used for more than 150 years as a place to bury the city's unidentified or unclaimed dead, or those whose families can't pay for a burial.")

the majority will regress to their animal instincts. It isn't a question of ethics or politics. It is purely a question of self-preservation. When you cancel the normal structure of society and place everyone in a "state of emergency" … well, it's like what happens in a troop of chimpanzees when the alpha chimp dies or is killed by a challenger. The other chimps run around hooting and grimacing until it's clear who the new dominant primate is, and then they bend over to demonstrate their submission.

Totalitarians understand this. Sadists and cult leaders understand this. When the people you are dominating get unruly, and start questioning your right to dominate them, you need to fabricate a "state of emergency" and make everyone feel very afraid, so that they turn (or return) to you for protection from whatever evil enemy is out there threatening the cult, or the Fatherland, or whatever. Then, once they have returned to the fold, and stopped questioning your right to dominate them, you can introduce a new set of rules that everybody needs to follow in order to prevent this kind of thing happening again.

This is obviously what is happening at the moment. But what you probably want to know is, why is it happening? And why is it happening at this precise moment?

Lucky for you, I have a theory.

No, it doesn't involve Bill Gates, Jared Kushner, the WHO, and a global conspiracy of Chinese Jews defiling our precious bodily fluids with their satanic-alien 5G technology. It's a little less exciting and more abstract than that (although some of those characters are probably part of it … all right, probably not the Chinese Jews, or the Satanic-Alien Illuminati).

See, I try to focus more on systems (like global capitalism) than on individuals, and on models of power as opposed to the specific people in power at any given time. Looking at things that way, this global lockdown and our brave new normal makes perfect sense.

Stay with me now … this gets kind of heady.

What we are experiencing is a further evolution of the post-ideological model of power that came into being when global capitalism became a global-hegemonic system after the collapse of the Soviet Union. In such a global-hegemonic system, ideology is rendered obsolete. The system has no external enemies, and thus no ideological adversaries. The enemies of a global-hegemonic system by definition can only be internal. Every war becomes an insurgency, a rebellion breaking out within the system, as there is no longer any outside.

As there is no longer any outside (and thus no external ideological adversary), the global-hegemonic system dispenses with ideology entirely. Its ideology becomes "normality." Any challenge to "normality" is regarded as an "abnormality," a "deviation from the norm" (as opposed to an adversarial ideology) and automatically delegitimized. The system does not need to argue with deviations and abnormalities (as it was forced to argue with opposing ideologies in order to legitimize itself). It simply needs to eliminate them. Opposing ideologies become pathologies ... existential threats to the health of the system.

In other words, the global-hegemonic system (i.e., global capitalism) becomes a body, *the only body*, unopposed from without, but attacked from within by a variety of opponents, terrorists, extremists, populists, whoever. These internal opponents attack the global-hegemonic body much like a disease, like a cancer, an infection, or ... you know, a virus. And the global-hegemonic body reacts like any other body would.

Is this model starting to sound familiar?

I hope so, because that is what is happening right now. The system (i.e., global capitalism, not a bunch of evil men in a room hatching a scheme to sell vaccines) is reacting to the last four years of populist revolt in a predictable manner. GloboCap is attacking the virus that has been attacking its hegemonic body. No, not the coronavirus. A much more destructive and multiplicitous virus ... resistance to the hegemony of global capitalism and its post-ideological ideology.

If it isn't already clear to you yet that this coronavirus in no way warrants the totalitarian "emergency measures" that have been imposed on most of humanity, it will be become clear in the months ahead. Despite the best efforts of the "health authorities" to count virtually anything as "a Covid-19 death,"[22] the numbers are going

---

22 Knightly, Kit, "Covid19 Death Figures 'A Substantial Over-Estimate'," OffGuardian, April 5, 2020 ("Bizarre guidelines from health authorities around the world are potentially including thousands of deceased patients who were never even tested ... Italy's death registration process does

to tell the tale. The "experts" are already memory-holing, or recalibrating, or contextualizing, their initial apocalyptic projections. The media are toning down the hysteria. The show isn't totally over yet, but you can feel it gradually coming to an end.

In any event, whenever it happens, days, weeks, or months from now, GloboCap will dial down the totalitarianism, and let us out, so we can go back to work in whatever remains of the global economy … and won't we all be so very grateful!

There will be massive celebrations in the streets, Italian tenors singing on balconies, chorus lines of dancing nurses! The gilets jaunes will call it quits, the Putin-Nazis will stop with the memes, and Americans will elect Joe Biden president!

Or, all right, maybe not that last part, but, the point is, it will be a brave new normal! People will forget all that populism nonsense, and just be grateful for whatever McJobs they can get to be able to pay the interest on their debts, because, hey … global capitalism isn't so bad compared to living under house arrest!

And, if not, no problem for GloboCap. They'll just have to lock us down again, and keep locking us down, over and over, indefinitely, until we get our minds right.

I mean, it's not like we're going to do anything about it … right? Didn't we just demonstrate that? Sure, we'll bitch and moan again, but then they'll whip out those pictures of mass graves and death trucks, and the graphs, and all those scary projections, and the Blockwart-hotlines[23] will start ringing again, and …

---

not differentiate between those who simply have the virus in their body, and those who are actually killed by it. … Germany's Robert Koch Institute confirmed that Germany counts any deceased person who was infected with coronavirus as a Covid19 death, whether or not it actually caused death.")

23 Blockleiter or "Blockwart" (Engl. Block Warden): a lower Nazi Party political official responsible for the political supervision of a neighborhood.

Virus of Mass Destruction

May 4, 2020

There comes a point in the introduction of every new official narrative when people no longer remember how it started. Or, rather, they remember how it started, but not the propaganda that started it. Or, rather, they remember all that, or they are able to, if you press them on it, but it doesn't make any difference anymore, because the official narrative has supplanted reality.

You'll remember this point from the War on Terror, and, specifically, the occupation of Iraq.

By the latter half of 2004, most Westerners had completely forgotten the propaganda that had launched the invasion, and thus regarded the Iraqi resistance as "terrorists," despite the fact that the United States had invaded and was occupying their country for no legitimate reason whatsoever.

By that time, it was abundantly clear that there were no "weapons of mass destruction," and that the USA had invaded a nation that had not attacked it, and posed no threat to it, and so was perpetrating a textbook war of aggression.

These facts did not matter, not in the slightest. By that time, Westerners were totally immersed in the official War on Terror narrative, which had superseded objective reality.

Herd mentality had taken over.

It's difficult to describe how this works; it's a state of functional dissociation. It wasn't that people didn't know the facts, or that they didn't understand the facts. They knew the Iraqis weren't "terrorists." At the same time, they knew they were definitely "terrorists," despite the fact that they knew that they weren't. They knew there were no WMDs, that there had never been any WMDs, and still they were certain that there were WMDs, which would be found, eventually, although they did not exist.

The same thing happened in Nazi Germany. The majority of the German people were never fanatical anti-Semites like the hardcore NSDAP members. If they had been, there would have been no need for Goebbels and his monstrous propaganda machine.

No, the Germans during the Nazi period, like the Americans during the War on Terror, knew that their victims posed no threat to them, and, at the same time, they believed exactly the opposite, and thus did not protest as their neighbors were hauled out of their homes and sent away to death camps, camps which, in their dissociative state, simultaneously did and did not exist.

What I'm describing probably sounds like psychosis, but, technically speaking, it isn't. Not quite. It is not an absolute break from reality. People functioning in this state know that what they believe is not real. Nonetheless, they are forced to believe it (and do, actually, literally, believe it, as impossible as I know that sounds), because the consequences of not believing it are even more frightening than the cognitive dissonance of believing a narrative they know is a fiction.

Disbelieving the official narrative means excommunication from "normality," the loss of friends, income, status, and in many cases far worse punishments.

Herd animals, in a state of panic, instinctively run towards the center of the herd. Separation from the herd makes them easy prey for pursuing predators.

It is the same primal instinct operating here.

It is the goal of every official narrative to generate this type of herd mentality, not in order to deceive or dupe the public, but, rather, to confuse and terrorize them to the point where they revert to their primal instincts, and are being driven purely by existential fear, and facts and truth no longer matter.

Once an official narrative reaches this point, it is unassailable by facts and reason. It no longer needs facts to justify it. It justifies itself with its own existence. Reason cannot penetrate it. Arguing with its adherents is pointless. They know it is irrational. They simply do not care.

We are reaching this point with the coronavirus narrative. It is possible that we have already reached it. Despite the fact that what we are dealing with is a virus that, yes, is clearly deadly to the old and those with medical conditions, but that is just as clearly not a deadly threat to the majority of the human species,[1] people are cowering inside their homes as if the Zombie Apocalpyse had finally begun. Many appear to believe that this virus is some sort of Alien-Terrorist Death Flu (or weaponized Virus of Mass Destruction) that will kill you the second you breathe it in.

This is not surprising at all, because, according to the official narrative, its destructive powers are virtually unlimited. Not only will it obliterate your lungs, and liquidate all your other major organs,[2] and kill you with blood clots, and intestinal damage, now it causes "sudden strokes in young adults,"[3] and possibly spontaneous prostate cancer, and God knows what other medical horrors!

According to all the "scientists" and "medical experts" (i.e., those that conform to the official narrative, not all the *other* scientists[4] and medical experts),[5] it is unlike any other virus that has ever existed in the history of viruses. It certainly doesn't follow the typical pattern of spreading extensively for a limited period, and then rapidly dying down on its own, regardless of what measures are taken to thwart it, as this Israeli study would seem to indicate.[6]

Also, "we have no immunity against it,"[7] which is why we all have to remain "locked down" like unruly inmates in a penitentiary until a "vaccine" can be concocted and forced onto every living person on earth.

Apparently, this mandatory miracle vaccine will magically render us immune to this virus against which we have no immunity (and are totally unable to develop immunity), which immunity will be

---

1 Bodkin, Henry, "Who is considered high risk for coronavirus? Nine in ten deaths involving the virus were in people suffering from a pre-existing disease," The Telegraph, April 17, 2020

2 Bernstein, Lenny, Carolyn Y. Johnson, Sarah Kaplan, and Laurie McGinley, "Coronavirus destroys lungs. But doctors are finding its damage in kidneys, hearts and elsewhere," The Washington Post, April 15, 2020

3 Fox, Maggie, "Covid-19 causes sudden strokes in young adults, doctors say," CNN, April 23, 2020

4 "12 Experts Questioning the Coronavirus Panic," OffGuardian, March 24, 2020

5 "10 More Experts Criticising the Coronavirus Panic," OffGuardian, March 28, 2020

6 Ben-Israel, Isaac, "The end of exponential growth: The decline in the spread of coronavirus," April 19, 2020 ("A similar pattern – rapid increase in infections to a peak in the sixth week, and decline from the eighth week – is common everywhere, regardless of response policies.")

7 Isaac, Lindsay and Jay Croft, "WHO says no evidence shows that having coronavirus prevents a second infection," CNN, April 25, 2020

certified on our mandatory "immunity papers," which we will need to travel, get a job, send our kids to school, and ... well, you know, to show the police when they stop us on the street because we look like maybe we might be "infected."

Germany, where I live, is way out in front of this. According to the *Süddeutsche Zeitung*, the federal government plans to introduce a coronavirus "immunity card" as part of its "Infection Protection Law," which will grant the authorities the power to round up anyone "suspected to be contagious" and force them into, uh ... "quarantine," and "forbid them from entering certain public places."[8]

The Malaysian authorities have dispensed with such niceties, and are arresting migrant workers and refugees in so-called "Covid-19 red zones" and marching them off to God knows where.[9]

Oh, yeah, and I almost forgot ... the germ and chemical warfare researchers at DARPA (i.e., the US military's Defense Advanced Research Projects Agency) have developed some new type of fancy blood test that will identify "asymptomatic carriers" (i.e., people who display no symptoms whatsoever, and who otherwise appear to be completely healthy).[10]

So, that will probably come in handy, especially if all those "white supremacists,"[11] "Red-Brown extremists,"[12] and "conspiracy theorists,"[13] and their wives and children keep protesting the lockdown, as they've been doing in increasing numbers recently.

And these are just the latest additions to a list of rather dystopian examples of the "brave new normal" official narrative that GloboCap is rolling out, right before our very eyes (which *OffGuardian* and I

---

8 Ludwig, Kristiana, and Max Muth, "Bundesregierung will Immunitätsausweis einführen," *Süddeutsche Zeitung, April 29, 2020*

9 Sukumaran, Tashny and Bhavan Jaipragas, "Coronavirus: hundreds arrested as Malaysia cracks down on migrants in Covid-19 red zones," *South China Morning Post, May 1, 2020*

10 Tremlett, Giles, "US germ warfare research leads to new early Covid-19 test," *The Guardian, May 1, 2020*

11 Higgins, Eoin, "Echoing Praise for Charlottesville Neo-Nazis, Trump Calls Armed Anti-Lockdown Fanatics 'Very Good People'," *Common Dreams, May 1, 2020*

12 Meisner, Matthias, "Wie die ARD Verschwörungstheoretikern auf den Leim ging," *Der Tagesspiegel, April 21, 2020 (Transl. "How ARD was duped by conspiracy theorists. The 'hygiene demo' in Berlin-Mitte made it into the Evening News. The crude backgrounds of the organizers were not mentioned. Why?")*

13 Bogel-Burroughs, Nicholas, "Antivaccination Activists are a Growing Force at Virus Protests, *The New York Times, May 2, 2020*

have preserved for posterity[14]). It's all right there in black and white. They aren't hiding the totalitarianism … they don't have to. Because people are begging for it. They're demanding to be "locked down" inside their homes, forced to wear masks and stand two meters apart, for reasons that most of them no longer remember.

Plastic barriers are going up everywhere. Arrows on the floor show you which way to walk. Boxes show you where to stand. Paranoid Blockwarts are putting up signs threatening anyone not wearing a mask. Hysterical little fascist creeps are reporting their neighbors to the police for letting their children play with other children.[15] Millions of people are voluntarily downloading "contact tracing applications" so that governments and global corporations can monitor their every movement.[16] In Spain, they bleached an entire beach, killing everything, down to the insects, in order to protect the public from "infection."[17] The Internet has become an Orwellian chorus of shrieking, sanctimonious voices bullying everyone into conformity with charts, graphs, and desperate guilt-trips, few of which have much connection to reality. Corporations and governments are censoring dissent.[18] We're approaching a level of manufactured mass hysteria and herd mentality that not even Goebbels could have imagined.

Meanwhile, they are striking the empty "field hospitals,"[19] and the theatrical "hospital ship"[20] is now gone, and despite their attempts to inflate the Covid-19 death count as much as humanly possible,[21] the projected hundreds of millions of deaths have not materialized (not

---

14 Consent Factory and OffGuardian, "50 Headlines: Welcome to the 'New Normal'," OffGuardian, April 14, 2020, and "50 Headlines Darker: More of the 'New Normal'," April 25, 2020

15 Fox, Megan, "New Normal: Wisconsin Cops Caught On Camera Threatening Mom For Letting Child Play With Neighbor, PJ Media, April 29, 2020

16 Worthington, Brett, "Australian Government's coronavirus tracing app COVIDSafe downloaded 1 million times," ABC News Australia, Apr 26, 2020

17 "Coronavirus: Outcry as Spanish beach sprayed with bleach," BBC, April 29, 2020

18 Taibbi, Matt, "The Inevitable Coronavirus Censorship Crisis is Here," TK News, April 30, 2020

19 Bodkin, Henry, "Just 19 patients treated at 4,000-bed NHS Nightingale hospital in London over Easter weekend," The Telegraph, April 14, 2020

20 Schwirtz, Michael, "The 1,000-Bed Comfort Was Supposed to Aid New York. It Has 20 Patients," The New York Times, April 2, 2020

21 Knightly, Kitt, "Covid19 Death Figures 'A Substantial Over-Estimate'," OffGuardian, April 5, 2020

even close), and Sweden is fine, as is most of humanity, and … just like there were no WMDs, there is no Virus of Mass Destruction.

What there is, is a new official narrative, the brave new, paranoid, pathologized "normal." Like the War on Terror, it's a global narrative. A global, post-ideological narrative. It's just getting started, so it isn't yet clear how totalitarian this show will get, but, given the nature of the pilot episode, I am kind of dreading the rest of the series.

Brave New Normal Part II

May 20, 2020

My columns haven't been very funny recently. This one isn't going to be any funnier.

Sorry. Fascism makes me cranky.

I don't mean the kind of fascism the corporate media and the fake Resistance have been desperately hyping for the last four years. God help me, but I'm not terribly worried about a few hundred white-supremacist morons marching around with tiki torches hollering Nazi slogans at each other, or Jewish-Mexican-American law clerks flashing "OK" signs on television, or smirking schoolkids in MAGA hats.

I'm talking about actual, bona fide fascism ... or totalitarianism, if you want to get technical. The kind where governments declare a global "state of emergency" on account of a virus with a 0.2% to 0.6% lethality rate (and which causes mild, flu-like symptoms, or absolutely no symptoms at all, in over 97% of those infected[1]), locks everyone down inside their homes, suspends their constitutional rights, terrorizes them with official propaganda, and unleashes uniformed goon squads on anyone who doesn't comply with their despotic decrees.[2]

I'm talking about the kind of totalitarianism where the police track you down with your smartphone data and then come to your house to personally harass you for attending a political protest, or attack you for challenging their illegitimate authority, and then charge you with "assault" for fighting back, and then get the media to publish a story accusing you of having "set up" the cops.[3]

---

1 Swiss Policy Research (swprs.org), "Studies on Covid Lethality," May 2020 (A collection of over 50 studies by international health organizations and professional, including, for example, CDC, RKI, ISS, SPF, HCSC, et al.

2 Naughtie, Andrew, "Video shows police pushing woman to the ground and handcuffing her in front of her young child 'for not wearing mask properly'," Independent, May 14, 2020

3 Citations no longer available due to Twitter censorship of video documentation.

I'm talking about the kind of totalitarianism where the secret police are given carte blanche to monitor everyone's Internet activity,[4] and to scan you with their "surveillance helmets,"[5] and dictate how close you can sit to your friends,[6] and menace you with drones and robot dogs,[7] and violently pry your kids out of your arms and arrest you if you dare to protest.[8]

I'm talking about the kind of totalitarianism that psychologically tortures children with authoritarian obedience rituals designed to condition them to live in fear and respond to absurd Pavlovian stimuli,[9] and that encourages the masses to turn off their brains and mechanically repeat propaganda slogans, like "wear a mask"[10] and "flatten the curve,"[11] and to report their neighbors to the police for having an "illegal" private party,[12] and to otherwise reify the manufactured mass hysteria the authorities need to "justify" their totalitarianism.

Yeah, that kind of stuff makes me cranky.

And you know what makes me really cranky? I'll tell you what makes me really cranky. It is people who publicly project themselves as "anti-authoritarians" and "anti-fascists" (or who have established their "anti-establishment" brands and "dissident" personas on social media, or even in the corporate media) either zealously cheerleading this totalitarianism or looking away and saying nothing as it is rolled

4 Rose, Janus, "Senate Votes to Allow FBI to Look at Your Web Browsing History Without a Warrant," Vice, May 13, 2020

5 Gosh, Shona, "Police in China, Dubai, and Italy are using these surveillance helmets to scan people for COVID-19 fever as they walk past and it may be our future normal," Business Insider, May 17, 2020

6 Eyewitness News, "Coronavirus News: NYC parks filled with people as police patrol social distancing," ABC7 New York, May 17, 2020

7 Randall, Ian, "Robots and drones equipped with infrared cameras could patrol holiday destinations and enforce social distancing rules under new EU plans to save the summer break," Daily Mail, May 14, 2020

8 Fowler, Bella, "Coronavirus Australia: Dramatic arrest of a mother protesting in Sydney shocks bystanders," News.com.au, May 10, 2020

9 Abrahamson, Rachel Paula, "Heartbreaking photo shows French preschoolers playing in chalk squares," TODAY, May 13, 2020

10 Taylor, Emma, "A fashion brand showcased a range of designer face masks at Paris Fashion Week amid the global spread of coronavirus," Insider, February 28, 2020

11 Rose, Joel, "U.S. Field Hospitals Stand Down, Most Without Treating Any COVID-19 Patients," NPR, All Things Considered, May 7, 2020

12 "Coronavirus: Hundreds of Level 3 Parties Busted by Police," Newshub.co.nz, May 3, 2020

out by the very authorities and media propagandists they pretend to oppose. I don't know exactly why, but that stuff makes me particularly cranky.

I'll provide you with a few examples.

The militant "Portland anti-fascists" who the corporate media fell in love with and made famous for bravely fighting off the Trump-loving Putin-Nazi Menace over the course of the last four years, as soon as the Corona-Fascism began, did what all true anti-fascists do when the state goes full-blown fascist … no, they did not "smash the state," or "occupy the streets," or anything like that. They masked-up and started making vegan hand sanitizer.[13]

Popular Internet "anti-imperialists" started accusing everyone opposing the lockdown of being part of some far-right Republican plot to "promote mass death under the banner of freedom," or to "normalize death" to benefit the rich, or being members of a "death cult," or something.[14]

Celebrity socialists took to Twitter to warn that we would "shortly have the blood of thousands of people on our hands,"[15] and call us "anti-vaxxers" and "flat earth fucks."[16] Indie political and military analysts patiently explained why governments needed to be able to pull people out of their homes against their will and quarantine them.[17] Anarchist anthropologists averred that the lockdown wasn't damaging the productive economy; it was only damaging the "bullshit economy," and those complaining about being out of work were people whose work is "largely useless."[18]

---

13 "The Oregonian, 'Portland anti-fascists are making hand sanitizer for essential workers, homeless residents'," Agency - An Anarchist PR Project, April 16, 2020

14 Khalek, Rania, "Anti-lockdown protests want to normalize mass death so we get used to the idea of our fellow citizens dying, all so the rich can get richer. They'd rather hundreds of thousands of us die than put in place even temporary welfare to stave off disaster. Sick!," Twitter, April 23, 2020

15 Galloway, George, "All those who have agitated for the collapse of the lockdown and quarantine whether of the 'left' or the 'right' will shortly have the blood of thousands of people on their hands. Mark my words, you will never be forgiven," Twitter, May 7, 2020

16 Galloway, George, "THIS THIS THIS you flat-earth fucks" (hysterically citing a tweet by Ranjeet Brar asserting that "Covid is real"), Twitter, April 14, 2020

17 Moon of Alabama, "China did this in phase 2 of the Wuhan quarantine because it was the only way to protect the families from their infected members. Without that policy Wuhan would not have ended the epidemic. Current test reliability is relativ high if test is immediate used when symptoms appear." Twitter, April 9, 2020

18 Graeber, David (R.I.P.)

Others simply looked away or sat by in silence as we were confined to our homes, and made to carry "permission papers" to walk to work or the corner grocery store,[19] and were beaten and arrested for not "social-distancing,"[20] and were otherwise bullied and humiliated for no justifiable reason whatsoever. (We are talking about a virus, after all, that even the official medical experts, e.g., the U.K.'s Chief Medic,[21] admit is more or less harmless to the vast majority of us, not the Bubonic Fucking Plague or some sort of Alien-Terrorist-Death-Flu … so spare me the "we-had-no-choice-but-to-go-totalitarian" rationalization.)

My intent is not merely to mock these people (i.e., these "radical," "anti-establishment" types who fell into formation and started goose-stepping because the media told us, "YOU'RE ALL GOING TO DIE!"), but also to use them as a clear example of how official narratives are born and take hold.

That's somewhat pertinent at the moment, because the "Brave New Normal" official narrative has been born, but it has not yet taken hold. What happens next will determine whether it does.

In order to understand how this works, imagine for a moment that you are one of these people who are normally skeptical of the government and the media, and that you consider yourself an anti-authoritarian, or at least a friend of the working classes, and now you are beginning to realize that there is no Alien-Terrorist-Death-Flu (just as there were no "WMDs," no "Russian hackers," no "pee-tape," etc.), and so it dawns on you that you've been behaving like a hysterical, brainwashed, fascist minion of the very establishment you supposedly oppose … or at the very least like an abject coward. Imagine how you might feel right now.

You would probably feel pretty foolish, right? And more than a little ashamed of yourself. So, OK, what would do about that?

19 "Coronavirus lockdown in France: Can you tick several boxes on your permission form?" ("There are seven legitimate reasons to leave home under France's current lockdown restrictions. They can all be found on the government's official permission form – accessible to print or on your smartphone – which people must carry on them at all times when outside."), The Local, April 6, 2020

20 Moore, Tina, Lee Brown and Aaron Feis, "Taser-wielding NYPD cop punches bystander during social-distancing bust," New York Post, May 3, 2020

21 Black, Catte, "WATCH: UK Chief Medic confirms (again) covid19 harmless to vast majority," OffGuardian, May 15, 2020

Well, you would have a couple of options.

Option Number One would be, admit what you did, apologize to whomever you have to, and try like hell not to do it again.

Not many people are going to choose this option.

Most people are going to choose Option Number Two, which is to desperately try to deny what they did, or desperately rationalize what they did (and in many cases are still actively doing).

Now, this is not as easy at it sounds, because doing that means they will have to continue to believe (or at least pretend to believe) that there *is* an Alien-Terrorist-Death-Flu which is going to kill hundreds of millions of people the moment we stop locking everyone down, and forcing them to "social distance," and so on. They will have to continue to pretend to believe that this Alien-Terrorist-Death-Flu exists, even though they know it doesn't.

And this is where that Orwellian "doublethink" comes in. People (i.e., these "anti-authoritarians," not to mention the majority of the "normal" public) are not going to want to face the fact that they have been behaving like a bunch of fascists, or cowards, for no justifiable reason whatsoever.

So what they are going to do, instead, is desperately pretend that their behavior was justified and that the propaganda they have been swallowing, and regurgitating, was not propaganda, but rather, "the Truth."

In other words, in order to avoid their shame, they are going to do everything in their power to reify the official narrative and delegitimize anyone attempting to expose it as the fiction that it is. They are going to join in with the corporate media that are calling us "extremists,"[22] "conspiracy theorists,"[23] "anti-vaxxers,"[24] and other such

---

22 Wilson, Jason and Robert Evans, "Revealed: major anti-lockdown group's links to America's far right," The Guardian, May 8, 2020

23 Baumgärtner, Maik, Felix Bohr, Roman Höfner, Timo Lehmann, Ann-Katrin Müller, Sven Röbel, Marcel Rosenbach, Jonas Schaible, Wolf Wiedmann-Schmidt and Steffen Winter, "Protests in Germany See Fringe Mix with the Mainstream, "Der Spiegel, May 14, 2020 ("At demonstrations and on the internet, both the far-left and the far-right have converged in their agitation against measures taken to limit the spread of the coronavirus. In a disturbing development, their conspiracy theories are also reaching the mainstream.")

24 Dearden, Lizzie, "Coronavirus protests: Jeremy Corbyn's brother among protesters arrested at Hyde Park 'mass gathering'," Independent, May 16, 2020 ("Conspiracy theorists and anti-vaxxers gathered at Speakers' Corner on Saturday for one of dozens of 'mass gatherings' organised across Britain to oppose lockdown restrictions.")

epithets. They are going to accuse those of us on the Left of aligning with "far-Right Republican militias,"[25] and "Boogaloo acceleration-ists,"[26] and of being members of the Russian-backed "Querfront,"[27] and assorted other horrible things meant to scare errant leftists into line.

Above all, they are going to continue to insist, notwithstanding all the evidence to the contrary, that we are "under attack" by a "kill-er virus" which could "strike again at any time," and so we have to maintain at least some level of totalitarianism and paranoia, or else … well, you know, "the terrorists win."

It is this reification of the official narrative by those too ashamed to admit what they did (and try to determine why they did it), and not the narrative or the propaganda itself, that will eventually es-tablish the "Brave New Normal" as "reality" (assuming the process works as smoothly as it did with the "War on Terror," the "War on Populism," and the "Cold War" narratives). The facts, the data, the "science" won't matter. Reality is consensus reality … and a new con-sensus is being formed at the moment.

There is still a chance (right now, not months from now) for these people (some of whom are rather influential) to stand up and say, "Whoops! I screwed up and went all Nazi there for a bit." But I seriously doubt that is going to happen.

It's much more likely that the Brave New Normal (or some inter-mittent, scaled-down version of it) will gradually become our new "reality."

People will get used to being occasionally "locked down," and being ordered to wear masks and not to touch each other, and to standing in designated circles and boxes, like they got used to the "anti-Terrorism measures," and believing that Trump is a "Russian asset."

25 Perkns, Tom, "Michigan: rightwing militia groups to protest stay-at-home orders," The Guard-ian, May 13, 2020

26 "This Week in Fascism #57: Boogaloo News Bears," It's Going Down, May 6, 2020 ("Welcome, fellow antifascists! This week, we've got Boogaloo accelerationists showing up to ReOpen protests, threatening to shoot the police, getting arrested with pipebombs, and networking with abor-tion-clinic bombers")

27 Meisner, Matthias, "Querfront-Protest vor der Volksbühne - Wie die ARD Verschwörungsthe-oretikern auf den Leim ging," Der Tagesspiegel, April 21, 2020 (Transl. "Third Position protest in front of the Volksbühne – How the ARD conspiracy theorists fell for it.")

The coming economic depression will be blamed on the Alien-Terrorist-Death-Flu, rather than on the lockdown that caused it. Millions of people will be condemned to extreme poverty, or debt-enslaved for the rest of their lives, but they'll be too busy trying to survive to mount any kind of broad resistance.

The children, of course, won't know any better. They will grow up with their "isolation boxes," and "protective barriers," and "contact tracing," and will live in constant low-grade fear of another killer virus, or terrorist attack, or Russian-backed white supremacist uprising, or whatever boogeyman might next appear to menace the global capitalist empire, which, it goes without saying, will be just fine.

Me, I'll probably remain kind of cranky, but I will try to find the humor in it all. Bear with me ... that might take a while.

The Minneapolis Putsch

June 1, 2020

Well, it looks like the Resistance's long-anticipated "Second Civil War" has finally begun … more or less exactly on cue.

Rioting has broken out across the nation. People are looting and burning stores and attacking each other in the streets. Robocops are beating, tear-gassing, and shooting people with non-lethal projectiles. State National Guards have been deployed, curfews imposed, "emergencies" declared. Secret Servicemen are fighting back angry hordes attempting to storm the White House. Trump is tweeting from an "underground bunker."[1] Opportunist social media pundits on both sides of the political spectrum are whipping people up into white-eyed frenzies. Americans are at each other's throats, divided by identity politics, consumed by rage, hatred, and fear.

Things couldn't be going better for the Resistance if they had scripted it themselves.

Actually, they did kind of script it themselves. Not the murder of poor George Floyd, of course. Racist police have been murdering Black people for as long as there have been racist police. No, the Resistance didn't manufacture racism. They just spent the majority of the last four years creating and promoting an official narrative which casts most Americans as "white supremacists" who literally elected Hitler president, and who want to turn the country into a racist dictatorship.

According to this official narrative, which has been relentlessly disseminated by the corporate media, the neoliberal intelligentsia, the culture industry, and countless hysterical, Trump-hating loonies, the Russians put Donald Trump in office with those DNC emails they never hacked and some division-sowing Facebook ads that supposedly hypnotized Black Americans into refusing to come out and vote for Clinton.

Putin purportedly ordered this personally, as part of his plot to "destroy democracy." The plan was always for President Hitler to embolden his white-supremacist followers into launching the "RaHoWa," or the "Boogaloo," after which Trump would declare martial law, dissolve the legislature, and pronounce himself Führer. Then they would start rounding up and murdering the Jews, and the Blacks, and Mexicans, and other minorities ... according to this twisted liberal fantasy.

I've been covering the roll-out and dissemination of this official narrative since 2016, and have documented much of it in my essays, so I won't reiterate all that here. Let's just say, I'm not exaggerating, much. After four years of more or less constant conditioning, millions of Americans believe this fairy tale, despite the fact that there is absolutely zero evidence whatsoever to support it.

Which is not exactly a mystery or anything. It would be rather surprising if they didn't believe it. We're talking about the most formidable official propaganda machine in the history of official propaganda machines.

And now the propaganda is paying off.

The protesting and rioting that typically follows the murder of an unarmed Black person by the cops has mushroomed into "an international uprising"[2] cheered on by the corporate media, corporations, and the liberal establishment, who don't normally tend to support such uprisings, but they've all had a sudden change of heart, or spiritual or political awakening, and are down for some serious property damage, and looting, and "preventative self-defense," if that's what it takes to bring about justice and restore America to the peaceful, prosperous, non-white-supremacist paradise it was until the Russians put Donald Trump in office.

In any event, the Resistance media have dropped their breathless coverage of the non-existent Corona-Holocaust to breathlessly cover the "revolution." The American police, who just last week were national heroes for risking their lives to beat up, arrest, and generally intimidate maskless "lockdown violators," are now the fascist foot soldiers of the Trumpian Reich.

The Nike corporation produced a commercial urging people to

---

2 McCurry, Justin, Josh Taylor, Eleanor Ainge Roy and Michael Safi, "George Floyd: protests take place in cities around the world," The Guardian, June 1, 2020

smash the windows of their Nike stores and steal their sneakers.[3] Liberal journalists took to Twitter, calling on rioters to "burn that shit down!" … until the rioters reached their gated community and started burning down their local Starbucks.[4]

Hollywood celebrities are masking up and going full-black bloc, and doing legal support.[5] Chelsea Clinton is teaching children about BLM David and Racist Goliath.[6] John Cusack's bicycle was attacked by the pigs.[7] I haven't checked on Rob Reiner yet, but I assume he is assembling Molotov cocktails in the basement of a Resistance safe house somewhere in Hollywood Hills.

Look, I'm not saying the neoliberal Resistance orchestrated or staged these riots, or "denying the agency" of the folks in the streets. Whatever else is happening out there, a lot of very angry Black people are taking their frustration out on the cops, and on anyone and anything else that represents racism and injustice to them.

This happens in America from time to time. America is still a racist society. Most African-Americans are descended from slaves. Legal racial discrimination was not abolished until the 1960s, which isn't that long ago in historical terms.

I was born in the segregated American South, with the segregated schools, and all the rest of it. I don't remember it — I was born in 1961 — but I do remember the years right after it. The South didn't magically change overnight in July of 1964. Nor did the North's variety of racism, which, yes, is subtler, but no less racist.

So I have no illusions about racism in America. But I'm not really talking about racism in America. I'm talking about how racism in America has been cynically instrumentalized, not by the Russians,

---

3 *Gallucci, Nicole, "Nike urges people to stand against racism in striking new ad," Mashable, May 30, 2020*

4 *"The Epitome of Rioting Irony and Ignorance in One Tweet - ESPN NBA Reporter Chris Martin Palmer made a fool out of himself with a pair of Tweets, one of which exploded in his face," Mish Talk, May 31, 2020*

5 *Alexander, Bryan, "Kanye, Banksy, Drake and more stars take action following George Floyd's death," USA Today, May 31, 2020*

6 *Clinton, Chelsea, "Getting ready for zoom Sunday school (lesson this week is David & Goliath) and talking to kids about why Marc and I are contributing daily to @bailproject. Please contribute to this and similar local efforts in your community if you're able to. #BlackLivesMatter #JusticeForGeorgeFloyd," Twitter, May 31, 2020*

7 *Haring, Bruce, "John Cusack Allegedly Attacked By Police While Filming – Watch Video Of Incident," Deadline, May 31, 2020*

but by the so-called Resistance, in order to delegitimize Trump and, more importantly, everyone who voted for him, as a bunch of "white supremacists" and "racists."

Fomenting racial division has been the Resistance's strategy from the very beginning. A quote attributed to Joseph Goebbels, "accuse the other side of that which you are guilty," is particularly apropos in this case. From the moment Trump won the Republican nomination, the corporate media and the rest of the Resistance have been telling us the man is literally Hitler, and that his plan is to foment racial hatred among his "white supremacist base," and eventually stage some sort of "Reichstag" event, declare martial law and pronounce himself dictator. They've been telling us this story over and over, on television, in the liberal press, on social media, in books, movies, and everywhere else they could possibly tell it.

So, before you go out and join the "uprising," take a quick look at the headlines today, turn on CNN or MSNBC, and think about that for just a minute. I don't mean to spoil the party, but they have preparing you for this for the last four years.

Not you Black folks. I'm not talking to you. I wouldn't presume to tell you what to do. I'm talking to white folks like myself, who are cheering on the rioting and looting, and coming out to "help" you with it, but who will be back home in their gated communities when the ashes have cooled, and the corporate media are gone, and the cops return to "police" your neighborhoods.

OK, and this is where I have to restate (for the benefit of my partisan readers) that I'm not a fan of Donald Trump, and that I think he's a narcissistic ass clown, and a glorified con man, and … blah blah blah, because so many people have been so polarized by insane propaganda and mass hysteria that they can't even read or think anymore, and so just scan whatever articles they encounter to see whose "side" the author is on and then mindlessly celebrate or excoriate it.

If you're doing that, let me help you out … whichever side you're on, I'm not on it.

I realize that's extremely difficult for a lot of folks to comprehend these days, which is part of the point I've been trying to make. I'll try again, as plainly as I can.

America is still a racist country, but America is no more racist today than it was when Barack Obama was president. A lot of American police are brutal, but they are no more brutal than when Obama was president.

America didn't radically change the day Donald Trump was sworn into office. All that has changed is the official narrative. And it will change back as soon as Trump is gone and the ruling classes have no further use for it.

And that will be the end of the War on Populism, and we'll switch back to the War on Terror, or maybe the Brave New Pathologized Normal ... or whatever Orwellian official narrative the folks at GloboCap have in store for us.

The New (Pathologized) Totalitarianism

June 29, 2020

It was always going to come to this … mobs of hysterical, hate-drunk brownshirts hunting down people not wearing masks and trying to get them fired from their jobs, "NO MASK, NO SERVICE" signs outside stores,[1] security staff stopping the mask-less from entering,[2] paranoid pod people pointing and shrieking at the sight of maskless shoppers in their midst,[3] goon squads viciously attacking and arresting them …[4]

Welcome to the Brave New Normal.

And it isn't just the Maskenpflicht-Sturmabteilung. The new official narrative is omnipresent. The corporate media are pumping out hysteria about "Covid-19 hospitalizations" (i.e., anyone admitted to a hospital, for any reason, who tested positive for the coronavirus)[5] and "major incidents" (i.e., people at the beach).[6] Police are manning makeshift social-distancing-monitoring watchtowers in London.[7] There are propaganda posters and billboards everywhere, repeating the same neo-Goebbelsian slogans, reinforcing the manufactured mass hysteria. Dissent and nonconformity are being pathologized, "diagnosed" as psychopathy and paranoia.[8]

---

1 Perry, David M., "No shirt, no shoes, no mask, no service," CNN, May 22, 2020

2 Woods, Amanda, "Man refusing to wear mask fights his way into Walmart in Florida," New York Post, June 22, 2020

3 Sheehy, Kate, "Viral video shows Staten Island store mob screaming at woman without mask," New York Post, May 25, 2020

4 Video no longer available; censored by YouTube.

5 Knightly, Kit, "Covid19 Death Figures 'A Substantial Over-Estimate'," OffGuardian, April 5, 2020

6 Mee, Emily, "Major incident declared in Bournemouth as thousands of people flock to beaches," Sky News, June 25, 2020

7 Johnson, Luke, "This is the latest lockdown lunacy from govt: police patrol towers on Oxford St pavement - enforcing 2m distancing," Twitter, June 26, 2020

8 Dolan, Eric W., "Psychopathic traits linked to non-compliance with social distancing guidelines amid the coronavirus pandemic," PsyPost, June 7, 2020

Mandatory vaccinations are coming.[9]

You didn't think they were kidding, did you, when they started introducing the Brave New Normal official narrative back in April and March? They told us, clearly, what was coming. They told us life was going to change, forever. They locked us down inside our homes. They ordered churches[10] and synagogues[11] closed. They ordered the police to abuse and arrest us if we violated their arbitrary orders.[12] They closed the schools, parks, beaches, restaurants, cafés, theaters, clubs, anywhere that people gather. They ripped children out of their mother's arms,[13] beat and arrested other mothers for the crime of "wearing their masks improperly,"[14] dragged maskless passengers off of public buses,[15] gratuitously beat and arrested people for not "social-distancing" on the sidewalk,[16] shackled people with ankle monitors,[17] and intimidated everyone with robots and drones.[18] They outlawed protests, and then hunted down people who attended them and harassed them at their homes.[19] They started tracking everyone's contacts and movements.[20] They drafted new "emergency" laws to allow them to forcibly quarantine people.[21]

9 Grant, Jason, "State Bar Group Calls for 'Mandatory' COVID-19 Vaccinations, Regardless of Objections," New York Law Journal, May 28, 2020

10 Guzman, Joseph, "Pastor arrested for holding church services despite coronavirus quarantine order," The Hill, March 30, 2020

11 "Coronavirus Update: 8 Arrested In Monsey For Violating Social Distancing Emergency Orders," CBS New York, April 9, 2020

12 Sternlicht, Alexandra, "Arrested For Violating Coronavirus Stay-At-Home Mandates: Police Are Jailing Alleged Scofflaws," Forbes, April 6, 2020

13 Fowler, Bella, "Coronavirus Australia: Dramatic arrest of a mother protesting in Sydney shocks bystanders," News.com.au, May 10, 2020

14 Naughtie, Andrew, "Video shows police pushing woman to the ground and handcuffing her in front of her young child 'for not wearing mask properly'," Independent, May 14, 2020

15 Murphy, Darryl C., "Police forcibly eject man without face mask from SEPTA bus," WHYY/PBS, April 10, 2020

16 Moore, Tina, Lee Brown and Aaron Feis, "Taser-wielding NYPD cop punches bystander during social-distancing bust," New York Post, May 3, 2020

17 Kallingal, Mallika, "Ankle monitors ordered for Louisville, Kentucky residents exposed to Covid-19 who refuse to stay home," CNN, April 3, 2020

18 Lutz, Eric, "Coronavirus Surveillance Is Entering Dystopian Territory," Vanity Fair, April 9, 2020

19 Video documentation no longer available; Aleshia Yates' account suspended by Twitter

20 Lewis, Paul, David Conn and David Pegg, "UK government using confidential patient data in coronavirus response," The Guardian, April 12, 2020

21 Knightly, Kit, "Coronavirus Crackdown," OffGuardian, March 21, 2020

They did all this openly. They publicized it. It's not like they were hiding anything. They told us exactly what was coming, and advised us to shut up and follow orders.

Tragically, most people have done just that.

In the space of four months, GloboCap has successfully imposed totalitarianism — pathologized totalitarianism — on societies across the world. It isn't traditional totalitarianism, with a dictator and a one-party system, and so on. It is subtler and more insidious than that. But it is totalitarianism nonetheless.

GloboCap could not have achieved this without the approval (or at least the acquiescence) of the vast majority of the masses. The coronavirus mass hysteria was a masterstroke of propaganda, but propaganda isn't everything. No one is really fooled by propaganda, or not for long, in any event. As Gilles Deleuze and Félix Guattari noted in the opening of *Anti-Oedipus*:

> "The masses were not innocent dupes. At a certain point, under a certain set of conditions, they wanted fascism, and it is this perversion of the desire of the masses that needs to be accounted for."

I am not going to explore the "perversion of the desire of the masses" here in this essay, but I do want to dig into the new pathologized totalitarianism a little bit.

Now, I'm going to assume that you understand that the official "apocalyptic pandemic" narrative is predicated on propaganda, wild speculation, and mass hysteria, and that by now you're aware that we are dealing with a virus that causes mild to moderate flu-like symptoms (or absolutely no symptoms at all) in about 95% of those infected, and that over 99.5% survive, and thus is clearly no cause for widespread panic or justification for the totalitarian "emergency measures" that have been imposed.

I am also going to assume that you watched as GloboCap switched off the "deadly pandemic" to accommodate the BLM protests, then switched it back on as soon as they subsided, and that you noted how the propaganda shifted to "cases" when the death count finally became a little too embarrassing to continue to hype.

So, I won't waste your time debunking the propaganda. Let's talk pathologized totalitarianism.

*

The genius of the new pathologized totalitarianism is like that old joke about the Devil; his best trick was convincing us that he does not exist. Pathologized totalitarianism appears to emanate from nowhere, and everywhere, simultaneously, and thus, technically, it does *not* exist. It cannot exist. Because no one is responsible for it … because everyone is responsible for it.

Mass hysteria is its lifeblood. It feeds on existential fear. "Science" is its rallying cry. Not actual science, not provable facts, but "Science" as a new kind of deity whose Name is invoked to silence heretics, or to ease the discomfort of the cognitive dissonance that results from desperately trying to believe the absurdities of the official narrative.

The other genius of it (from GloboCap's perspective) is that it is inexhaustible, endlessly recyclable.

Unlike previous official enemies, the "deadly virus" could be *any* virus, or any pathogen whatsoever. All they have to do from now on is "discover" some "novel" micro-organism that is highly contagious (or that mimics some other micro-organism that we already have), and wave it in front of people's faces. Then they can crank up the Fear Machine, and start projecting hundreds of millions of deaths if everyone doesn't do exactly as they're told. They can run this schtick … well, pretty much forever, anytime the working classes get restless, or an unauthorized president gets elected, or just for the sheer sadistic fun of it.

Look, I don't mean to be depressing, but, seriously, spend an hour on the Internet, or talk to one of your hysterical friends that wants to make mask-wearing mandatory, permanently. This is the mentality of the Brave New Normal … irrationally paranoid and authoritarian. So, no, the future isn't looking very bright for anyone not prepared to behave as if the world were one big infectious disease ward.

I have interacted with a number of very paranoid corona-totalitarians recently, just as a kind of social experiment. They behave exactly like members of a cult.

When challenged with facts and basic logic, first, they bombard you with media propaganda and speculation from "medical experts." Then, after you debunk that nonsense, they attempt to emotionally manipulate you by sharing their heartbreaking personal accounts of the people their therapists' brother-in-laws' doctors had to helplessly watch as they died in agony when their lungs and hearts mysteriously exploded. Then, when you don't bite down on that, they start hysterically shrieking paranoia at you ("JUST WAIT UNTIL THEY INTUBATE YOU!" "KEEP YOUR SPITTLE AWAY FROM ME!") and barking orders and slogans at you ("JUST WEAR THE GODDAMN MASK, YOU BABY!" ... "NO SHOES, NO SHIRT, NO MASK, NO SERVICE!")

Which, OK, that would be kind of funny (or terribly sad), if these paranoid people were not just mouthpieces echoing the voice of the official power (i.e., GloboCap) that is transforming what is left of society into a paranoid, pathologized, totalitarian nightmare right before our very eyes. They're kind of like the "woman in red" in *The Matrix*. When you are talking to them, you're not talking to them. You're talking to the agents. You're talking to the machines. Try it sometime. You'll see what I mean. It's like talking to a single algorithm that is running in millions of people's brains.

I can't lie to you. I'm not very hopeful. No one who understands the attraction (the seduction) of totalitarianism is. Much as we may not like to admit it, it is exhilarating, liberating, being part of the mob, surrendering the burden of personal autonomy and individual responsibility, fusing with a fanatical movement that is ushering in a new "reality" backed by the sheer brute force of the state ... or the supranational global-capitalist empire.

It is irresistible, that attraction, to most of us. The chance to be a part of something like that, to unleash one's hatred on those who refuse to go along with the new religion ... to publicly ridicule them, to humiliate them, to segregate them from normal society, to hunt them down and get them fired from their jobs, to cheer as the police abuse and arrest them, to diagnose them as "abnormal" and "inferior," these social deviants, these subhuman "others," who dare to challenge the authority of the Party, or the Church, or the State, or the Reich, or "Science."

Plus, in the eyes of GloboCap and their millions of fanatical, slogan-chanting followers, such non-mask-wearing deviants are dangerous. They are like a disease. An infestation. A sickness in the social body. If they refuse to conform, they will have to be dealt with ... you know, quarantined, or something like that. Or they can just surrender, join the "New Normal," and stop acting like babies and "wear a goddamn mask."

After all, it's just a harmless piece of cloth.

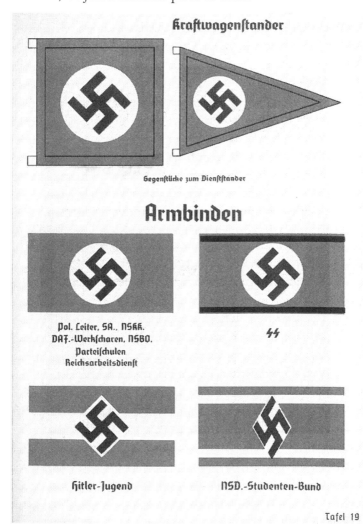

GloboCap Über Alles

July 20, 2020

So, how are you enjoying the "New Normal" so far? Is it paranoid and totalitarian enough for you? If not, well, hold on, because it's just getting started. There's plenty more totalitarianism and paranoia still to come.

I know, it feels like forever already, but, in fact, it has only been a few months since GloboCap started rolling out the new official narrative. We're still in the early stages of it.

The phase we're in now is kind of like where we were back in February of 2002, a few months after the 9/11 attacks, when everyone was still in shock, the Patriot Act was just a few months old, and the Department of Homeland Security hadn't even been created yet.

You remember how it was back then, when GloboCap was introducing the official "War on Terror" narrative, don't you?

OK, maybe you do and maybe you don't. Maybe you're too young to remember, or you were caught up in the excitement of the moment and weren't paying attention to the details.

But some of us remember it clearly. We remember watching (and futilely protesting) as GloboCap prepared to invade, destabilize, and restructure the Middle East, as countries throughout the global capitalist empire implemented "emergency security measures" (which, 18 years later, are still in effect), as the corporate media bombarded us with official propaganda, jacked up The Fear, and otherwise prepared us for the previous "New Normal" … some of us remember all that clearly.

Personally, I remember listening to a liberal academic on NPR calmly speculating that, just hypothetically, at some point in the not-too-distant future, we might need to "sacrifice our principles" a bit, and torture some people, to "keep America safe."

I recounted this to other Americans at the time, among my many other concerns about where the post-9/11 mass hysteria was heading. Most of them told me I was being paranoid, or that they didn't care, because we needed to do whatever was "necessary" to protect Americans, and, in any event, "the terrorists deserved it."

Shortly thereafter, I started making plans to get the hell out of the country.

I mention that, not to signal my "virtue" — leaving the USA didn't achieve anything, except for improving my standard of living — but to jog your memory, and maybe prompt you to compare that period to the one we are in now.

The parallels are overwhelming. The "state of emergency." The official propaganda. The mass hysteria. The mob mentality. The exaggeration of the actual threat. The police-state atmosphere. The suppression of dissent. The constant repetition of the new official narrative. The exhortative catchphrases and meaningless slogans. The confusion. The chaos. The existential fear. And so on.

It is all so very familiar.

I'm referring to the simulated pandemic, of course, but also to the racialized civil unrest and identitarian polarization that GloboCap has fomented throughout the USA, and, to varying degrees, the rest of the empire. I've been covering the War on Populism and GloboCap's "Trump-is-literally-Hitler" propaganda since 2016, so the civil unrest isn't terribly surprising. But, I confess, I did not see the fake plague coming. And running the two psy-ops together was brilliant.

The effect on people has been devastating. Everyone is either depressed or enraged, or in some stage of paranoid paralysis. Some have been so thoroughly terrorized that they are literally refusing to leave their houses. Others are lining up at gun shops. White people are getting down on their knees and publicly washing Black people's feet in "symbolic demonstrations of forgiveness."[1] Condiments are changing their names.[2]

It's like we're all trapped in a gratuitously didactic Netflix zombie-apocalypse series set in the world of *The Handmaid's Tale*, written, directed, and produced by Spike Lee.

---

1 Reimann, Nicolas, "No, Police Officers Didn't Wash Protesters' Feet In North Carolina," *Forbes*, June 14, 2020 ("The foot washing was done by white religious leaders—not police—as part of a ceremony that 'was a symbolic demonstration of forgiveness, solidarity and justice for all mankind.'"

2 Kesslen, Ben, "Aunt Jemima brand to change name, remove image that Quaker says is 'based on a racial stereotype'," *NBC News*, June 17, 2020

The official propaganda could not be more Orwellian, nor could people's willingness to go along with it. It doesn't even have to appear to make sense. Doublethink has taken over.

For example, most of the developed world has been in some form of totalitarian lockdown, and subjected to other police-state measures, like being beaten and arrested for not wearing a mask,[3] for no justifiable reason whatsoever, for going on the last five months, but, according to the corporate media and the millions of people they have apparently brainwashed, it's only now that Trump has sent his Homeland Security goons into Portland that, suddenly, "democracy is under attack!"[4]

But wait ... no, I take it back, the Orwellianism gets even more Orwellian. According to GloboCap and its sanctimonious minions, that sentence I just wrote about Portland is racist, because nearly everything you can imagine is racist, or a potential threat to public health.

Calling riots "riots" is racist.[5] Silence is racist.[6] Free speech is racist.[7] Refusing to wear a mask is racist.[8] The BLM protesters are immune to the virus, but other large gatherings (which, it goes without saying, are probably racist) all have to be banned.[9] Normality, as Americans knew it, is over, and it is never, ever, coming back, because white supremacy caused the pandemic.[10] Sweden, Norway,

---

3 *Video documentation no longer available; BeachMilk account deplatformed by Twitter.*

4 *Olmos, Sergio, Mike Baker, and Zolan Kanno-Youngs, "Federal Agents Unleash Militarized Crackdown on Portland," The New York Times, July 17, 2020*

5 *Steinmetz, Katy, "'A War of Words.' Why Describing the George Floyd Protests as 'Riots' Is So Loaded," TIME, June 8, 2020*

6 *Capatides, Christina, "White silence on social media: Why not saying anything is actually saying a lot," CBS News, June 3, 2020*

7 *Bragg, Billy, "'Cancel culture' doesn't stifle debate, but it does challenge the old order," The Guardian, July 10, 2020*

8 *"Letters to the Editor: How racism, bigotry and elitism may be driving mask resistance," Los Angeles Times, June 30, 2020*

9 *Schwartz, Ian, "NYC Mayor De Blasio: All Large Gatherings Banned Except For Black Lives Matter Protests, Real Clear Politics, July 9, 2020*

10 *Mac, Leslie, "I think now is a good time to start preparing ourselves for this intensive need for social distancing, masks, etc at least until Jan 2022. By prepare I mean mentally too because I know a lot of us have been clinging to some semblance of relief in 2021. It's not happening ... we are in the midst of the largest public health and financial crisis in history ... and make no mistake. White supremacy got us here lock, stock and barrel. White supremacy set these conditions, it brought this country directly from slavery to Trump." Twitter, July 13, 2020*

Denmark, and Finland (where life has been going on without mass hysteria) do not exist. They have never existed, and, if they ever did, they were probably racist. Talking on public transportation is deadly.[11] Interacting with children is potentially deadly, [12] as are most other forms of human interaction ... unless you're tearing down a racist statue, or burning down a local family business, while wearing a designer anti-racism mask.

Seriously, though, just like in 2002, when GloboCap was rolling out the official "War on Terror" narrative, the facts are all available to anyone who cares.[13] The falsification of Covid death statistics and hospital capacity figures, the unreliability of the tests, and so on ... it has all been repeatedly documented.

Anyone with a positive test result who later dies of any cause (including a fatal motorcycle accident[14]) is counted as a "Covid death."[15] Anyone admitted to a hospital for anything who tests positive for the virus is a "Covid hospitalization." And, I'm sorry to disappoint my liberal friends (assuming I have any left at this point), but systematic racism and police brutality did not suddenly begin in 2016.

What suddenly began in 2016 was a concerted effort on the part of GloboCap to put down a growing populist backlash against global capitalism and its soulless ideology. Yes, most of that backlash is neo-nationalist in character, but it also includes a significant number of old-fashioned lefty-types like myself, and a lot of other un-woke folks who aren't quite ready to embrace their new identities as interchangeable human commodities.

---

11 Andrews, Luke, "Wales BANS public transport users from talking on mobile phones, reading newspapers, eating food or running for the bus in new Covid rules," Daily Mail Online, July 16, 2020

12 O'Donovan, Caroline, "Back To School: Teachers Are Ready To Quit Rather Than Put Their Lives At Risk," Buzzfeed News, July 17, 2020

13 Knightly, Kit, "UK government (finally) admits Covid statistics are inaccurate," OffGuardian, July 17, 2020

14 "Florida Man Killed in Motorcycle Accident Recorded as 'COVID Death'," 21st Century Wire, July 19, 2020

15 Loke, Yoon K. and Carl Heneghan, "Why no-one can ever recover from COVID-19 in England – a statistical anomaly," The Centre for Evidence-based Medicine, July 16, 2020 ("By this Public Health England (PHE) definition, no one with COVID in England is allowed to ever recover from their illness. A patient who has tested positive, but successfully treated and discharged from hospital, will still be counted as a COVID death even if they had a heart attack or were run over by a bus three months later.")

We are experiencing the culmination of that effort (or what they hope is the culmination of that effort) to put down this motley populist insurgency and ensure that it never happens again.

GloboCap is teaching us a lesson. The lesson is:

> "This is what you get when you fuck around with GloboCap. This is what voting for Trump, Brexit, and all the rest of that 'populist' nonsense gets you … global pandemics, civil race wars, riots, lockdowns, economic depression, societal collapse, chaos, fear. Go ahead, fuck around with us some more. We will make you wear ridiculous face masks forever. We will paint little arrows and boxes on the floor to show you where to walk and stand. We will bankrupt your businesses, shut down your schools, psychologically torture your children. We'll inject them with any fucking thing we want. There is nothing you can do about it. We will make you get down on your knees and apologize for ever fucking with us, or we will stigmatize you as a 'racist,' sic our mobs of fanatics on you, and 'cancel' you and your entire family."

This, essentially, is the message that GloboCap is delivering to disobedient populists … left or right, it makes no difference. (GloboCap doesn't care which political labels we cling to or slap on each other.) It is our final warning to quit playing grab-ass, get with the global capitalist program, and start behaving, and thinking, as we're told … unless we want to get locked down again, ordered to wear things on our faces, and be otherwise ritually humiliated.

See, the so-called "New Normal" (i.e., the new ideological narrative that GloboCap is rolling out) is actually not that new at all. Or, OK, the pathologization part is — and I'll be paying close attention to that aspect of it — but, basically, it's just plain old totalitarianism.

It isn't state-totalitarianism, because our world isn't ruled by nation-states. It is ruled by global capitalism. We are being reminded of that fact at the moment … and being shown what happens if we start to forget it.

Where we go from here is anyone's guess. My hunch is, it is only going to get worse until they can get Trump out of office, which Americans are liable to help them do, simply to make the whole nightmare stop.

Once he's gone, they will probably retire the fake pandemic, call off the riots, and stage some sort of international celebration of the "Rebirth of Democracy," after which they can finally get back to the business of ruthlessly destabilizing, restructuring, and privatizing the planet, sanitizing history, curing humanity of racism, hatred, and other pathologies, and otherwise enforcing rigid conformity to global capitalist ideology.

partially correct predictions

Maybe they could get the *Hamilton* composer to write them a hip-hop *Deutschlandlied* to use as a supranational anthem. They could call it *GloboCap Über Alles* … it kind of has a ring to it, doesn't it?

The White Black Nationalist Color Revolution

July 29, 2020

So, the White Black Nationalist Color Revolution ("made possible in part by your friends at GloboCap") appears to be going extremely well. According to *Foreign Policy* magazine,[1] the Trump regime is clinging to power, but it's only a matter of time until the identitarian moderate rebels drive the Putin-backed fascists out of office and restore democracy to the Western world.

Yes, that's right, just when it looked like the corporate-sponsored, totally organic, peaceful uprising against racism was over, and the Russo-fascist Trump regime had survived, the Global Capitalist Anarchists of Portland and other militant "Resistance" cells have launched a devastating counter-attack against assorted fascist building facades, fascist fences, and stores, and so on, and are now going mano-a-mano in the streets with heavily-armed Putin-Nazi goon squads.

According to *The Guardian*,[2] and other members of the underground "Resistance" media, peaceful protesters in Portland have been attacking the fascists with rocks, bottles, improvised explosive devices, and other peaceful anti-racist projectiles. In Oakland, they peacefully set fire to the courthouse.[3] In Austin, Texas, a peaceful protester armed with an AK-47-style rifle was shot to death by a suspected fascist whose vehicle was peacefully swarmed by a mob

---

1 Snyder, Timothy, "In Portland, the Baby Fascists Have Shown Their Face," Foreign Policy, July 23, 2020

2 McGreal, Chris, "Portland: protesters bring down fence as confrontation with Trump agents rises," the Guardian, July 26, 2020

3 "Oakland protesters set fire to courthouse and vandalize," ABC News/Associated Press, July 26, 2020

after he "tried to aggressively drive past protesters."[4] In Los Angeles, peaceful anti-racism protesters have been whipped up into such a frenzy of righteous anti-fascist fervor that they are performing flying tackles on the cops, who then promptly beat the snot out of them.[5]

And so on … I think you get the picture.

Portland, Oregon, where just under 6% of the population is Black, has of course been at the vanguard of the revolution, as it has since the Russians stole the election from Hillary Clinton in 2016 by "in-fluencing" gullible African-Americans with a handful of ridiculous Facebook ads[6] and then installed Donald Trump and the rest of the Putin-Nazi Occupation Government in office.

Not only have local Antifa militants been tirelessly fighting gangs of neo-nationalist boneheads you've probably never heard of more or less around the clock since then, Portland is also the headquarters of most of the militant Antifa intelligentsia (characters like Alexander Reid Ross, an anti-fascist geography lecturer who inculcates kids with his paranoid theories about the international Duginist-Red-Brown conspiracy to take over the whole world and mass-murder the Jews).

So, naturally, Portland is now the epicenter of the White Black Nationalist Color Revolution.

But this isn't just the usual Portlandia silliness. This White Black Nationalist Color Revolution has been in the works for the last four years. Since the moment Trump won the Republican nomination, the global-capitalist ruling classes have been fomenting racialized polarization, Putin-Nazi paranoia, and other forms of mass hysteria in anticipation of the events of this summer.

The official propaganda has remained consistent. Both the liberal corporate media and the alternative left media have been predicting that Trump is going to go full-Hitler, impose martial law, proclaim himself *Führer*, and perpetrate some sort of racialized holocaust … for reasons they've never quite been able to explain.

---

4 *Danner, Chaz, "What We Know About the Austin BLM Protest Shooting," New York Magazing, Intelligencer, July 27, 2020*

5 *"Violent clashes broke out among police and demonstrators in downtown L.A. amid protests at City Hall and the Federal Building," KTLA News, July 26, 2020*

6 *Shane, Scott and Sheera Frankel, "Russian 2016 Influence Operation Targeted African-Americans on Social Media," The New York Times, December 17, 2018*

He hasn't, of course, so the global-capitalist ruling classes had no choice but to unleash a shit-storm of civil unrest to goad him into overreacting … which, no surprise, he was stupid enough to do.

Ordering the goon squads into the streets might delight his hard-core right-wing base, but it will alienate the majority of "normal" Americans, who aren't especially fond of goon squads (unless they're doing their thing in some faraway country). Most importantly, it will motivate all those non-Clinton-voting Obama voters to go out and vote for "Slappy" Joe Biden, or whichever corporate puppet the Democrats have replaced him with by November 3.

That seems to be the general strategy.

Now, regardless of whether they can pull this off (and whatever your feelings about GloboCap as a de facto hegemonic empire), you have to at least admire their audacity. The part where the mayors of major cities stood down and otherwise hamstrung their cops, and let the "peaceful protesters" run amok, was particularly audacious, in my opinion.

That was a serious gamble on GloboCap's part. Trump could have resisted the urge to go totalitarian and just called their bluff. He could have made a speech explaining to Americans exactly how these color revolutions work, how this one is going right by the book, and why he wasn't going to take the bait, and left the cities in question to their own devices (until the mayors were forced to restore order themselves). But no, tactical genius that he is, he had to order in the goon squads, which, of course, is exactly what the "Resistance" wanted. Now he's got cities like Philadelphia threatening to order their police to confront and attempt to arrest the federal agents.[7]

I assume you see where all this is heading.

The other part that was particularly tricky was segueing from the original protests following the murder of George Floyd by the cops, most of which were authentic expressions of frustration and outrage by actual Black people about systemic racism and police brutality (both of which are very real, of course) to the orchestrated civil unrest that followed, most of which is being coordinated, funded, and carried out by White people.

---

7 Mock, Brenton, *"Philadelphia's Top Prosecutor Is Prepared to Arrest Federal Agents,"* Bloomberg *News, July 22, 2020*

That was also a rather bold move, but, as the generous folks at The Ford Foundation put it back in July of 2016 when they announced that they would be overseeing the funneling of $100 million to organizations in the Black Lives Matter movement:[8]

"We want to nurture bold experiments."

Oh, and speaking of bold experiments, what better setting could there be for a White Black Nationalist Color Revolution than a fake apocalyptic plague that has wrecked the economies of most Western countries, terrorized the masses into mindless obedience, and destabilized entire societies to the point where fanatical, GloboCap-brainwashed brownshirts are macing people in the face for not wearing masks at outdoor picnics[9] and wishing death on families if the mothers won't put masks on their kids?[10]

No, credit where credit is due to GloboCap. At this point, not only the United States but countries all throughout the global-capitalist empire are in such a state of mass hysteria and so hopelessly politically polarized that hardly anyone can see the textbook color revolution that is being executed, openly, right in front of our faces.

Or … OK, actually, most Trump supporters see it, but most of them, like Trump himself, have mistaken Antifa, Black Lives Matter, and the Democratic Party and their voters for the enemy, when they are merely pawns in GloboCap's game.

Most liberals and leftists cannot see it at all, literally, as in they cannot perceive it. Like Dolores in the HBO *Westworld* series, "it doesn't look like anything" to them. They actually believe they are fighting fascism, that Donald Trump, a narcissistic, word-salad-spewing former game show host, is literally the Return of Adolf Hitler, and that somehow (presumably with the help of Putin) he has staged the current civil unrest, like the Nazis staged the Reichstag fire![11] (*The New York Times* will never tire of that one, nor will their liberal and

---

8 Black, Gabriel, *"Billionaires back Black Lives Matter," World Socialist Web Site, October 11, 2016*

9 *"Mask Insanity - Horrible Woman Maces Couple Enjoying Picnic," TMZ, July 25, 2020*

10 *Tweet no longer available, SallyKP account suspended.*

11 Cohen, Roger, *"American Catastrophe Through German Eyes," The New York Times, July 24, 2020*

leftist readers, who have been doing battle with an endless series of imaginary Hitlers since ... well, since Hitler.)

I've been repeating it my columns for the last four years, and I'm going to repeat it once again. What we are experiencing is not the "return of fascism." It is the global-capitalist empire restoring order, putting down the populist insurgency that took them by surprise in 2016.

The White Black Nationalist Color Revolution, the fake apocalyptic plague, all the insanity of 2020 ... it has been in the pipeline all along. It has been there since the moment Trump won the election.

No, it is not about Trump, the man. It has never been about Trump, the man, no more than the Obama presidency was ever about Obama, the man. GloboCap needs to crush Donald Trump, and moreover, to make an example of him, not because he is a threat to the empire (he isn't), but because he became a symbol of populist resistance to global capitalism and its increasingly aggressive "woke" ideology. It is this populist resistance to its ideology that GloboCap is determined to crush, no matter how much social chaos and destruction they unleash in the process.

In one of my essays from last October, *Trumpenstein Must Be Destroyed*, I made this prediction about the year ahead:

> "2020 is for all the marbles. The global capitalist ruling classes either crush this ongoing populist insurgency or God knows where we go from here. Try to see it through their eyes for a moment. Picture four more years of Trump ... second-term Trump ... Trump unleashed. Do you really believe they're going to let that happen, that they are going to permit this populist insurgency to continue for another four years? They are not. What they are going to do is use all their power to destroy the monster, not Trump the man, but Trump the symbol. They are going to drown us in impeachment minutiae, drip, drip, drip, for the next twelve months. The liberal corporate media are going to go full-Goebbels. They are going to whip up so much mass hysteria that people won't be able to think. They are going to pit us one against the other, and force us onto

one or the other side of a simulated conflict (Democracy versus the Putin-Nazis) to keep us from perceiving the actual conflict (Global Capitalism versus Populism). They are going to bring us to the brink of civil war ..."

OK, I didn't see the fake plague coming, but, otherwise, how's my prediction holding up?

Invasion of the New Normals

August 9, 2020

They're here! No, not the pod people from *Invasion of the Body Snatchers*. We're not being colonized by giant alien fruit. I'm afraid it is a little more serious than that. People's minds are being taken over by a much more destructive and less otherworldly force, a force that transforms them overnight into aggressively paranoid, order-following, propaganda-parroting totalitarians.

You know the people I'm talking about. Some of them are probably your friends and family, people you have known for years, and who had always seemed completely rational, but who are now convinced that we need to radically alter the fabric of human society to protect ourselves from a virus that causes mild to moderate flu-like symptoms (or absolutely no symptoms whatsoever) in over 95% of those infected and that over 99.6% survive ... which, it goes without saying, is totally insane.

I have been calling them "corona-totalitarians," but I'm going to call them the "New Normals" from now on, as that more accurately evokes the pathologized-totalitarian ideology that they are systematically spreading.

At this point, I think it is important to do that, because, clearly, their ideological program has nothing to do with any actual virus, or any other actual public health threat. As is glaringly obvious to anyone whose mind has not been taken over yet, the "apocalyptic coronavirus pandemic" was always just a Trojan horse, a means of introducing the "New Normal," which they've been doing since the very beginning.

The official propaganda started in March and reached full intensity in early April. Suddenly, references to the "New Normal" were everywhere, not only in the leading corporate media (e.g., CNN,[1]

1 Sanchez, Ray, "America's 'new normal' will be anything but ordinary," CNN, April 17, 2020

NPR,[2] CNBC,[3] *The New York Times*,[4] *The Guardian*,[5] *The Atlantic*,[6] *Forbes*,[7] et al.), the IMF and the World Bank Group,[8] the WEF,[9] UN,[10] WHO,[11] CDC[12] (and the list goes on), but also on the blogs of athletic organizations,[13] global management consulting firms,[14] charter school websites,[15] and random YouTube videos.[16]

The slogan has been relentlessly repeated (in textbook totalitarian "big lie" fashion) for going on the past six months. We have heard it repeated so many times that many of us have forgotten how insane it is, the idea that the fundamental structure of society needs to be drastically and irrevocably altered on account of a virus that poses no threat to the vast majority of the human species.

And, make no mistake, that is exactly what the "New Normal" movement intends to do. "New Normalism" is a classic totalitarian movement (albeit with a pathological twist), and it is the goal of every totalitarian movement to radically, utterly transform society, to remake the world in its monstrous image.

2 Aubrey, Allison, "New Normal: How Will Things Change In Post Pandemic World, National Public Radio, Morning Edition, April 27, 2020

3 Higgins-Dunn, Noah, "New York moves to a 'new normal' as Gov. Cuomo outlines gradual reopening of businesses," CNBC, April 15, 2020

4 Fisher, Max, "What Will Our New Normal Feel Like? Hints Are Beginning to Emerge," The New York Times, April 21, 2020

5 Meek, James, "Our new normal: why so many of us feel unprepared for lockdown life," The Guardian, April 3, 2020

6 Friedersdorf, Conor, "You Will Adjust to the New Normal," The Atlantic, March 12, 2020

7 Meister, Jeanne, "The Impact Of The Coronavirus On HR And The New Normal Of Work," Forbes, March 31, 2020

8 Dewan, Sabina and Ekkehard Ernst, "Rethinking the World of Work," International Monetary Fund, Winter 2020

9 Lacina, Linda, "Prepare for a 'new normal' as lockdown restrictions ease: Monday's COVID-19 WHO briefing," World Economic Forum, April 14, 2020

10 "A new normal: UN lays out roadmap to lift economies and save jobs after COVID-19," The United Nations, Africa Renewal, April 27, 2020

11 "Transition to a 'new normal' during the COVID-19 pandemic must be guided by public health principles," Statement to the press by Dr Hans Henri P. Kluge, WHO Regional Director for Europe, Copenhagen, Denmark, World Health Organization, April 16, 2020

12 Ruhle, Stephanie, "Former CDC Director: We need a 'new normal'," CNBC, April 17, 2020

13 Mulkeen, Jon and Bob Ramsak, "The New Normal: Life in the time of coronavirus," World Athletics Organization, March 23, 2020

14 Sneader, Kevin and Shubham Singhal, "Beyond coronavirus: The path to the next normal," McKinsey & Company, March 23, 2020

15 "March 2020 Update: A New Normal," Diverse Charter Schools Coalition, March, 2020

16 "The New Normal," Guilty Feminist, April 20, 2020

That is what totalitarianism is, this desire to establish complete control over everything and everyone, every thought, emotion, and human interaction. The character of its ideology changes (i.e., Nazism, Stalinism, Maoism, etc.), but this desire for complete control over people, over society, and ultimately life itself, is the essence of totalitarianism … and what has taken over the minds of the New Normals.

In the New Normal society they want to establish — as in every totalitarian society — fear and conformity will be pervasive. Their ideology is a pathologized ideology (as opposed to, say, the racialized ideology of the Nazis), so its symbology will be pathological. Fear of disease, infection, and death, and obsessive attention to matters of health will dominate every aspect of life. Paranoid official propaganda and ideological conditioning will be ubiquitous and constant.

Everyone will be forced to wear medical masks to maintain a constant level of fear and an omnipresent atmosphere of sickness and death, as if the world were one big infectious disease ward. Everyone will wear these masks at all times, at work, at home, in their cars, everywhere. Anyone who fails or refuses to do so will be deemed "a threat to public health," and beaten and arrested by the police,[17] or swarmed by mobs of New Normal vigilantes.[18]

Cities, regions, and entire countries will be subjected to random police-state lockdowns,[19] which will be justified by the threat of "infection." People will be confined to their homes for up to 23-hours a day, and allowed out only for "essential reasons." Police and soldiers will patrol the streets, stopping people, checking their "papers,"[20] and beating and arresting anyone out in public without the proper documents, or walking or standing too close to other people, like they are doing in Melbourne, Australia, currently.[21]

---

17 Naughtie, Andrew, "Video shows police pushing woman to the ground and handcuffing her in front of her young child 'for not wearing mask properly'," Independent, May 14, 2020

18 "This unknown woman using a walker was confronted by the group currently outside East Precinct and paint was strewn all over her," Portland Police Department, Twitter, August 7, 2020

19 Picheta, Rob, "Victoria declares 'state of disaster,' locking down millions in Melbourne to fight a soaring coronavirus outbreak, CNN, August 3, 2020

20 Molloy, Shannon, "Coronavirus Victoria: Daniel Andrews announces permit system for Melbourne," News.com.au, August 4, 2020

21 Graham, Ben, "Dramatic footage has emerged of a Melbourne mum being pinned to the ground by three police officers after she allegedly broke lockdown rules," News.com.au, August 7, 2020

The threat of "infection" will be used to justify increasingly insane and authoritarian edicts, compulsory demonstration-of-fealty rituals, and eventually the elimination of all forms of dissent. Just as the Nazis believed they were waging a war against the "subhuman races," the New Normals will be waging a war on "disease," and on anyone who "endangers the public health" by challenging their ideological narrative.

Like every other totalitarian movement, in the end, they will do whatever is necessary to purify society of "degenerate influences" (i.e., anyone who questions or disagrees with them, or who refuses to obey their every command). They are already aggressively censoring the Internet[22] and banning their opponents' political protests,[23] and political leaders and the corporate media are systematically stigmatizing those of us who dare to challenge their official narrative as "extremists,"[24] "Nazis,"[25] "conspiracy theorists,"[26] "covidiots,"[27] "coronavirus deniers," "anti-vaxxers," and "esoteric" freaks. One German politican even went so far as to demand that dissidents be deported[28] … presumably on trains to somewhere in the East.

Despite this increasing totalitarianization and pathologization of virtually everything, the New Normals will carry on with their

22 Taibbi, Matt, "The Inevitable Coronavirus Censorship Crisis is Here," TK News, April 30, 2020

23 Impelli, Matthew, "Anti-Lockdown, Anti-Mask Protesters Are Getting Arrested in Australia," Newsweek, August 7, 2020

24 Pleitgen, Frederik, "Thousands gather in Berlin to protest against Covid-19 restrictions," CNN, August 1, 2020 ("A large crowd of far-right groups gathered for a "sit-in" at Berlin's iconic Brandenburg Gate on Saturday to protest against the German government's coronavirus restrictions.")

25 "This was the scene in Berlin, where an estimated 17,000 people defied social-distancing and mask requirements to join a protest supported by neo-Nazi groups, conspiracy theorists and others who said they were fed up with the restrictions," The New York Times, Twitter, August 1, 2020

26 Connolly, Kate, "Berlin protests against coronavirus rules divide German leaders," The Guardian, August 3, 2020 ("The demonstrators spanned a wide range of interest groups, from left to rightwing extremists, including members of the neo-Nazi NPD party and Reichsbürger or Citizens of the Reich – who reject the legitimacy of the German state – as well as followers of QAnon, the rightwing conspiracy theory group, members of the Querdenken or Lateral Thinkers movement, followers of the anti-Islam protest group Pegida, anti-vaxxers and self-declared esotericists.")

27 "German minister brands anti-virus measure protesters 'Covidiots'," The National News, August 2, 2020 ("Thousands of extremists and conspiracy theorists marched to decry the government's Covid-19 safety measures.")

28 Bozkurt, Aziz, "I demand: tougher laws to be able to deport these life-endangering people. No matter how. Does not matter where. Just get out of my country. #b0108 #COVIDIOTS," Twitter, August 1, 2020 (N.B. Aziz Bozkurt was Chairman of the Migration and Diversity Working Group, SPD, at the time of this tweet.)

lives as if everything were … well, completely normal. They will go out to restaurants and the movies in their masks. They will work, eat, and sleep in their masks. Families will go on holiday in their masks, or in their "Personal Protective Upper-Body Bubble-Wear."[29] They will arrive at the airport eight hours early, stand in their little color-coded boxes, and then follow the arrows on the floor to the "health officials" in the hazmat suits, who will take their temperature through their foreheads and shove ten-inch swabs into their sinus cavities. Parents who wish to forego this experience will have the option to preventatively vaccinate themselves and their children with the latest experimental vaccine (after signing a liability waiver, of course) within a week or so before their flights, and then present the officials with proof of vaccination (and of their compliance with various other "health guidelines") on their digital Identity and Public Health Passports, or subdermal biometric chips.

Children, as always, will suffer the worst of it. They will be terrorized and confused from the moment they are born,[30] by their parents, their teachers, and by the society at large. They will be subjected to ideological conditioning and paranoid behavioral modification at every stage of their socialization … with fanciful reusable corporate plague masks branded with loveable cartoon characters,[31] paranoia-inducing picture books for toddlers,[32] and paranoid "social distancing" rituals,[33] among other forms of psychological torture.

This conditioning (or torture) will take place at home, as there will be no more schools, or rather, no *public* schools. The children of the wealthy will attend private schools, where they can be cost-effectively "socially-distanced." Working class children will sit at home, alone, staring into screens, wearing their masks, their hyperactivity and anxiety disorders stabilized with anti-depressant medications.

29 *Rowan Kelleher, Suzanne, "Can This 'Hazmat Suit For Flying' Save Air Travel?" Forbes, July 18, 2020*

30 *Carlisle, Madeleine, "Hospital in Thailand Gives Newborn Babies Tiny Face Shields as Protection From Coronavirus," TIME, April 11, 2020*

31 *Bryson Taylor, Derrick, "This Year's Must-Have Back-to-School Item: Masks for Children," The New York Times, August 6, 2020 ("Crayola, Old Navy and Disney are among the brands making colorful masks for children. Child psychologists see this a positive step toward 'normalcy.'")*

32 *Kamin, Deborah, "These new books are here to teach your kids about social distancing, masks and covid-19," The Washington Post, September 1, 2020*

33 *"French children traumatised by coronavirus crisis, expert warns," RFI, August 7, 2020*

And so on … I think you get the picture. I hope so, because I don't have the heart to go on.

I pray this glimpse into the New Normal future has terrified and angered you enough to rise up against it before it is too late. This isn't a joke, folks. The New Normals are serious. If you cannot see where their movement is headed, you do not understand totalitarianism. Once it starts, and reaches this stage, it does not stop, not without a fight. It continues to its logical conclusion. The way that usually happens is, people tell themselves it isn't happening, it can't be happening, not to us. They tell themselves this as the totalitarian program is implemented, step by step, one seemingly harmless step at a time. They conform, because, at first, the stakes aren't so high, and their conformity leads to more conformity, and the next thing they know they're telling their grandchildren that they had no idea where the trains were going.

If you have made it through to the end of this essay, your mind hasn't been taken over yet. (The New Normals clicked off around paragraph 2.) What that means is that it is your responsibility to speak up, and to do whatever else you can, to stop the New Normal future from becoming a reality.

You will not be rewarded for it. You will be ridiculed, castigated, and demonized for it. Your New Normal friends will hate you for it. Your New Normal family will forsake you for it. The New Normal police might arrest you for it. It is your responsibility to do it anyway … as, of course, it is also mine.

The "Storming of the Reichstag Building" on 29 August, 2020

September 2, 2020

On March 21, 1933, the Nazi-controlled Reichstag passed a new law making it a crime to speak out against the government. *Die Verordnung des Reichspräsidenten gegen heimtüchische Angriffe auf de Regierung der nationalen Erhebung* ("The Regulations of the Reich President for Defense from Treacherous Attacks against the Government of the National Uprising") rendered even the slightest expression of dissent from Nazi ideology a criminal offense.

This new law, among other totalitarian measures, was part of a process known as *Gleichschaltung* … the process of achieving rigid and total ideological coordination and uniformity in politics, culture, and private communication by forcibly repressing (or eliminating) independence and freedom of thought and expression.

GloboCap hasn't done anything that heavy-handed in the course of rolling out the New Normal totalitarianism, but that's mainly because they do not have to. When you control the vast majority of the global corporate media, you don't need to pass a lot of ham-fisted laws banning all dissent from your totalitarian ideology. This isn't the 1930s, after all. Over the last ninety years, the arts of propaganda, disinformation, and perception management have advanced to a point that even Goebbels couldn't have imagined.

The skill with which GloboCap and the corporate media delegitimized the anti-New Normal demonstrations in Berlin, London, and other cities last weekend is a perfect example of the state of those arts. I'll focus on Berlin, as that's where I live, and the so-called "Storming of the Reichstag" incident, but it works pretty much the same way everywhere.

In the weeks leading up to the demonstration in Berlin, government officials and corporate-media propagandists did what officials and propagandists do. They relentlessly repeated their official narrative, namely, that anyone protesting the New Normal (or doubting the official Coronavirus narrative) is a "violent neo-Nazi extremist," or "conspiracy theorist," or some other type of existential "threat to democracy."

This official narrative was originally disseminated following the August 1 demonstrations in Berlin, the scale of which took the authorities by surprise. Tens or hundreds of thousands of people (depending on whose narrative you believe) gathered in the city to protest the New Normal and its increasingly absurd "emergency measures." The German media,[1] CNN,[2] *The New York Times*,[3] and other "respectable news outlets" uniformly condemned them as "neo-Nazis," or insinuated that they were "neo-Nazi-sympathizers."

Despite the finding of Germany's Federal Office for the Protection of the Constitution that only "individual members of far-right-groups" had taken part in the August 1 protests, and that "far-right extremists had no formative influence on the demos,"[4] both the German and international corporate media pumped out story after story about the ultra-violent neo-Nazi hordes that were about to descend on Berlin, again!

Der Tagespiegel, a major German newspaper, reported that the demo was being "infiltrated by Nazis." Die Tagesschau, the German BBC, shrieked "the neo-Nazis are mobilizing!"[5] RBB, another public

1 Richter, Christine, "Geisel: Corona-Demos als Kontaktbörse für Rechtsextreme" ("Corona demos as a networking hub for right-wing extremists"), Berliner Morgenpost, August 12, 2020

2 Pleitgen, Frederik, "Thousands gather in Berlin to protest against Covid-19 restrictions," CNN, August 1, 2020 ("A large crowd of far-right groups gathered for a "sit-in" at Berlin's iconic Brandenburg Gate on Saturday to protest against the German government's coronavirus restrictions.")

3 "This was the scene in Berlin, where an estimated 17,000 people defied social-distancing and mask requirements to join a protest supported by neo-Nazi groups, conspiracy theorists and others who said they were fed up with the restrictions," The New York Times, Twitter, August 1, 2020

4 Eppelsheim, Philip, "Wenige Rechtsextreme bei Corona-Demo" ("Few right-wing extremists at Corona-Demo"), Franfurter Allgemeine Zeitung, August 8, 2020 ("According to the assessment of the Federal Office for the Protection of the Constitution, only 'individual members' from the extreme right-wing spectrum took part in the Corona demonstration last Saturday in Berlin. Before the event, various people and organizations from this spectrum had been mobilized. But: 'They did not have a formative influence on the demonstration march or the entire rally,' stated the Federal Office for the Protection of the Constitution.")

5 Betchska, Julius, "So will die extreme Rechte den Corona-Protest unterwandern" ("This is how

broadcaster, reported that the "traveling circus of Corona-deniers"[6] was heading straight for the city![7] Ver.di, the German journalists union, warned their members that they were expecting reporters to suffer "double-digit physical attacks."[8]

And these are just a few of countless examples.

The US and UK corporate media also did their Gleichschaltung duty, disseminating the official "The Nazis are Coming!" narrative. (I don't need to do the citations, do I?) And, of course, Antifa joined in the chorus.[9]

On Wednesday, three days before the demo, having successfully whipped the New Normal masses up into a state of wide-eyed panic over the imminent neo-Nazi invasion, the Berlin government banned the protests.[10] The New Normal masses celebrated. A few concerns about ... you know, democracy, were perfunctorily voiced, but they were quickly silenced when Interior Senator Andreas Geisel explained that abrogating the people's constitutional rights to freedom of assembly and speech was not in any way a totalitarian act, but was purely a matter of "protecting the public health."

For good measure, Geisel also added:

> "I'm not willing to accept a second time that Berlin is abused as a stage for Corona deniers, Reichsbürger, and right-wing extremists."

the extreme Right plans to infiltrate the protest"), Der Tagesspiegel, August 25, 2020 ("The Stuttgart-based "Querdenken 711" group is mobilizing throughout Germany for the protest, coaches are chartered ... security officials expect 'the complete spectrum' of the New Right in Berlin.")

6 Sundermeyer, Olaf, "Wanderzirkus der Corona-Leugner kommt in die Stadt" ("A Traveling Circus of Corona Deniers is Coming to the City"), Radio Berlin Brandenburg, RBB24, July 31, 2020

7 N.B. Any reference to any kind of "deniers" in Germany naturally evokes Holocaust deniers, i.e., Nazis

8 Reichel, Jörg, Managing Director of the German Union of Journalists (dju) in Berlin-Brandenburg, "#b2908 We strongly advise journalists against accreditation via hp #Querdenken711 . We expect a double-digit number of attacks by participants in the demonstration on journalists over the weekend, up to and including bodily harm," Twitter, August 23, 2020

9 New York City Antifa, "This weekend in Berlin, fascists and the Far Right are joining up w/ anti-maskers & chuds who think coronavirus is a hoax. 'Compact' magazine, an extreme Far Right rag w/ AfD ties (apparently pro-Qanon) and Austrian fascist Martin Sellner of 'Generation Identity' are there today," Twitter, August 28, 2020

10 "Berliner Senat verbietet Corona-Demonstration," ("Berlin Senate bans Corona-Demonstration"), Der Spiegel, August 26, 2020

Then, in a particularly Orwellian twist, although the protest itself had now been banned, the Berlin government decided to approve a "counter-protest" against the banned protest.[11]

I'm not quite sure how that was supposed to work.

The night before the demo, an administrative court overturned the protest ban. It didn't really matter, as the authorities knew they couldn't stop the demo in any event. Banning the protest was just part of the show (and the Gleichschaltung process the show was part of), meant to emphasize the existential threat posed by the bloodthirsty Nazi legion that was on its way to sack the city.

On Saturday, hundreds of thousands of people (the overwhelming majority of whom were not neo-Nazis, or Nazi-sympathizers, or any other kind of monsters) poured into the streets of central Berlin. The police surrounded them, trapping them on the avenues, closed off the side streets so they couldn't get out, and, once again, tried to ban the protest on the grounds that they weren't "social distancing." Everyone sat down in the street. Cops stalked around in their masks and body armor, sweating heavily, and occasionally pushing people. Lawyers made phone calls. It was very hot.

Eventually, the court instructed the police to let the demonstration go ahead. And the rest is history ... except that it isn't.

According to the official narrative, there were no hundreds of thousands of protesters. There were "tens of thousands," and they were all "neo-Nazis," "Nazi-sympathizers," "Coronavirus deniers," and "stark-raving mad conspiracy theorists." (Full disclosure: I was there with them, and, yes, indeed, there were some neo-Nazis among the hundreds of thousands of people in the streets, but, just like at the August 1 protest, these far-right boneheads were a small minority, and were not at all welcomed by the majority of the participants, no more than the Trotskyists and anti-Semites were welcomed at the 2003 anti-war protests before the US invasion of Iraq, although, yes, they were definitely there.)

In any event, hundreds of thousands of protesters made their way down Unter den Linden, through the iconic Brandenburg Gate, and onward to the main demonstration, filling the Straße des 17. Juni

---

11 *"Gegenproteste zu verbotener Anti-Corona-Demo in Berlin dürfen stattfinden"* (*"Counter-protest against banned Anti-Corona demonstration allowed to take place,"*), Welt, August 26, 2020

from the Brandenburg Gate to the Siegessäule. By now, I assume you've seen the pictures. Or maybe you haven't. It's actually fairly hard to find any photos in the media that give you any real perspective.

And, finally, we have come to the main event … which, of course, was not this enormous gathering of totally non-violent, non-Nazi people peacefully protesting New Normal totalitarianism, nor the speech of Robert F. Kennedy, Jr. No, the "story," the official main event, was the "Storming of the Reichstag building by Nazis."

I'll let Mathias Bröckers handle this part. Here's an excerpt from his recent blog post:[12]

Storming of Reichstag Averted – Democracy Saved!

"How do you manage to delegitimize a peaceful mass protest against the corona measures in such a way that the media report not about a protest by hundreds of thousands, but about the "storming" of the Reichstag? Quite simply: you approve an application by a group of Reichsbürger to assemble directly in front of the Reichstag *(N.B. the official applicant for this assembly was Ex-NPD-member Rüdiger Hoffmann[13])* and station only three policemen in front of the west entrance despite the large police presence everywhere in the area. Then you let a crazy Q-Anon-chick scream into the microphone that 'Donald Trump has declared freedom,' that 'the police have laid down their weapons,' and that 'everyone should now occupy the steps of the Reichstag,' and, presto, you have the images you need to dominate the coverage … a mob of a few dozen people with Reichsbürger flags 'storming the Reichstag.'"

---

12 Bröckers, Mathias, "Reichtagssturm abgewehrt – Demokratie gerettet!" ("Storming of Reichstag Averted – Democracy Saved!"), Broekers.com, August 31, 2020

13 "Bundesverfassungsgericht bestätigt Verbot von Protestcamp" ("Federal Constitutional Court confirms ban on protest camp"), Welt, August 30, 2020 (Update, 4:51 PM: "The 'Reich citizen' and former NPD functionary Rüdiger Hoffmann is holding a rally in front of the Reichstag … according to the police, participants crashed a barrier and stormed onto the lawn in front of the Reichstag. They are now being expelled from there – with lawn sprinklers.")

Never mind that the massive demonstration at the Siegesäule (i.e., the Victory Column) organized by Querdenken 711 had absolutely nothing to do with this incident, which was carried out by a right-wing-extremist splinter group. The demonstration had already been demonized as a protest staged by Reichsbürger extremists and tin-foil-hat lunatics in the days leading up to it, and now the visual "confirmation" was provided.

In a video of the lead-up to the "Reichstag storming" incident,[14] Tamara K., a natural health practitioner, and pretty obviously a far-right wacko, is the "crazy Q-Anon-chick" in question. You can clearly hear her advising the crowd that "there are no more police here," which the video confirms. Or rather, the few police that were there had left the building completely unguarded and pulled back to well behind this assembly of obviously far-right-extremist-type clowns, who, remember, had been granted official permission to stage their assembly at the steps of the Reichstag. This, despite the days and weeks of warnings of an imminent "neo-Nazi invasion" from government officials and the corporate media.

Go ahead, call me a "conspiracy theorist."

Anyway, once the Reichstag steps were thoroughly occupied by these far-right loonies and the Reichsbürger flags were in the right positions, the police finally arrived to mount their defense. It was touch-and-go there for a while, but at the end of the day, democracy triumphed. Naturally, there were plenty of journalists on hand to capture this historic drama and broadcast it all around the world.

And there you have it, the official narrative, which Saskia Esken, SPD co-leader, succinctly squeezed into a tweet:

> "Tens of thousands of far-right radicals, Reichsbürger, QAnon followers, Holocaust deniers, anti-Semitic conspiracy theorists, and esoterics, who declare the media, science, and politicians 'guilty' and openly call for the storming of the Reichstag and a coup d'état. That is the 29 August Berlin demonstration."[15]

---

14 *Video no longer available; censored by YouTube*
15 *Esken, Saskia, Twitter, August 30, 2020*

Oh, and yesterday, as I was writing this column, I saw that the Berlin Senate had passed a new regulation requiring the participants of any future protests to all wear medical-looking masks[16] … so I take back what I wrote in the beginning. It looks like GloboCap, or at least its German branch, has some ham-fisted totalitarianism left in it.

I'll keep you posted on the Gleichschaltung process, and the advance of New Normal totalitarianism, generally. In the meantime, remember, this is just about a virus! And the Nazis really are coming this time! And looting is a powerful tool to bring about real, lasting change in society[17] … oh, yeah, and the chocolate ration has been increased!

16 "Berliner Senat beschließt Maskenpflicht für Demonstrationen" ("Berlin Senate passes Mask Mandate for Demonstrations"), Radio Berlin Brandenburgh, RBB24, September 1, 2020

17 Escobar, Natalie, "One Author's Controversial View: 'In Defense Of Looting'," National Public Radio, August 27, 2020

The War on Populism: The Final Act

September 20, 2020

So, it appears the War on Populism[1] is building toward an exciting climax. All the proper pieces are in place for a Class-A GloboCap color revolution, and maybe even civil war.

You got your unauthorized Putin-Nazi president, your imaginary apocalyptic pandemic, your violent identitarian civil unrest, your heavily-armed politically-polarized populace, your ominous rumblings from military quarters ...

You couldn't really ask for much more.

OK, the plot is pretty obvious by now (as it is in all big-budget action spectacles, which is essentially what color revolutions are), but that won't spoil our viewing experience. The fun isn't in guessing what is going to happen. Everybody knows what's going to happen. The fun is in watching Bruce, or Sigourney, or "the moderate rebels," or the GloboCap "Resistance," take down the monster, or the "terrorists," or "Hitler," and save the world, or democracy, or whatever.

The show-runners at GloboCap understand this, and they are sticking to the classic Act III formula (i.e., the one they teach in all those scriptwriting seminars, which, full disclosure, I have taught a few of those). They've been running the War on Populism right by the numbers since the very beginning.

I'm going to break that down in just a moment, act by act, plot point by plot point, but, first, let's quickly cover the basics.

The first thing every big Hollywood action picture (or GloboCap color revolution) needs is a solid logline to build the plot around. The logline is the spine of the entire picture. The logline shows us: (1) our protagonist, (2) what our protagonist is trying to do, and (3) our antagonist or antagonistic force.

---

1 Hopkins, C. J., *"The War on Populism: Consent Factory Essays, Vol. II, (2018-2019), Consent Factory Publishing, September 2020*

For example, here's one everyone will recognize:

> "A computer hacker learns from mysterious rebels about the true nature of his reality and his role in the war against its controllers."

In our case, the logline writes itself:

> "After America is taken over by an evil, Russian-backed, Hitlerian dictator, the forces of democracy unite to depose the tyrant and save the free world."

Donald Trump is our antagonist, of course. And what an antagonist he has been! As the deep-state spooks and the corporate media have been relentlessly repeating for the last four years, the man is both a Russian-backed traitor and literally the resurrection of Hitler!

In terms of baddies, it doesn't get any better.

It goes without saying that our protagonist is GloboCap (i.e., the non-existent global-capitalist empire), or "democracy," as it is known in the entertainment business.

Now, we're in the middle of Act III already, and, as in every big-budget action movie, our protagonist suffered a series of mounting losses all throughout Act II, and the baddie was mostly driving the action. So, now it's time for the Final Push, but, before all the action gets underway, here's a quick recap of those previous acts.

Ready? All right, here we go …

Act I
(status quo/inciting incident)

So, there democracy (i.e., GloboCap) was … peacefully operating its de facto global-capitalist empire like a normal global hegemon (i.e., destabilizing, restructuring, and privatizing everything it hadn't already destabilized and privatized, and … OK, occasionally murdering, torturing, and otherwise mercilessly oppressing people), when out of nowhere it was viciously attacked by Donald Trump and his Putin-Nazi "populists," who stole the 2016 election from Clinton with those insidious Facebook ads. (For you writers, this was the Inciting Incident.)

(new situation/predicament/lock-in)

GloboCap did not take this well. The deep state and the corporate media started shrieking about a coming "Age of Darkness,"[2] "The death of globalization at the hands of white supremacy,"[3] "racial Orwellianism,"[4] "Zionist anti-Semitism,"[5] the "Bottomless Pit of Fascism,"[6] and so on. Liberals festooned themselves with safety pins and went out looking for minorities to hide in their attics throughout the occupation.[7] According to GloboCap, every "populist" that voted for Trump (or just refused to vote for Clinton) was a genocidal white supremacist undeserving of either empathy or mercy.[8]

Somewhere in there, the "Resistance" was born. (This is the plot point known as the Lock-In, where the protagonist commits to the struggle ahead.)

Act II (a)
(progress/obstacles)

As is traditional at the opening of Act II, things were looking promising for GloboCap. The "Resistance" staged those pink pussy-hat protests, and the corporate media were pumping out Russia and Hitler propaganda like a Goebbelsian piano. Yes, there were obstacles, but the "Resistance" was growing.

---

2 Freedland, Jonathan, "If Donald Trump wins, it'll be a new age of darkness," The Guardian, November 1, 2016

3 Mason, Paul, "Globalisation is dead, and white supremacy has triumphed," The Guardian, November 9, 2016

4 Blow, Charles M., "Trump: Making America White Again," The New York Times, November 21, 2016

5 Gjeltin, Tom, "Could A Trump Presidency Be Pro-Israel And White Nationalist At The Same Time?" National Public Radio, Morning Edition, November 21, 2016

6 Olberman, Keith, "Should We Give Donald Trump a Chance?" The Resistance with Keith Olberman, GQ, November 16, 2016

7 Abad-Santos, Alex, "A small way to show solidarity after Donald Trump's presidential win, inspired by Brexit," Vox, November 14, 2016

8 Bouie, Jamelle, "There's No Such Thing as a Good Trump Voter," Slate, November 15, 2016

And then, in May of 2017, special counsel Robert Mueller was appointed, and "Russiagate" was officially launched. It appeared that Donald Trump's days were numbered!

(rising action/first culmination)

But, no, it was never going to be that easy. (If it was, feature films would be less than an hour long, not to mention incredibly boring.) There was plenty of action (and an endless series of "bombshells") throughout the ensuing two years, but, by the end of March 2019, "Russiagate" had blown up in GloboCap's face.

"Populism" was still on the rise! It was time for GloboCap to get serious. (This was the classic first culmination, sometimes known as The Point of No Return.)

Act II (b)
(complications/subplots/higher stakes)

In the aftermath of the "Russiagate" fiasco, the GloboCap "Resistance" flailed around for a while. An assortment of ridiculous subplots unfolded, Obstructiongate, Ukrainegate, Pornstargate (and I'm probably forgetting some "gates"), white-supremacist non-terrorist terrorism, brain-devouring Russian-Cubano crickets, Russian spy whales, and other such nonsense.

Meanwhile, the forces of "populism" were running amok all across the planet. The gilets jaunes were on the verge of taking down Macron in France, and gangs of neo-nationalist boneheads had launched a series of frontal assaults on Portlandia, GloboCap Anti-Fascist HQ, which Antifa was barely holding off.

(second culmination/major setback)

All wasn't totally lost, however. GloboCap sprang back into action, Hitlerizing Jeremy Corbyn, the leader of British leftist "populism," thus preventing the mass exodus of Jews from Great Britain.

And now the US elections were on the horizon. Trump was still Russian-agent Hitler, after all, so he wasn't going to be too hard to beat. All that GloboCap had to do was put forth a viable Democratic candidate, then let the corporate media do their thing.

OK, first, they had to do Bernie Sanders (because he was another "populist" figurehead, and the point of the entire War on Populism has been to crush the "populist" resistance to global capitalism from both the Left and the Right), but the DNC made short work of that.

So, everything was looking hunky-dory until (and you screenwriters saw this coming, didn't you?) the pivotal plot-point at the end of Act II ... The Major Setback, or The Dark Night of the Soul, when all seems lost for our protagonist.

Yes, implausible as it probably still seems, the Democratic Party nominated Joe Biden, a clearly cognitively-compromised person who literally sucked his wife's fingers on camera and who can't get through a two-minute speech without totally losing his train of thought and babbling non-sequiturial gibberish.

Exactly why they did this will be debated forever, but, obviously, Biden was not GloboCap's first choice. The man is as inspiring as a head of lettuce. There is an actual campaign group called "Settle for Biden!"[9]

GloboCap was now staring down the barrel of certain swing-voter death. And, as if things weren't already dire enough, the "populists" rolled out a catchy new slogan, "TRUMP 2020, BECAUSE FUCK YOU AGAIN!"

Act III

So, all right, this is part where Neo orders up "guns ... lots of guns." Which is exactly what our friends at GloboCap did. The time for playing grab-ass was over. Faced with four more years of Trump and this "populist" rebellion against global capitalism and its increasingly insufferable woke ideology, the entire global capitalist machine went full-totalitarian all at once. Suddenly, a rather undeadly virus (as far as deadly pestilences go) became the excuse for GloboCap to lock down most of humanity for months, destroy the economy, unleash the goon squads, terrorize everyone with hysterical propaganda, and otherwise remake society into a global totalitarian police state.

9 settleforbiden.org

And that wasn't all … oh no, far from it. GloboCap was just getting started. Having terrorized the Western masses into a state of anus-puckering paranoia over an imaginary apocalyptic plague and forced everyone to perform a variety of humiliating ideological-compliance rituals, they unleashed the identitarian civil unrest. Because what would a color revolution be without rioting, looting, wanton destruction, clouds of tear gas, robocops, and GloboCap-sponsored "moderate rebels" and "pro-regime forces" shooting each other down in the streets on television? (In an homage to Orwell's Ministry of Truth, the corporate media, with totally straight faces, have been describing this rioting as "mostly peaceful."[10])

That brings us up to speed, I think. The rest of Act III should be pretty exciting, despite the fact that the outcome is certain.

One way or another, Trump is history. Or do you seriously believe that GloboCap is going to let him serve another term? Not that Trump is any actual threat to them. As I have said repeatedly over the past four years, Donald Trump is not a populist. Donald Trump is a narcissistic ass clown who is playing president to feed his ego. He is not a threat to global capitalism, but the people who elected him are. In order to teach these people a lesson, GloboCap needs to make an example of Trump. Odds are, it's not going to be pretty.

See, they have him between a rock and a hard place. As CNN's Fareed Zakaria explained,[11] on election night, Trump will appear to have won (because the Democrats will all be mailing in their votes, due to the apocalyptic plague), but later, once the mail-in votes are counted, which may take weeks or even months, it will turn out that Biden really won.

But, by then, it won't matter who really won, because one of two scenarios will have already played out.

In Scenario Number One, Trump declares victory before all the mail-in votes have been counted and is "removed from office" for "attempting a coup." In Scenario Number Two, he doesn't declare

10 Wulfsohn, Joseph A., "CNN panned for on-air graphic reading 'fiery but mostly peaceful protest' in front of Kenosha fire," FOX News, August 27, 2020

11 Zakaria, Fareed, "We need to prepare for a 'deeply worrying scenario' on November 3 as mail-in ballots may delay the presidential election results. Will President Trump accept the outcome if Joe Biden wins?" CNN, September 13, 2020

victory, and the country enters a state of limbo, which the Democrats will prolong as long as possible.

Either way, rioting breaks out. Serious rioting, not "peaceful" rioting. Rioting that makes the "BLM protests" we have witnessed so far look like a game of touch football.

And this is where the military comes in. I'll leave you with just a few of the many ominous headlines that GloboCap has been generating:

"This Election Has Become Dangerous for the U.S. Military" — *Foreign Policy*[12]

"Al Gore suggests military will remove Trump from office if he won't concede on election night" — Fox News[13]

"Former ambassador warns of election violence" — *The Guardian*[14]

"All Enemies, Foreign and Domestic": An Open Letter to Gen. Milley" — *Defense One*[15]

"Is Trump Planning a Coup d'État?" — *The Nation*[16]

"What happens if Trump loses but refuses to concede?" — *Financial Times*[17]

"What If Trump Won't Leave?" — *The Intercept*[18]

12 Feaver, Peter, "This Election Has Become Dangerous for the U.S. Military," Foreign Policy, September 9, 2020

13 Henney, Meagan, "Al Gore suggests military will remove Trump from office if he won't concede on election night," FOX News, August 26, 2020

14 Borger, Julian, "The US feels very volatile': Former ambassador warns of election violence," The Guardian, September 15, 2020

15 Nagl, John and Paul Yingling, "All Enemies, Foreign and Domestic": An Open Letter to Gen. Milley," Defense One, August 11, 2020

16 Abramsky, Sasha, "Is Trump Planning a Coup d'État?" The Nation, September 7, 2020

17 Manson, Katrina and Kadhim Shubber, "What happens if Trump loses but refuses to concede?" Financial Times, September 14, 2020

18 Piven, Frances Fox, "What If Trump Won't Leave?" The Intercept, August 11 2020

"White Supremacists, Domestic Terrorists Pose Biggest Threat Of 'Lethal Violence' This Election, DHS Assessment Finds" — *Forbes*[19]

"Trump's Attacks Put Military In Presidential Campaign Minefield" — NPR[20]

"Trump's Election Delay Threat Is a Coup in the Making" — *Common Dreams*[21]

"How to Plan a Coup" — *Bill Moyers on Democracy*[22]

"It can happen here: A Trump election coup?" — *Wall Street International Magazine*[23]

Does it sound like GloboCap is bluffing to you? Because it doesn't sound like that to me. I could be totally wrong, of course, and just letting my imagination run away with itself, but if I were back home in the USA, instead of here in Berlin, I wouldn't bet on it.

In any event, whatever is coming, whether this is really the end of the War on Populism or just the beginning of a new, more dramatic phase of it, the next two months are going to be exciting. So, go grab your popcorn, or your AR-15, and your mask, or full-body anti-virus bubble suit (which you might want to have retrofitted with Kevlar), and sit back and enjoy the show!

---

19 McEvoy, Jemima, "White Supremacists, Domestic Terrorists Pose Biggest Threat Of 'Lethal Violence' This Election, DHS Assessment Finds," Forbes, September 7, 2020

20 Bowman, Tom, "Trump's Attacks Put Military In Presidential Campaign Minefield," National Public Radio, September 10, 2020

21 Weissman, Robert, "Trump's Election Delay Threat Is a Coup in the Making," Common Dreams, July 30, 2020

22 Richardson, Heather Cox, "How to Plan a Coup," Bill Moyers on Democracy, September 15, 2020

23 Gardner, Hal, "It can happen here: A Trump election coup?" Wall Street International Magazine, September 18, 2020

The Covidian Cult

October 13, 2020

One of the hallmarks of totalitarianism is mass conformity to a psychotic official narrative. Not a regular official narrative, like the "Cold War" or the "War on Terror" narratives. A totally delusional official narrative that has little or no connection to reality and that is contradicted by a preponderance of facts.

Nazism and Stalinism are the classic examples, but the phenomenon is better observed in cults and other sub-cultural societal groups. Numerous examples will spring to mind: the Manson family, Jim Jones' People's Temple, the Church of Scientology, Heavens Gate, etc., each with its own psychotic official narrative: Helter Skelter, Christian Communism, Xenu and the Galactic Confederacy, and so on.

Looking in from the dominant culture (or back through time in the case of the Nazis), the delusional nature of these official narratives is glaringly obvious to most rational people. What many people fail to understand is that to those who fall prey to them (whether individual cult members or entire totalitarian societies) such narratives do not register as psychotic. On the contrary, they feel entirely normal. Everything in their social "reality" reifies and reaffirms the narrative, and anything that challenges or contradicts it is perceived as an existential threat.

These narratives are invariably paranoid, portraying the cult as threatened or persecuted by an evil enemy or antagonistic force which only unquestioning conformity to the cult's ideology can save its members from. It makes little difference whether this antagonist is mainstream culture, body thetans, counter-revolutionaries, Jews, or a virus. The point is not the identity of the enemy. The point is the atmosphere of paranoia and hysteria the official narrative generates, which keeps the cult members (or the society) compliant.

In addition to being paranoid, these narratives are often internally inconsistent, illogical, and … well, just completely ridiculous. This does not weaken them, as one might suspect. Actually, it increases their power, as it forces their adherents to attempt to reconcile their inconsistency and irrationality, and in many cases utter absurdity, in order to remain in good standing with the cult. Such reconciliation is of course impossible, and causes the cult members' minds to short circuit and abandon any semblance of critical thinking, which is precisely what the cult leader wants.

Moreover, cult leaders will often radically change these narratives for no apparent reason, forcing their cult members to abruptly forswear (and often even denounce as "heresy") the beliefs they had previously been forced to profess, and behave as if they had never believed them, which causes their minds to further short circuit, until they eventually give up even trying to think rationally, and just mindlessly parrot whatever nonsensical gibberish the cult leader fills their heads with.

Also, the cult leader's nonsensical gibberish is not as nonsensical as it may seem at first. Most of us, upon encountering such gibberish, assume that the cult leader is trying to communicate, and that something is very wrong with his brain. The cult leader isn't trying to communicate. He is trying to disorient and control the listener's mind.

Listen to Charlie Manson "rapping."[1] Not just to what he says, but how he says it. Note how he sprinkles bits of truth into his stream of free-associated nonsense, and his repetitive use of thought-terminating clichés, described by Robert J. Lifton as follows:

> "The language of the totalist environment is characterized by the thought-terminating cliché. The most far-reaching and complex of human problems are compressed into brief, highly selective, definitive-sounding phrases, easily memorized and easily expressed. They become the start and finish of any ideological analysis."
> — Robert J. Lifton, *Thought Reform and the Psychology of Totalism: A Study of "Brainwashing" in China*, 1961

If all this sounds familiar, good. Because the same techniques that

---

1 *"Charles Manson speaks the truth," Lord Santa, YouTube, May 1, 2014*

most cult leaders use to control the minds of the members of their cults are used by totalitarian systems to control the minds of entire societies: Milieu Control, Loaded Language, Sacred Science, Demand for Purity, and other standard mind-control techniques. It can happen to pretty much any society, just as anyone can fall prey to a cult, given the right set of circumstances.

It is happening to most of our societies right now.

An official narrative is being implemented. A totalitarian official narrative. A totally psychotic official narrative, no less delusional than that of the Nazis, or the Manson family, or any other cult.

Most people cannot see that it is happening, for the simple reason that it is happening to them. They are literally unable to recognize it. The human mind is extremely resilient and inventive when it is pushed past its limits. Ask anyone who has struggled with psychosis or has taken too much LSD. We do not recognize when we are going insane. When reality falls apart completely, the mind will create a delusional narrative, which appears just as "real" as our normal reality, because even a delusion is better than the stark raving terror of utter chaos.

This is what totalitarians and cult leaders count on, and exploit to implant their narratives in our minds, and why actual initiation rituals (as opposed to purely symbolic rituals) begin by attacking the subject's mind with terror, pain, physical exhaustion, psychedelic drugs, or some other means of obliterating the subject's perception of reality. Once that is achieved, and the subject's mind starts desperately trying to construct a new narrative to make sense out of the cognitive chaos and psychological trauma it is undergoing, it is relatively easy to "guide" that process and implant whatever narrative you want, assuming you have done your homework.

And this is why so many people — people who are able to easily recognize totalitarianism in cults and foreign countries — cannot perceive the totalitarianism that is taking shape now, right in front of their faces (or, rather, right inside their minds). Nor can they perceive the delusional nature of the official "Covid-19" narrative, no more than those in Nazi Germany were able to perceive how completely delusional their official "master race" narrative was. Such people are neither ignorant nor stupid. They have been successfully initiated into a cult, which is essentially what totalitarianism is, albeit on a societal scale.

Their initiation into the Covidian Cult began in January, when the medical authorities and corporate media turned on The Fear with projections of hundreds of millions of deaths[2] and fake photos of people dropping dead in the streets.[3] The psychological conditioning has continued for months. The global masses have been subjected to a constant stream of propaganda, manufactured hysteria, wild speculation, conflicting directives, exaggerations, lies, and tawdry theatrical effects. Lockdowns. Emergency field hospitals and morgues. The singing-dancing NHS staff. Death trucks. Overflowing ICUs. Dead Covid babies. Manipulated statistics. Goon squads. Masks. And all the rest of it.

Eight months later, here we are. The Head of the Health Emergencies Program at the WHO has basically confirmed an IFR of 0.14%,[4] roughly the same as the seasonal flu. And here are the latest survival rate estimates from the Center for Disease Control:[5]

> Age 0-19 … 99.997%
> Age 20-49 … 99.98%
> Age 50-69 … 99.5%
> Age 70+ … 94.6%

The "science" argument is officially over. An increasing number of doctors and medical experts are breaking ranks and explaining how the current mass hysteria over "cases" (which now includes perfectly

---

2 Lovelace Jr., Berkeley and Noah Higgins-Dunn, "WHO says coronavirus death rate is 3.4% globally, higher than previously thought," CNBC, March 3 2020

3 Agence France-Presse, "A man lies dead in the street: the image that captures the Wuhan coronavirus crisis, The Guardian, January 31, 2020 ("'These days, many have died,' says bystander as image shows workers in protective suits and masks taking body away.")

4 Knightly, Kit, "WHO (Accidentally) Confirms Covid is No More Dangerous Than Flu," Off-Guardian, October 8, 2020 ("The global population is roughly 7.8 billion people, if 10% have been infected that is 780 million cases. The global death toll currently attributed to Sars-Cov-2 infections is 1,061,539. That's an infection fatality rate of roughly or 0.14%. Right in line with seasonal flu and the predictions of many experts from all around the world. 0.14% is over 24 times LOWER than the WHO's 'provisional figure' of 3.4% back in March. This figure was used in the models which were used to justify lockdowns and other draconian policies.")

5 "COVID-19 Pandemic Planning Scenarios," Centers for Disease Control and Prevention, September 10, 2020

healthy people) is essentially meaningless propaganda, for example, in this segment on ARD, one of the big mainstream German TV channels.[6]

And then there is the existence of Sweden, and other countries which are not playing ball with the official Covid-19 narrative, which makes a mockery of the ongoing hysteria.

I'm not going to go on debunking the narrative. The point is, the facts are all widely available. Not from "conspiracy theorist" websites. From mainstream outlets and medical experts. From the Center for Fucking Disease Control.

Which does not matter in the least, not to the members of the Covidian Cult. Facts do not matter to totalitarians and cult members. What matters is loyalty to the cult or the party.

Which means we have a serious problem, those of us to whom facts still matter, and who have been trying to use them to convince the Covidian cultists that they are wrong about the virus for going on eight months at this point.

While it is crucial to continue reporting the facts and sharing them with as many people as possible — which is becoming increasingly difficult due to the censorship of alternative and social media — it is important to accept what we are up against. What we are up against is not a misunderstanding or a rational argument over scientific facts. It is a fanatical ideological movement. A global totalitarian movement … the first of its kind in human history.

It isn't national totalitarianism, because we're living in a global capitalist empire, which isn't ruled by nation-states, but rather, by supranational entities and the global capitalist system itself. And thus, the cult/culture paradigm has been inverted. Instead of the cult existing as an island within the dominant culture, the cult has become the dominant culture, and those of us who have not joined the cult have become the isolated islands within it.

I wish I could be more optimistic, and maybe offer some sort of plan of action, but the only historical parallel I can think of is how

6 *"ARD: German Scientists Call for Second Corona Phase," Frank Hoogerbeets, Odysee, October 8, 2020 (lbry://@hobeets#0/ard-scientists-call-for-second-phase#7) ("In a broadcast from German ARD TV network, scientists call for the second phase in the corona pandemic, which should focus on protecting the elderly and end the government's containment strategy which continue to undermine society as a whole.")*

Christianity "converted" the pagan world ... which doesn't really bode so well for us. While you're sitting at home during the "second wave" lockdowns, you might want to brush up on that history.

THE WAR IS OVER ... GLOBOCAP TRIUMPHS!

November 10, 2020

OK, so, that was not cool. For one terrifying moment there, it actually looked like GloboCap was going to let Russian-Asset Hitler win.

Hour after hour on election night, states on the map kept turning red, or pink, or some distinctly non-blue color. Wisconsin. Michigan. Georgia. Florida. It could not be happening, and yet it was. What other explanation was there?

The Russians were stealing the election again!

But, of course, GloboCap was just playing with us. They're a bunch of practical jokers, those GloboCap guys. Naturally, they couldn't resist the chance to wind us up just one more time.

Seriously, though, while I enjoy a good prank, I still have a number of liberal friends, many of whom were on the verge of suffering major heart attacks as they breathlessly waited for the corporate media to confirm that they had successfully voted a "literal dictator" out of office.[1] (A few of them suffer from IBS or other gastrointestinal disorders, so, in light of the current toilet paper shortage caused by the Return of the Apocalyptic Plague, toying with them like that was especially cruel.)

But, whatever. That's water under the bridge. The good news is, the nightmare is over![2] Literal Hitler and his underground army of Russia-loving white supremacists have been vanquished! Decency has been restored![3] Globalization has risen from the dead![4]

---

1 "Obama compares Trump to a 'two-bit dictator' who lies 'every single day'," Associated Press/The Guardian, November 3, 2020

2 Milbank, Dana, "Our Long National Nightmare is Over," The Washington Post, November 7, 2020

3 Prignano, Christina, "Biden calls for America to 'marshal the forces of decency'," Boston Globe, November 7, 2020

4 Mason, Paul, "Globalisation is dead, and white supremacy has triumphed," The Guardian, November 9, 2016

And, of course, the most important thing is, racism in America is over … again!

Yes, that's right, folks, no more racism! Kiss all those Confederate monuments goodbye! The Democrats are back in the White House! According to sources, domestic staff are already down in the West Wing basement looking for that bust of MLK that Trump ordered removed and desecrated the moment he was sworn into office.[5] College kids are building pyres of racist and potentially racist books, paintings, films, and other degenerate artworks. Jussie Smollet can finally come out of hiding.[6]

OK, granted, they're not going to desegregate liberal cities or anything crazy like that, or stop "policing" Black neighborhoods like an occupying army, or stop funding public schools with property taxes, but Kamala Harris is Black, mostly, and Grampa Joe will tell us more stories about "Corn Pop," the razor-wielding public-pool gangster,[7] and other dangerous Black people he hasn't yet incarcerated,[8] so that should calm down all those BLM folks.

In the meantime, the official celebrations have begun.

Assorted mass-murdering GloboCap luminaries, government leaders, and the corporate media are pumping out hopey-changey propaganda like it was 2008 all over again. Pundits are breaking down and sobbing on television.[9] Liberal mobs are ritualistically stomping Cheetos to death in the streets of Brooklyn.[10] Slaphappy hordes of Covidian Cultists are amassing outdoors, masks around their necks, sharing bottles of champagne and French-kissing each

5 Mullin, Benjamin, "Time editor on MLK bust: We regret the error," Poynter, January 24, 2017 ("Nancy Gibbs, the editor of Time magazine, issued an apology on Tuesday for an error that the Trump administration has repeatedly used to criticize the press in the last week. In doing so, she pushed back against claims from the administration that the magazine made a deliberate error when reporter Zeke Miller incorrectly reported that the White House had removed a bust of civil rights hero Martin Luther King, Jr. from the Oval Office.")

6 Onibada, Ane, "Jussie Smollett Said He Didn't Fake A Hate Crime Against Himself," Buzzfeed News, September 10, 2020

7 Hains, Tim, "Joe Biden Recalls Terrifying 1960s Public Pool Confrontation With Razor-Wielding Gangster Named 'Corn Pop'," Real Clear Politics, September 15, 2019

8 Sullum, Jacob, "Biden Tries To Gloss Over His Long History of Supporting the Drug War and Draconian Criminal Penalties," Reason, October 16, 2020

9 "CNN's Van Jones brought to tears as Joe Biden wins US election," The Guardian, November 7, 2020

10 Plitman, Jacob, "People are ritualistically stomping on cheetos here in crown heights," Twitter, November 7, 2020 (tweeting a photo of the Cheetos-stomping mob)

other,[11] protected from the virus by the Anti-Trump Force Field that saved the BLM protesters last Summer. It's like V-Day, the fall of the Berlin wall, and the bin Laden assassination all rolled into one!

All of which is understandable, given all the horrors of these last four years, the concentration camps,[12] the wars of aggression,[13] the censorship,[14] the secret CIA kill lists,[15] the show trials,[16] and all that other dictator stuff. On top of which, there was all that white supremacy and anti-Semitism,[17] and that horrible wall that transformed America into an "apartheid state" where people were imprisoned in an open-air ghetto[18] and gratuitously abused and murdered. (Whoops, I think I screwed up my citations … maybe double-check those footnotes.)

But let's not dwell on all those horrors right now. There will be plenty of time for all that later, when Donald Trump is hauled into court and tried for his crimes against humanity, like all our previous war-criminal presidents.

No, this is a time for looking ahead to the Brave New Global-Capitalist Normal, in which everyone will sit at home in their masks surfing the Internet on their toasters with MSNBC playing in the background … well, OK, not absolutely everyone. The affluent will still need to fly around in their private jets and helicopters, and take vacations on their yachts, and, you know, all the usual affluent stuff. But the rest of us won't have to go anywhere or meet with anyone in person, because our lives will be one never-ending Zoom meeting carefully monitored by official fact-checkers to ensure we're not being

---

11 "Photos: Fireworks, Champagne and dancing in the streets of L.A. as Biden and Harris win," Los Angeles Times, November 7, 2020

12 Mark, Michelle, "Obama officials rushed to explain photos from 2014 that went viral showing locked-up immigrant children — and Trump's facilities look the same," Insider, June 19, 2018

13 Taibbi, Matt, "16 Years Later, How the Press That Sold the Iraq War Got Away With It" (An excerpt from Hate Inc.), Rolling Stone, March 22, 2019

14 Greenwald, Glenn, "Facebook and Twitter Cross a Line Far More Dangerous Than What They Censor," The Intercept, October 16, 2020 ("Just weeks before the election, the tech giants unite to block access to incriminating reporting about their preferred candidate.")

15 Becker, Jo and Scott Shane, "Secret 'Kill List' Proves a Test of Obama's Principles and Will," The New York Times, May 29, 2012

16 Hopkins, C. J., "A Russiagate Requiem," Consent Factory, April 2, 2019

17 Cortes, Steve, "Trump Didn't Call Neo-Nazis 'Fine People.' Here's Proof," Real Clear Politics, March 21, 2019

18 "It's Been a Decade. Open Gaza, the Palestinian Ghetto," Haaretz (Editorial), May 17, 2016

"misinformed" or exposed to "dangerous conspiracy theories" which could potentially lead to the agonized deaths (or the mild-to-moderate flu-like illnesses[19]) of hundreds of millions of innocent people.

But let's not count our chickens just yet. As much as you're probably looking forward to life in the Brave New GloboCap Normal, or the Great Reset,[20] or whatever they end up calling the new pathologized totalitarianism, it isn't a fait accompli quite yet … not until Russian-Asset Hitler has been thoroughly humiliated and removed from office, and anyone who voted for him, or didn't believe he was literally Hitler, or a Russian asset, or who otherwise refused to take part in the mindless, corporate-media-generated Anti-Trump Hate-Fest, has been demonized as a "racist," a "traitor," an "anti-Semite," a "conspiracy theorist," or some other type of "far-right extremist."

That's probably going to take another couple months.

I'm pretty certain the plan is still to goad Trump into overreacting and trying to resist his removal from office. And I do not mean just in the courts. No, after all the money, time, and effort that GloboCap has invested over the last four years, they are going to be extremely disappointed if he just slinks away without going full-Hitler and starting a Second Civil War.

As I've been saying, over and over, since he won the election, GloboCap needs to make an example of Trump to put down the widespread populist rebellion against global capitalism and its ideology that erupted back in 2016 … and, no, it doesn't make any difference whether Donald Trump is actually a populist, or whether people realize that it is global capitalism and not "Cultural Marxism" that they are rebelling against.

According to the script, this is the part where Trump refuses to respect "democracy" and has to be forcibly dragged out of office by the Secret Service or elements of the military, ideally "live" on international television. It may not end up playing out that way (Trump is probably not as dumb as I think), but that's the Act III scenario for GloboCap: the "attempted Trump coup," then the "perp walk." They need the public and future generations to perceive him as an "illegitimate president," a "usurper," an "intruder," an "imposter," an "invader" ... which, he is. (Merely being rich and famous does not make you a member of the GloboCap Power Club.)

The corporate media are already at work manufacturing this version of reality, not only in the content of their "reporting," but also with the unbridled contempt they are showing for a sitting president. The networks actually cut him off in the middle of his post-election address.[21] The Twitter Corporation is censoring his tweets.[22]

What could possibly be more humiliating, and indicative of who is really in charge?

Meanwhile, the GloboCap propaganda has reached some new post-Orwellian level. After four long years of "RUSSIA HACKED THE ELECTION!" ... now, suddenly, "THERE IS NO SUCH THING AS ELECTION FRAUD IN THE USA!"

That's right, once again, millions of liberals, like that scene in 1984 where the Party switches official enemies right in the middle of the Hate-Week speech, have been ordered to radically revise their "reality," and hysterically deny the existence of the very thing they have been hysterically alleging for four solid years ... and they are actually doing it!

At the same time, the Trumpians have been reduced to repeating, over and over, and over, "THE MEDIA DOES NOT SELECT THE PRESIDENT," and "BIDEN IS NOT THE PRESIDENT ELECT," and other versions of "THIS CAN'T BE HAPPENING."

I hate to rub salt into anyone's wounds, particularly those whose faces are currently being stomped on by GloboCap's enormous boot, but, yes, this is actually happening.

Second Civil War or no Second Civil War, this is the end for Donald Trump. As Biden and the corporate media keep telling us, we are looking at a "very dark winter,"[23] on the other side of which a new reality awaits us ... a new, pathologized, totalitarian reality.

---

21 Bauder, David, "Networks cut away from Trump's White House address," AP News, November 6, 2020

22 Steinbuch, Yaron, "Trump slams Twitter as 'out of control' for censoring his tweets," New York Post, November 6, 2020

23 "Dark Winter ... a senior-level war game examining the national security, intergovernmental, and information challenges of a biological attack on the American homeland," conducted June 22-23, 2001, Johns Hopkins Center for Health Security

Call it the "New Normal" if you want. Pretend that "democracy has triumphed" if you want. Wear your mask. Mask your children. Terrorize them with pictures of "death trucks," and tales of "Russian hackers" and "white-supremacist terrorists." Live in fear of an imaginary plague (or perhaps a non-imaginary plague if that "very dark winter" comes to pass). Censor all dissent. Ban all protests. Do not attempt to adjust your telescreen. Click on the link to join the Zoom meeting. Have your password and your identity papers ready. Watch your pronouns. Get down on your knees.

It's GloboCap Fucking Über Alles!

The Germans Are Back!

November 22, 2020

Break out the Wagner ... the Germans are back! No, not the warm, fuzzy, pussified, peace-loving, post-war Germans. The *Germans*! You know the ones I mean. The "I didn't know where the trains were going" Germans. The "I was just following orders" Germans. The other Germans.

Yeah ... *those* Germans.

In case you missed it, on November 18, the German parliament passed a new law, revising the so-called "Infection Protection Act" (*"Das Infektionsschutzgesetz"* in German), that formally granted the government the authority to issue whatever edicts it wants under the guise of protecting the public health.[1]

The government has been doing this anyway, ordering lockdowns, curfews, travel bans, banning demonstrations, raiding homes and businesses, ordering everyone to wear medical masks, harassing and arresting dissidents, etc., but now it has been "legitimized" by the Bundestag, enshrined into law, and presumably stamped with one of those intricate official stamps that German bureaucrats like to stamp things with.

Now, this revised "Infection Protection Act," approval of which was rushed through the parliament, is not in any way comparable to the "Enabling Act of 1933,"[2] which formally granted the Nazi

---

1 *"The Law for the Protection of the Population in an Epidemic Situation of National Importance of March 27, 2020" is an article law that was enacted on the occasion of the outbreak of the COVID-19 pandemic caused by the novel coronavirus SARS-CoV-2 in Germany. The Act revised the "Infection Protection Act" (IfSG). Some of the changes apply for a limited period, some for an unlimited period. On November 3, 2020, the parliamentary groups of the CDU/CSU and SPD introduced the draft of a third law to protect the population in an epidemic situation of national importance to the German Bundestag. On November 18, 2020, the Bundestag passed the law. 415 MPs voted for, 236 against, 8 abstained. On the same day, the Federal Council approved the law in a special session with 49 yes votes out of a total of 69. Federal President Frank-Walter Steinmeier enacted the law on the same day.*

2 *"The Enabling Act allowed the Reich government to issue laws without the consent of Germany's parliament, laying the foundation for the complete Nazification of German society. The law was passed on March 23, 1933, and published the following day. Its full name was the "Law to Remedy the Distress of the People and the Reich," United States Holocaust Memorial Museum*

government the authority to issue whatever edicts it wanted under the guise of remedying the distress of the people.

Yes, I realize that sounds quite similar, but, according to the government and the German media, there is absolutely no equivalence whatsoever, and anyone who even suggests there is is "a far-right AfD extremist," or "a neo-Nazi conspiracy theorist," or "an anti-vax esotericist" … or whatever.

As this revised "Protection Act" was being passed (i.e., the current one, not the one in 1933), tens of thousands of anti-totalitarian protesters gathered in the streets, many of them carrying copies of the *Grundgesetz* (i.e., the constitution of the Federal Republic of Germany), which the parliament was in the process of abrogating. They were met by thousands of riot police, who declared the demonstration "illegal" (because many of the protesters were not wearing masks), beat up and arrested hundreds of them, then hosed down the rest with water cannons.

The German media (which are totally objective, and not at all like Goebbels' Ministry of Propaganda in the Nazi era) dutifully reminded the German public that these protesters were all "Corona Deniers," "far-right extremists," "conspiracy theorists," "anti-vaxxers," "neo-Nazis," and so on, so they probably got what they deserved.

Also, a spokesperson for the Berlin police (who bear absolutely no resemblance to the Gestapo, or the Stasi, or any other notorious official-ideology-enforcing goons) pointed out that their water cannons were only being used to "irrigate" the protesters (i.e., not being aimed directly at them) because there were so many "Corona Denier" children in their ranks.

According to the government, the German media, the intelligentsia, and, basically, anyone in public life who wants to remain there, these "Corona Deniers" are becoming a problem. They are spreading baseless "conspiracy theories" that are threatening the public health and causing distress to the German people (e.g., that the vast majority of those infected suffer only mild to moderate flu symptoms or, more commonly, no symptoms at all, and that over 99.7% survive).[3] They are walking around without medical-looking masks, which is

3 Black, Catte, "UK Chief Medic confirms (again) covid19 harmless to vast majority," *OffGuardian, May 15, 2020*

making a mockery of the government and media's efforts to convince the public that they are under attack by an apocalyptic plague. They are posting scientific facts on the Internet.[4] They are staging these protests and otherwise challenging the government's right to declare a "health emergency," suspend the German constitution indefinitely, and rule society by decree and force.

Despite the German government and media's efforts to demonize anyone not obediently parroting the official "New Normal" narrative as a "dangerous neo-Nazi Corona Denier," the "Corona Denialism" movement is growing, not just in Germany, but all throughout Europe.[5] Clearly, the time is coming for Germany to take stronger measures against this threat. The health of the Vater ... uh, the nation, is at stake!

Fortunately, this revised "Infection Protection Act" will provide the government with the authority it needs to conceive and carry out some kind of ... well, you know, solution. Allowing these degenerate anti-social deviants to run around challenging the German government's absolute power is not an option, not in a time of national health emergency! These "Nazi-sympathizing Corona Deniers" must be rooted out and dealt with, mercilessly!

I'm not privy to the details, of course, but, it being Germany, I imagine some sort of Special Task Force has been set up to efficiently deal with the "Corona Denier Problem." Steps are clearly already being taken.

Alternative media outlets are being deplatformed (because, according the state and corporate media, they are "Querfront," i.e., "Third Position" magazines).[6] In April, a well-known dissident lawyer was forcibly committed to a psychiatric ward (but the authorities and the media assured us that it had nothing to do with her dissident views, or with the lawsuits she was filing against the government; she just coincidentally became completely paranoid).[7] Heavily-armed police are arresting YouTubers (although it isn't clear exactly what for, as

4 "Facts about Covid-19," Swiss Policy Research (swprs.org)

5 "Anti-Lockdown Protests All Across Europe," OffGuardian, November 19, 2020

6 Hurtz, Simon, "Falsch, aber faszinierend" ("False, but fascinating"), Süddeutsche Zeitung, May 11, 2020

7 "German lawyer sent to psychiatric ward after mounting serious resistance to 'unconstitutional' Covid-19 lockdown," RT, April 15, 2020

the authorities have released no details and the mainstream media is not reporting it).[8]

In the run-up to the 29 August demonstration, at which the government granted some neo-Nazis de-facto permission to "storm the Reichstag," so the media could film it and discredit the real protest,[9] one German politician went so far as to call for "Corona Deniers" to be deported, presumably on trains, somewhere to the east.[10]

But seriously, I don't mean to pick on the Germans. I love the Germans. I live in Germany. And they are hardly the only ones implementing the new pathologized totalitarianism. It's just that, given their not-too-distant history, it is rather depressing, and more than a little frightening, to watch as Germany is once again transformed into a totalitarian state, where the police are hunting down the maskless on the streets, raiding restaurants, bars, and people's homes, where goose-stepping little Good German citizens are peering into the windows of Yoga studios to see if they are violating "social distancing rules," where I can't take a walk or shop for groceries without being surrounded by hostile, glaring, sometimes verbally-abusive Germans, who are infuriated that I'm not wearing a mask, and otherwise mindlessly following orders, and who robotically remind me, "Es ist Pflicht! Es ist Pflicht!"

Yes, I am fully aware that it is "Pflicht." If I had any doubt as to whether it was "Pflicht," the Berlin Senat cleared that up when they commissioned and ran this charming advert instructing me to fuck myself if I don't want to follow their "Corona orders" and profess my belief in their new Big Lie.[11]

---

8 Romero, Luiz, "German chemist was not killed by 'government operatives' after revealing 'secret' about vaccine," Politifact/The Poynter Institute, December 10, 2021 ("Followers of German chemist Andreas Noack's conspiracy theories are claiming that 'government operatives' killed him after he purportedly revealed that Pfizer's COVID-19 vaccine contains graphene. Noack died from a heart attack, according to his partner. Austrian police said he died of natural causes. German authorities had raided Noack's apartment a year earlier, but the operation was unrelated to him, according to German police. The Pfizer vaccine doesn't contain graphene.")

9 Hopkins, C. J., "The Storming of the Reichstag Building on 29 August, 2020," Consent Factory, September 2, 2020

10 Bozkurt, Aziz, SPD, Federal Chairman of the Working Group on Migration and Diversity, "I demand tougher laws to be able to deport these life-threatening people. no matter how. does not matter where. just get out of my country. COVIDIOTS," Twitter, August 1, 2020

11 Olterman, Philip, "Berlin gives middle finger to anti-maskers in tourism agency ad," The Guardian, October 14, 2020

DER ERHOBENE ZEIGEFINGER FÜR ALLE OHNE MASKE.

Wir halten die Corona-Regeln ein.

#BERLINGEGENCORONA   BERLIN

And OK, before the Literalist Society starts flooding me with outraged emails, no, I'm not calling these Germans "Nazis." I am calling them "totalitarians." Which, at this point, given everything we know, if you're still pretending that this coronavirus in any way warrants the increasingly ridiculous "emergency measures" we are being subjected to, I'm sorry, but that is what you are.

You may not believe that is what you are … totalitarians never do, not until it is far too late.

It functions like a cult, totalitarianism. It creeps up on you, little by little, little lie by little lie, accommodation by accommodation, rationalization by rationalization ... until one day you find yourself taking orders from some twisted little narcissistic nihilist on a mission to remake the entire world.

You don't surrender to it all at once. You do it over the course of weeks and months. Imperceptibly, it becomes your reality. You do not recognize that you are in it, because everything you see is part of it, and everyone you know is in it ... except for the others, who are not part of it. The "deniers." The "deviants." The "foreigners." The "strangers." The "Covidiots." The "virus spreaders."

See, although the narratives and symbols may change, totalitarianism is totalitarianism. It doesn't really matter which uniform it wears, or which language it speaks ... it is the same abomination.

It is an idol, a simulacrum of the hubris of man, formed from the clay of the minds of the masses by megalomaniacal spiritual cripples who want to exterminate what they cannot control. And what they want to control is always everything. Everything that reminds them of their weakness and their shame. You. Me. Society. The world. Laughter. Love. Honor. Faith. The past. The future. Life. Death. Everything that will not obey them.

Unfortunately, once this kind of thing gets started, and reaches the stage we are currently experiencing, more often than not, it does not stop, not until cities lie in ruins or fields are littered with human skulls. It might take us ten or twelve years to get there, but, make no mistake, that's where we're headed, where totalitarianism is always headed ... if you don't believe me, just ask the Germans.

Year Zero

December 16, 2020

2020 was GloboCap Year Zero ... the year when the global capitalist ruling classes did away with the illusion of democracy and reminded everyone who is actually in charge, and exactly what happens when anyone challenges them.

In the relatively short span of the last ten months, societies throughout the world have been radically transformed beyond all recognition. Constitutional rights have been suspended.[1] Protest has been banned.[2] Dissent is being censored.[3] Government officials are issuing edicts restricting the most basic aspects of our lives ... where we can go, when we can go there, how long we are allowed to spend there, how many friends we are allowed to meet there, whether and when we can spend time with our families, what we are allowed to say to each other, who we can have sex with, where we have to stand, how we are allowed to eat and drink,[4] etc.

The list goes on and on.

The authorities have assumed control of the most intimate aspects of our daily lives. We are being managed like inmates in a prison, told when to eat, sleep, exercise, granted privileges for good behavior, punished for the slightest infractions of an ever-changing set of arbitrary rules, forced to wear identical, demeaning uniforms (albeit only on our faces), and otherwise relentlessly bullied, abused, and humiliated to keep us compliant.

None of which is accidental, or has anything to do with any actual virus, or any other type of public health threat. Yes, before some of you go ballistic, I *do* believe there is an actual virus, which a number

---

1 Hopkins, C. J., *"The Germans Are Back!" Consent Factory, November 22, 2020*

2 *"Berlin bans protest against coronavirus curbs," Reuters, August 26, 2020*

3 Taibbi, Matt, *"The YouTube Ban Is Un-American, Wrong, and Will Backfire - Silicon Valley couldn't have designed a better way to further radicalize Trump voters," TK News, December 11, 2020*

4 *"Die Apfel- Polizei," YouTube (https://www.youtube.com/watch?v=pSlCkEgI_ZU) (In Frankfurt, the police ordered this man to eat his apple faster, in order to comply with the Corona-Apple-Eating-Speed Regulations ... seriously, not a joke.)*

of people have actually died from, or which at least has contributed to their deaths, but there is absolutely no evidence whatsoever of any authentic public health threat that remotely justifies thc totalitarian emergency measures we are being subjected to or the damage that is being done to society. Whatever you believe about the so-called "pandemic," it really is as simple as that. Even if one accepts the official "science," you do not transform the entire planet into a pathologized-totalitarian nightmare in response to a health threat of this nature.

The notion is quite literally insane.

GloboCap is not insane, however. They know exactly what they are doing ... which is teaching us a lesson, a lesson about power. A lesson about who has it and who doesn't. For students of history it's a familiar lesson, a standard in the repertoire of empires, not to mention the repertoire of penal institutions.

The name of the lesson is "Look What We Can Do to You Any Time We Fucking Want." The point of the lesson is self-explanatory. The USA taught the world this lesson when it nuked Hiroshima and Nagasaki. GloboCap (and the US military) taught it again when they invaded Iraq and destabilized the entire Greater Middle East. It is regularly taught in penitentiaries when the prisoners start to get a little too unruly and remember that they outnumber the guards. That's where the "lockdown" concept originated. It isn't medical terminology. It is penal institution terminology.

As we have been experiencing throughout 2020, the global capitalist ruling classes have no qualms about teaching us this lesson. It's just that they would rather not to have to unless it's absolutely necessary. They would prefer that we believe we are living in "democracies," governed by the "rule of law," where everyone is "free," and so on. It's much more efficient and much less dangerous than having to repeatedly remind us that they can take away our "democratic rights" in a heartbeat, unleash armed goon squads to enforce their edicts, and otherwise control us with sheer brute force.

People who have spent time in prison or have lived in openly totalitarian societies are familiar with being ruled by brute force. Most Westerners are not, so it has come as a shock. The majority of them still can't process it. They cannot see what is staring them in the face.

They cannot see it because they can't afford to see it. If they did, it would completely short-circuit their brains. They would suffer massive psychotic breakdowns and become entirely unable to function, so their psyches will not allow them to see it.

Others, who see it, can't quite accept the simplicity of it (i.e., the lesson being taught), so they are proposing assorted complicated theories about what it is and who is behind it ... the Great Reset, China, the Illuminati, Transhumanism, Satanism, Communism, whatever. Some of these theories are at least partially accurate. Others are utter bull-goose lunacy.

They all obscure the basic point of the lesson.

The point of the lesson is that GloboCap — the entire global-capitalist system acting as a single global entity — can, virtually any time it wants, suspend the Simulation of Democracy,[5] and crack down on us with despotic force. It can (a) declare a "global pandemic" or some other type of "global emergency," (b) cancel our so-called "rights," (c) have the corporate media bombard us with lies[6] and propaganda[7] for months, (d) have the Internet companies censor any and all forms of dissent and evidence challenging said propaganda, (e) implement all kinds of new intrusive "safety" and "security" measures, including but not limited to the physical violation of our bodies[8] ... and so on.

I think you get the picture.

And the "pandemic" is only one part of the lesson. The other part is being forced to watch (or permitted to watch, depending on your perspective) as GloboCap makes an example of Trump, as they made examples of Corbyn and Sanders, as they made examples of Saddam and Gaddafi, and other "uncooperative" foreign leaders, as they will make an example of any political figurehead that challenges their power. It does not matter to GloboCap that such political figureheads pose no real threat. The people who rally around them do. Nor

---

5 Hopkins, C. J., "The Simulation of Democracy," Consent Factory, May 23, 2018

6 Greenwald, Glenn, "With News of Hunter Biden's Criminal Probe, Recall the Media Outlets That Peddled the 'Russian Disinformation' Lie," Substack, December 11, 2020

7 Richardson, Hayley, "Nightmare before Christmas: Doctors battle to save Santa's life in emotional new NHS charity advert (just don't let the children see!)," The Daily Mail, December 9, 2020

8 N.B. The violation of our bodies is important, which is why they love "cavity searches" in prison, and why the torture-happy troops at Abu Ghraib were obsessed with sexually violating their victims.

does it make the slightest difference whether these figureheads or the folks who support them identify as "left" or "right." GloboCap could not possibly care less. The figureheads are just the teaching materials in the lesson that they are teaching *us*.

And now, here we are, at the end of the lesson, not the end of the War on Populism, just the end of this critical Trumpian part of it. Once the usurper has been driven out of office, the War on Populism will be folded back into the War on Terror, or the War on Extremism, or whatever GloboCap decides to call it. The name hardly matters. It is all the same war.

Whatever they decide to call it, this is GloboCap Year Zero. It is time for reeducation, my friends. It is time for cultural revolution. No, not communist cultural revolution ... global capitalist cultural revolution. It is time to flush the aberration of the last four years down the memory hole, and implement global "New Normal" *Gleichschaltung*, to make sure that this never happens again.

Oh, yes, things are about to get "normal." Extremely "normal." Suffocatingly "normal." Unimaginably, oppressively "normal." And I'm not just talking about the "Coronavirus measures." This has been in the works for the last four years.

Remember, back in 2016, when everyone was so concerned about "normality," and how Trump was "not normal," and must never be "normalized?"

Well, here we are. This is it. This is the part where GloboCap restores "normality," a "new normality," a pathologized-totalitarian "normality," a "normality" which tolerates no dissent and demands complete ideological conformity.

From now on, when the GloboCap Intelligence Community and their mouthpieces in the corporate media tell you something happened, that thing will have happened, exactly as they say it happened, regardless of whether it actually happened, and anyone who says it didn't will be labeled an "extremist," a "conspiracy theorist," a "denier," or some other meaningless epithet. Such un-persons will be dealt with ruthlessly. They will be censored, deplatformed, demonetized, decertified, rendered unemployable, banned from traveling, socially ostracized, hospitalized, imprisoned, or otherwise erased from "normal" society.

You will do what you are told. You will not ask questions. You will believe whatever they tell you to believe. You will believe it, not because it makes any sense, but simply because you have been ordered to believe it.

They aren't trying to trick or deceive anybody. They know their lies don't make any sense. And they know that you know they don't make any sense. They want you to know it. That is the point. They want you to know they are lying to you, manipulating you, openly mocking you,[9] and that they can say and do anything they want to you, and you will go along with it, no matter how insane.

If they order you to take a fucking vaccine, you will not ask what is in the vaccine, or start whining about the "potential side effects." You will shut up and take the fucking vaccine. If they tell you to put a mask on your kid, you will put a fucking mask on your fucking kid.[10] You will not go digging up Danish studies[11] proving the pointlessness of putting masks on kids.[12] If they tell you the Russians rigged the election, then the Russians rigged the fucking election. And, if four years later they turn around and tell you that rigging an election is impossible, then rigging an election is fucking impossible. It isn't an invitation to debate. It is a GloboCap-verified fact-checked fact. You will stand (or kneel) in your designated, color-coded, social-distancing box and repeat this verified fact-checked fact, over and over, like a fucking parrot, or they will discover some new mutant variant of virus and put you back in fucking "lockdown." They will do this until you get your mind right, or you can live the rest of your life on Zoom, or tweeting content that no one but the Internet censors will ever see into the digital void in your fucking pajamas.

The choice is yours. It's is all up to you!

Or, I don't know, this is just a crazy idea, you could turn off the fucking corporate media, do a little fucking research on your own,

9 Hart, Justin, "Our officials are just stupid everywhere. Here's a DOJ official putting on his mask backstage so he can walk out with it on and take it off," Twitter, December 12, 2020

10 Feis, Aaron, "Family kicked off United Airlines flight after toddler refuses to wear mask," New York Post, December 13, 2020

11 Heneghan, Carl and Tom Jefferson, "Landmark Danish study finds no significant effect for facemask wearers," The Spectator, November 19, 2020

12 "Are Face Masks Effective? The Evidence," Swiss Policy Research, July 2020 ("So far, most studies found little to no evidence for the effectiveness of face masks in the general population, neither as personal protective equipment nor as a source control.")

grow a little intestinal fortitude, and join the rest of us "dangerous extremists" who are trying to fight back against the New Normal.

Yes, it will cost you, and we probably won't win, but you won't have to torture your kids on airplanes, and you don't even have to "deny" the virus!

That's it, my last column of 2020 ... happy totalitarian holidays!

2021

"History has stopped. Nothing exists except an endless present in which the Party is always right." — George Orwell, *1984*

That's All Folks!

January 24, 2021

As Porky Pig used to say at the end of those wacky *Looney Tunes* cartoons, that's all folks! The show is over.

Literal Russian-Asset Hitler, the Latest Greatest Threat to Western Democracy, the Monster of Mar-a-Lago, Trumpzilla, Trumpenstein, the Ayatollah of Orange Shinola, has finally been humiliated and given the bum-rush out of Washington by the heroic forces of the GloboCap "Resistance" (with a little assistance from the US military).

The whole thing went exactly to script.

Well, OK, not quite exactly to script. Despite four years of dire warnings by the corporate media, the Intelligence Community, Hollywood celebrities, the Democratic Party, faux anti-fascists, fake-Left pundits, and pretty much every utterly deluded, Trump-obsessed liberal with an Internet connection, there was no Hitlerian "Reichstag Fire," no Boogaloo, no Civil War II, no coup, no white-supremacist uprising. Nothing. The man simply got on a chopper and was flown away to his Florida resort.

I know, you're probably thinking, "wow, how embarrassing for the GloboCap 'Resistance,' being exposed as a bunch of utterly shameless, neo-Goebbelsian propagandists, and liars, and hysterical idiots, and such!" And, in any other version of reality, you'd have a point, but not in this one.

No, in this reality, "Democracy Has Prevailed!"[1] Yes, it was touch and go there for a while, as there was no guarantee that the Intelligence Community, the military-industrial complex, Western governments, the corporate media, supranational corporations, Internet oligarchs, and virtually every other component of the global-capitalist empire could keep one former game-show host with no real political power whatsoever from taking over the entire world.

---

1 Farrer, Martin, "'Democracy has prevailed': front pages across world hail Joe Biden's inaugura-tion - Newspapers focus on healing words of the new US president and his call to end America's 'uncivil war'," *The Guardian, January 21, 2021*

Still, Trump's failure to go full-Hitler, or even half-Hitler, was somewhat awkward. I mean, you can't whip millions of people into a four-year frenzy of fear and hatred of a clearly powerless ass-clown president, and portray him as a Russian Intelligence asset, and the Son of Hitler, and all the rest of it, and then just drop the act cold and laugh in their faces. That would leave them feeling like total morons who had just spent the last four years of their lives being lied to and emotionally manipulated ... or like members of a cult, or something.

Fortunately, for GloboCap, this was not a problem. All they had to do was produce a cheap simulation of "Trump going full-Hitler." It didn't even have to be convincing. They just needed a semi-dramatic event to plug into the official narrative, something they could call "an attempted coup," "an insurrection," "an attack," and so on, which millions of credulous liberals could hysterically shriek about on the Internet.

The "Storming of the Capitol" did the trick.

They held a dress rehearsal in Berlin last August,[2] and then gave the real performance in the Capitol Building. This time it was for all the money, so they went ahead and got a couple people killed.

It wasn't very hard to pull off. All they actually had to do, in both Berlin and DC, was allow a small fringe group of angry protesters to gain access to the building, film it, and then pump out the "attempted coup" narrative. It made no difference whatsoever that the "domestic terrorists" (in both Berlin and Washington) were a completely unorganized, unarmed mob that posed absolutely zero threat of "staging a coup" and "overthrowing the government." It also made not the slightest difference that Trump didn't actually "incite" the mob (yes, I put myself through the agony of reading every word of his speech, which was the usual word salad from start to finish). We're talking propaganda here, not reality.

The so-called "Violent Storming of the Capitol" set the stage for the main event, which was the show of force we have all just witnessed. Someone — I'm not entirely clear who[3] — ordered in the

2 Hopkins, C. J., "The Storming of the Reichstag Building on 29 August, 2020," Consent Factory, September 2, 2020

3 Trump was still Commander in Chief at the time.

troops, tens of thousands of them, locked down Washington, erected fences, set up road blocks and military check points, and otherwise occupied the government district.[4]

It looked like any other US-military post-"regime-change" occupation, because that's what it was, which was precisely the point. As I have been repeating for … well, for over four years now, it was always going to end this way, with GloboCap making an example of Trump and reminding everyone who is really in charge. .

Look, let's be clear about these last four years, because there are all kinds of crazy theories going around (not to mention the official GloboCap narrative), but what actually happened is pretty simple.

Here's the whole story, as concise as I can make it.

*

In 2016, the American people, sick to the gills of global capitalism and its increasingly oppressive ideology, elected an unauthorized, narcissistic ass-clown to the highest office in the land. They did this for a variety of reasons, but mostly it was just a big "fuck you" to the establishment. It was an act of rebellion against a government which they know is owned by unaccountable, supranational corporations and supercilious oligarchs who openly detest them. It was an act of rebellion against a system of government they know they have no influence over, and are not going to have any influence over. It was an act of rebellion against global capitalism, the unopposed, global-hegemonic system which has dominated the world for the last thirty years … whether they realized what they were rebelling against or not.

This act of rebellion happened on the heels of Brexit (another such act of rebellion) and in the context of the rise of assorted "populist" movements in Western and Eastern Europe. When Trump actually won in 2016, the global capitalist ruling classes realized they had a serious problem, a "populist" rebellion in the heart of the empire. So they suspended the Global War on Terror and launched the War on Populism.

---

4 *Schwartz, Matthew S., "Up To 25,000 Troops Descend On Washington For Biden's Inauguration," National Public Radio, January 16, 2021*

The ultimate objective of the War on Populism was to neutralize this "populist" rebellion and remind the public who is actually running things. Think of the Trump era as a prison riot. In any maximum security prison, the prisoners know they can't escape, but they can definitely raise a little hell now and then, which they tend to do when they get really tired of being abused and neglected by the prison guards. Most prison riots run out of steam on their own, but if they go on too long or get too ugly, the penal authorities typically respond by shooting a few prisoners (usually the ringleaders), and reminding the inmates that they are in a prison, and that the owners and staff of the prison have guns, whereas they have shivs made out of spoons and toothbrushes.

This, basically, is what we've just experienced. The global capitalist ruling classes have just reminded us who is really in charge, who the US military really answers to, and how quickly they can strip away the facade of democracy and the rule of law.

They have reminded us of this for the last ten months, by putting us under house arrest, beating and arresting us for not following orders, for not wearing masks, for taking walks without permission, for having the audacity to protest their decrees, for challenging their official propaganda, about the virus, the election results, etc. They are reminding us currently by censoring dissent, and deplatforming anyone they deem a threat to their official narratives and ideology.

In other words, GloboCap is teaching us a lesson. I don't know how much clearer they could make it. They just installed a new puppet president, who can't even simulate mental acuity, in a locked-down, military-guarded ceremony which no one was allowed to attend, except for a few members of the ruling classes. They got some epigone of Albert Speer to convert the Mall (where the public normally gathers) into a "field of flags" symbolizing "unity."[5] They even did the Nazi "Cathedral of Light" thing. To hammer the point home, they got Lady Gaga to dress up as a *Hunger Games* character with a "Mockingjay" brooch and sing the National Anthem.[6]

5 *"'Field of Flags' lighting ceremony honors U.S. states and territories ahead of Biden's inauguration," PBS News Hour, January 18, 2021*

6 Zornosa, Laura, *"The mysterious case of the Lady Gaga inauguration bird and 'The Hunger Games'," Los Angeles Times, January 20, 2021*

They broadcast this spectacle to the entire world.

And the lesson isn't quite over yet … it won't be over for a while. The "War on Populism" will simply morph into the "New Normal War on Domestic Terror," which will become one more theater in the "Global War on Terror," which has been on hiatus, and which will now resume.

As I have pointed out repeatedly over the past four years, we appear to be headed toward a dystopian future in which there will basically be two classes of people: (a) "normals" (i.e., those who conform to global-capitalist ideology and decrees); and (b) the "extremists" (i.e., those who don't).

It will make no difference whatsoever what type of "extremists" these "extremists" are … religious-fundamentalist extremists, Muslim extremists, Christian extremists, right-wing extremists, left-wing extremists, white-supremacist or Black-nationalist extremists, virus deniers, anti-vaxxers, conspiracy theorists, anti-maskers, recalcitrant transphobians, anti-transhumanists, pronoun resisters, defiant oppositionalists … or whatever. The names don't really matter.

The point is, conform or be labelled an "extremist," a "domestic terrorist," or some other type of "antisocial person" or "social deviant," or "potential threat to public health."

I don't claim to know every detail, but one thing seems abundantly clear. We are not going back to the way things were. GloboCap has been explaining this to us, over and over, for almost a year. They couldn't have made it any more explicit. When they warned us to get ready because a "New Normal" was coming, they meant it.

And now … well … here it is.

The New Normal War on Domestic Terror

February 8, 2021

If you enjoyed the Global War on Terror, you are going to love the new War on Domestic Terror! It's just like the original Global War on Terror, except that this time the "Terrorists" are all "Domestic Violent Extremists" ("DVEs"), "Homegrown Violent Extremists" ("HVEs"), "Violent Conspiracy-Theorist Extremists" ("VCTEs"), "Violent Reality Denialist Extremists" (VRDEs"), "Insurrectionary Micro-Aggressionist Extremists" ("IMAEs"), "People Who Make Liberals Feel Uncomfortable" ("PWMLFUs"), and anyone else the Department of Homeland Security wants to label an "extremist" and slap a ridiculous acronym on.

According to the "National Terrorism Advisory System Bulletin"[1] issued by the DHS on January 27, 2021, these DCEs, HVEs, VCTEs, VRDEs, IMAEs, and PWMLFUs are "ideologically-motivated violent extremists with objections to the exercise of governmental authority" and other "perceived grievances fueled by false narratives." They are believed to be "motivated by a range of issues, including anger over Covid-19 restrictions, the 2020 election results, police use of force," and other dangerous "false narratives" (e.g., the existence of the "deep state," "herd immunity," "biological sex," "God," and so on).

"Inspired by foreign terrorist groups" and "emboldened by the breach of the US Capitol Building," this diabolical network of "domestic terrorists" is "plotting attacks against government facilities," "threatening violence against critical infrastructure" and actively "citing misinformation and conspiracy theories about Covid-19." For all we know, they might be huddled in the "Wolf's Lair" at Mar-a-Lago right now, plotting a devastating terrorist attack with those WMDs we never found in Iraq, or generating population-adjusted death-

---

1 Levine, Mike, "DHS uses federal alert system for 1st time in a year to warn of domestic terrorist threat," ABC News, January 27, 2021

rate charts going back 20 years,[2] or posting pictures of "extremist frogs" on the Internet.[3]

The Department of Homeland Security is "concerned," as are its counterparts throughout the global-capitalist empire. The New Normal War on Domestic Terror isn't just a war on American "domestic terror." The "domestic terror" threat is international. France has just passed a "Global Security Law"[4] banning citizens from filming the police beating the living snot out of people (among other "anti-terrorist" provisions). In the Netherlands, the police are cracking down on the VCTEs, VRDEs, and other "angry citizens who hate the system," who have been protesting over nightly curfews.[5]

Suddenly, everywhere you look (or at least if you are looking in the corporate media), "global extremism networks are growing." It's time for Globocap to take the gloves off again, root the "terrorists" out of their hidey holes, and roll out a new official narrative.

Actually, there's not much new about it. When you strip away all the silly new acronyms, the New Normal War on Domestic Terror is basically just a combination of the "War on Terror" narrative and the "New Normal" narrative, i.e., a militarization of the so-called "New Normal" and a pathologization of the "War on Terror." Why would GloboCap want to do that, you ask?

I think you know, but I'll go ahead and tell you.

See, the problem with the original "Global War on Terror" was that it wasn't actually all that global. It was basically just a war on Islamic "terrorism" (i.e., resistance to global capitalism and its post-ideological ideology), which was fine as long as GloboCap was just destabilizing and restructuring the Greater Middle East.

It was put on hold in 2016, so that GloboCap could focus on defeating "populism" (i.e., resistance to global capitalism and its post-ideological ideology), make an example of Donald Trump, and demonize everyone who voted for him (or just refused to take

---

2 *Chart unavailable; Alex Berenson deplatformed by Twitter. See, e.g., "Covid-19 Mortality: A Global Overview," Swiss Policy Research, May 2021*

3 *"Pepe the Frog," ADL.org*

4 *Bell, Melissa, "French lawmakers pass controversial bill that restricts the publication of images of police," CNN, November 25, 2021*

5 *Walsh, David, "'Angry citizens who hate the system': Why the riots in the Netherlands go beyond a COVID curfew," Euronews, January 28, 2021*

part in their free and fair elections),[6] which they have just finished doing, in spectacular fashion. So, now it's back to "War on Terror" business, except with a whole new cast of "terrorists," or, technically, an expanded cast of "terrorists." (I rattled off a list in my previous column.)

In short, GloboCap has simply expanded, recontextualized, and pathologized the "War on Terror" (i.e., the war on resistance to global capitalism and its post-ideological ideology).

This was always inevitable, of course. A globally-hegemonic system (e.g., global capitalism) has no external enemies, as there is no territory "outside" the system. Its only enemies are within the system, and thus, by definition, are insurgents, also known as "terrorists" and "extremists." These terms are utterly meaningless, obviously. They are purely strategic, deployed against anyone who deviates from GloboCap's official ideology ... which, in case you were wondering, is called "normality" (or, in our case, currently, "New Normality").

In earlier times, these "terrorists" and "extremists" were known as "heretics," "apostates," and "blasphemers." Today, they are also known as "deniers," e.g., "science deniers," "Covid deniers," and recently, more disturbingly, "reality deniers."

This is an essential part of the pathologization of the "War on Terror" narrative. The new breed of "terrorists" do not just hate us for our freedom; they hate us because they hate "reality." They are no longer our political or ideological opponents; they are suffering from a psychiatric disorder. They no longer need to be argued with or listened to; they need to be "treated," "reeducated," and "deprogrammed," until they accept "Reality."

If you think I'm exaggerating the totalitarian nature of the "New Normal/War on Terror" narrative ... well, I refer you to *The New York Times*, in which a recent op-ed explores the concept of an official government "Reality Czar" to deal with our "Reality Crisis."[7]

And this is just the beginning, of course. The consensus (at least in GloboCap circles) is, the New Normal War on Domestic Terror

---

6 Ball, Molly, *"The Secret History of the Shadow Campaign that Saved the 2020 Election,"* TIME, February 5, 2021

7 Roose, Kevin, *"How the Biden Administration Can Help Solve our Reality Crisis,"* The New York Times, February 2, 2021

will probably continue for the next 10 to 20 years,[8] which should provide the global-capitalist ruling classes with more than enough time to carry out the "Great Reset,"[9] destroy what's left of human society, and condition the public to get used to living like cringing, neo-feudal peasants who have to ask permission to leave their houses. We're still in the initial "shock and awe" phase (which they will have to scale back a bit eventually), but just look at how much they've already accomplished.

The economic damage is literally incalculable. Millions have been plunged into desperate poverty, countless independent businesses have been crushed, whole industries crippled, developing countries rendered economically dependent (i.e., compliant) for the foreseeable future, as billionaires amassed over $1 trillion in wealth[10] and supranational corporate behemoths consolidated their dominance across the planet.

And that's just the economic damage. The attack on society has been even more dramatic. GloboCap, in the space of one year, has transformed the majority of the global masses into an enormous, paranoid totalitarian cult that is no longer capable of even rudimentary reasoning. (I'm not going to go on about it here … at this point, you either recognize it or you're in it.)

They're actually lining up in parking lots, the double-masked members of this Covidian Cult, to be injected with an experimental genetic "vaccine" that they believe will save the human species from a virus that causes mild to moderate common-cold or flu-like symptoms in roughly 95% of those "infected," and that over 99% of the "infected" survive.[11]

So, it's no big surprise that these same mindless cultists are gung-ho for the New Normal War on Domestic Terror, and the upcoming globally-televised show trial of Donald Trump for "inciting insurrection," and the ongoing corporate censorship of the Internet, and

8 Demirjian, Karoun, "Bipartisan support emerges for domestic-terror bills as experts warn threat may last '10 to 20 years'," The Washington Post, February 4, 2021

9 Winter Oak, "Klaus Schwab and His Great Fascist Reset – An Overview," Wrong Kind of Green, October 5, 2020

10 Beer, Tommy, "Report: American Billionaires Have Added More Than $1 Trillion in Wealth During Pandemic," Forbes, January 26, 2021

11 "Facts about Covid," Swiss Policy Research, April 2020 (updated March 2022)

can't wait to be issued their "Freedom Passports,"[12] which will allow them to take part in "New Normal" life — double-masked and socially-distanced, naturally — while having their every movement and transaction, and every word they write on Facebook, or in an email, or say to someone on their smartphones, or in the vicinity of their 5G toasters, recorded by GloboCap's Intelligence Services and their corporate partners, subsidiaries, and assigns.

These people have nothing at all to worry about, as they would never dream of disobeying orders, and could not produce an original thought, much less one displeasing to GloboCap, if you held a fake apocalyptic plague to their heads.

As for the rest of us "extremists," "domestic terrorists," "heretics," and "reality deniers," (i.e., anyone criticizing global capitalism, or challenging its official narratives, and its increasingly totalitarian ideology, regardless of our specific DHS acronyms), I wish I had something hopeful to tell you, but, the truth is, things aren't looking so good. I guess I'll see you in a quarantine camp, or in the psych ward, or an offshore detention facility … or, I don't know, maybe I'll see you in the streets.

---

12 *Mzezewa, Tariro, "Coming Soon: The Vaccine Passport," The New York Times, February 4, 2021*

The Vaccine (Dis)Information War

February 23, 2021

Good news, folks! It appears that GloboCap's Genetic Modification Division has come up with a miracle vaccine for Covid! It's an absolutely safe, non-experimental, messenger-RNA vaccine that teaches your cells to produce a protein that triggers an immune response, just like your body's immune-system response ... only better, because it's made by corporations!

OK, technically, it hasn't been approved for use — that process normally takes several years — so I guess it's slightly "experimental," but the US Food and Drug Administration and the European Medicines Agency have issued "Emergency Use Authorizations," and it has been "tested extensively for safety and effectiveness," according to Facebook's anonymous "fact checkers," so there's absolutely nothing to worry about.

This non-experimental experimental vaccine is truly a historic development, because apart from saving the world from a virus that causes mild to moderate flu-like symptoms (or, more commonly, no symptoms whatsoever) in roughly 95% of those infected, and that over 99% of those infected survive, the possibilities for future applications of messenger-RNA technology, and the genetic modification of humans, generally, is virtually unlimited at this point.

Just imagine all the diseases we can "cure," and all the genetic "mistakes" we can fix, now that we can reprogram people's genes to do whatever we want ... cancer, heart disease, dementia, blindness, not to mention the common cold! We could even cure psychiatric disorders, like "antisocial personality disorder," "oppositional defiant disorder," and other "conduct disorders" and "personality disorders." Who knows? In another hundred years, we will probably be able to genetically cleanse the human species of age-old scourges, like racism, sexism, anti-Semitism, homophobia, transphobia, etcetera, by reprogramming everyone's defective alleles, or implanting some kind of nanotechnological neurosynaptic chips into our brains. The only thing standing in our way is people's totally irrational resistance to letting corporations redesign the human organism, which, clearly, was rather poorly designed, and thus is vulnerable to all these horrible diseases, and emotional and behavioral disorders.

But I'm getting a little ahead of myself.

The important thing at the moment is to defeat this common-flu-like pestilence that has no significant effect on age-adjusted death rates and the mortality profile of which is more or less identical to the normal mortality profile,[1] but which has nonetheless left the global corporatocracy no choice but to "lock down" the entire planet, plunge millions into desperate poverty, order everyone to wear medical-looking masks, unleash armed goon squads to raid people's homes, and otherwise transform society into a pathologized-totalitarian nightmare. And, of course, the only way to do that (i.e., save humanity from a flu-like bug) is to coercively vaccinate every single human being on the planet Earth!

OK, you're probably thinking that doesn't make much sense, this crusade to vaccinate the entire species against a relatively standard respiratory virus, but that's just because you're still thinking critically. You really need to stop thinking like that. As *The New York Times* just pointed out, "critical thinking isn't helping."[2] In fact, it might be symptomatic of one of those "disorders" I just mentioned above.[3] Critical thinking leads to "vaccine hesitancy," which is why corporations are working with governments to immediately censor any and all content that deviates from the official Covid-19 narrative[4] and deplatform the authors of such content,[5] or discredit them as "anti-vax disinformationists."[6]

1 *"Studies on Covid Lethality,"* Swiss Policy Research, May 2020

2 Warzel, Charlie, *"Don't Go Down the Rabbit Hole,"* The New York Times, February 18, 2021

3 Stieg, Cory, *"Sociopathic traits linked to not wearing a mask or social distancing during pandemic: study,"* CNBC, September 2 2020

4 O'Neill, Jesse, *"White House working with social media giants to silence anti-vaxxers,"* New York Post, February 19, 2021

5 Iyengar, Rishi, *"Robert F. Kennedy Jr. has been banned from Instagram,"* CNN, February 11, 2021

6 Bose, Nandita, *"White House working with Facebook and Twitter to tackle anti-vaxxers,"* Reuters, February 19, 2021

For example, Children's Health Defense,[7] which has been reporting on so-called "adverse events" and deaths in connection with the Covid vaccines, despite the fact that, according to the authorities, "there are no safety problems with the vaccines"[8] and "there is no link between Covid-19 vaccines and those who die after receiving them."[9] In fact, according to the "fact-checkers" at *Reuters*, these purported "reports of adverse events" "may contain information that is incomplete, inaccurate, coincidental, or unverifiable!"[10]

Yes, you're reading between the lines right. The corporate media can't come right out and say it, but it appears that the "anti-vax disinformationists" are fabricating "adverse events" out of whole cloth and hacking them into the VAERS database and other such systems around the world. Worse, they are somehow infiltrating these made-up stories into the mainstream media in order to lure people into "vaccine hesitancy" and stop us from vaccinating every man, woman, and child in the physical universe, repeatedly, on an ongoing basis, for as long as the "medical experts" deem necessary.[11]

Here are just a few examples of their handiwork …

> In Norway, 23 elderly people died after receiving the Pfizer vaccine.[12] However, according to *Reuters'* "fact-checkers," it turns out that old people just die sometimes, especially in nursing homes, from a variety of causes, unless they haven't been vaccinated, in which case they definitely died of Covid, regardless of what they actually died of.

7 Children's Health Defense, "One-Third of Deaths Reported to CDC After COVID Vaccines Occurred Within 18 Hours of Vaccination," The Defender, February 19, 2021

8 Reuters, "CDC says no safety problems with Pfizer, Moderna Covid vaccines after first month," NBC News, February 19, 2021

9 Widmer, Stephanie, "Fact-check: No link between COVID-19 vaccines and those who die after receiving them, ABC News, February 3, 2021

10 "Fact check: Reports of adverse effects in US database aren't confirmed to be linked to vaccination," Reuters, February 14, 2021

11 O'Reilly, Luke, "Boris Johnson tells G7 summit 'whole world' must be vaccinated," Evening Standard, February 14, 2021

12 "Fact check: Discussion of deaths in elderly vaccine recipients in Norway lacks context," Reuters, January 20, 2021

For example, a 99-year-old man suffering from dementia and emphysema, who tested negative for the virus three times, was added to the "Covid deaths" figures[13] because a nursing home doctor "assumed" it was Covid (which GloboCap has expressly instructed him to do).[14]

In Germany, 13 of 40 residents of one nursing home died after being vaccinated, but this was just a "tragic coincidence," which had absolutely nothing to do with the vaccine.[15]

In Spain, in another "tragic coincidence," 46 nursing home residents who received the Pfizer-BioNTech vaccine died within the course of one month.[16] A further 28 of the 94 residents and 12 staff members subsequently tested positive.

In Florida, a healthy middle-aged doctor died from an unusual blood disorder two weeks after receiving the vaccine, but, according to the experts, the sudden onset of this rare immunological blood disorder "should not be interpreted as linked to the vaccine," and was probably just a total coincidence.[17]

In California, a 60-year-old X-ray technologist received a second dose of the Pfizer vaccine. A few hours later he had trouble breathing. He was hospi-

13 Mooney, Bel, "My dad Ted passed three Covid tests and died of a chronic illness yet he's officially one of Britain's 120,000 victims of the virus and is far from alone... so how many more are there?" The Daily Mail, February 19, 2021

14 Hitchens, Peter, "How Covid deaths are recorded," Mail Online, February 4, 2021

15 Hilser, Stefan, "Elf Todesfälle im Seniorenwohnpark: Laut Bürgermeister ein „tragischer Zufall" und ohne Zusammenhang zum Impftermin" ("Eleven deaths in a senior citizens' home: According to the mayor, a "tragic coincidence" unrelated to their vaccinations"), Südkurier, January 25, 2021

16 McGovern, Celeste, "46 Nursing Home Residents in Spain Die Within 1 Month of Getting Pfizer COVID Vaccine," The Defender, February 16, 2021

17 D'Ambrosio, Amanda, "Officials Investigate Physician's Death After COVID Vaccination," MedPage Today, January 27, 2021

talized and died four days later.[18] His widow says she's not ready at this point to link her husband's death to the vaccine. "I'm not putting any blame on Pfizer," she said.[19] So, probably just another coincidence.

A 78-year-old woman in California died immediately after being vaccinated, but her death was not related to the vaccine, health officials assured the public.[20] "[She] received an injection of the Covid-19 vaccine manufactured by Pfizer around noon. While seated in the observation area after the injection, [she] complained of feeling discomfort and while being evaluated by medical personnel she lost consciousness." Despite the sudden death of his wife, her husband intends to receive a second dose.

A former Detroit news anchor died just one day after receiving the vaccine, but it was probably just a coincidental stroke, which the "normal side effects of the vaccine may have masked."[21]

Also in Michigan, a 90-year-old man died the day after receiving the vaccine, but, again, this was just a tragic coincidence.[22] As Dr. David Gorski explained, "the baseline death rate of 90-year-olds is high because they're 90 years old," which makes perfect sense, unless, of course, they died of Covid, in which case their age and underlying conditions make absolutely no difference whatsoever.

18 "Coronavirus vaccine: OC health care worker dies days after receiving 2nd shot, report says," ABC Chanel 7 Eyewitness News, January 29, 2021

19 Cabrera, Tony, "Family of OC man who died days after vaccination say they remain proponents of vaccine," ABC Chanel 7 Eyewitness News, January 29, 2021

20 "78-Year-Old Woman Dies After Receiving COVID-19 Vaccine; No Link Suspected," NBC Chanel 4 News, February 13, 2021

21 Garger, Kenneth, "Former Detroit news anchor dies one day after receiving COVID-19 vaccine," New York Post, February 18, 2021

22 Shamus, Kristen Jordan, "Macomb County man, 90, dies after COVID-19 vaccine — but doctors say shots are safe," Detroit Free Press, February 18, 2021

In Kentucky, two nuns at a monastery died, and more than two dozen others tested positive, in a sudden "Covid-19 outbreak" that began two days after the nuns were vaccinated. The monastery had been completely closed to visitors and Covid-free up to that point, but the nuns were old and had "health issues," and so on.[23]

In Virginia, a 58-year-old grandmother died within minutes after receiving the vaccine,[24] but, as Facebook's "fact checkers" prominently pointed out, it had to be just another coincidence, because the "vaccines have been tested for safety extensively."

And then there are all the people on Facebook sharing their stories of loved ones who have died shortly after receiving the Covid vaccine, who the Facebook "fact checkers" are doing their utmost to discredit with their official-looking "fact-check notices."[25]

OK, I know it's uncomfortable to have to face things like that (i.e., global Internet corporations like Facebook implying that these people are lying, or are using the sudden deaths of their loved ones to discourage others from getting vaccinated), especially if you're just trying to follow orders and parrot official propaganda (even the most fanatical Covidian Cultists probably still have a shred of human empathy buried deep in their cold little hearts). But there's an information war on, folks![26] You're either with the Corporatocracy or against it! This is no time to get squeamish, or ... you know, publicly exhibit an ounce of compassion.

What would your friends and colleagues think of you?!

---

23 Goffinet, Jared, "2 nuns die, 28 test positive for COVID-19 at NKY monastery," FOX19 Now, February 8, 2021

24 Donovan, Chelsea, "No autopsy performed after Gloucester woman's death minutes after receiving Pfizer vaccine," WTKR, February 16, 2021

25 "Approved COVID-19 vaccines have been tested extensively for safety and effectiveness. Source: World Health Organization."

26 Bland, Archie, "The information warriors fighting 'robot zombie army' of coronavirus sceptics," The Guardian, January 25, 2021

No, report these anti-vaxxers to the authorities, shout them down on social media, switch off your critical-thinking faculties, and get in line to get your vaccination! The fate of the human species depends on it! And, if you're lucky, maybe GloboCap will even give you one of those nifty numerical Covid-vaccine tattoos for free![27]

27 George, Bethany, "People Are Getting COVID Vaccine Tattoos to Celebrate Getting Their Shot," *Shape, May 26, 2021*

The "Unvaccinated" Question

March 29, 2021

So, the New Normals are discussing "the Unvaccinated Question." What is to be done with us? No, not those who haven't been "vaccinated" *yet*. Us. The "Covidiots." The "Covid deniers." The "science deniers." The "reality deniers." Those who refuse to get "vaccinated," ever.

There is no place for us in New Normal society. The New Normals know this and so do we. To them, we are a suspicious, alien tribe of people. We do not share their ideological beliefs. We do not perform their loyalty rituals, or we do so only grudgingly, because they force us to do so. We traffic in arcane "conspiracy theories," like "pre-March-2020 science," "natural herd immunity," "population-adjusted death rates," "Sweden," "Florida," and other heresies.

They do not trust us. We are strangers among them. They suspect we feel superior to them. They believe we are conspiring against them, that we want to deceive them, confuse them, cheat them, pervert their culture, abuse their children, contaminate their precious bodily fluids, and perpetrate God knows what other horrors.

So they are discussing the need to segregate us, how to segregate us, when to segregate us, in order to protect society from us. In their eyes, we are no more than criminals, or, worse, a plague,[1] an infestation. In the words of someone (I can't quite recall who), "getting rid of the Unvaccinated is not a question of ideology. It is a question of cleanliness," or something like that.

In Israel, Estonia, Denmark, Germany, the USA, and other New Normal countries, they have already begun the segregation process. In the UK, it's just a matter of time.[2]

---

1 *"A Plague Of Denial," Eugene Weekly, December 3, 2020*

2 *Kershner, Isabel, "As Israel Reopens, 'Whoever Does Not Get Vaccinated Will Be Left Behind',"
The New York Times, February 18, 2021; "Estonia and WHO to jointly develop digital vaccine*

The WEF, WHO, EU, and other transnational entities are helping to streamline the new segregation system, which, according to
the WEF, "will need to be harmonized by a normative body, such as
the WHO, to ensure that is ethical."[3]

Here in Germany, the government is considering banning us from
working outside our homes.[4] We are already banned from flying on
commercial airlines.[5] (We can still use the trains, if we dress up like
New Normals, i.e., by wearing a medical-looking mask.) In the village of Potsdam, just down the road from Wannsee (which name
you might recall from your 20th-Century history), we are banned
from entering shops and restaurants.[6] (I'm not sure whether we can
still use the sidewalks, or whether we have to walk in the gutters.)
In Saxony, our children are forbidden from attending school.[7] The
Berliner Ensemble (the theater founded by Bertolt Brecht and
Helene Weigel, lifelong opponents of totalitarianism and fascism),
has banned us from attending New Normal performances.

In the USA, we are being banned by universities.[8] Our children
are being banned from public schools.[9]

In New York, the new "Excelsior Pass" will allow New Normals to
attend cultural and sports events (and patronize bars and restaurants,

certificate to strengthen COVAX," World Health Organization, October 7, 2020; dos Santos,
Nina, Antonia Mortensen and Susanne Gargiulo, "Covid passports could deliver a 'summer of joy,'
Denmark hopes," CNN, February 13, 2021; Grenier, Elizabeth, "Berlin launches pilot project for
theaters as new COVID wave starts, Deutsche Welle, March 20, 2021 ("Cultural venues want to
be able to plan their safe reopening. Berlin is holding a series of events to develop a new strategy:
Tickets come with a COVID test."); Reynolds, Tim, "[Miami] Heat to open vaccinated-only
sections for fans on April 1," Associated Press, March 24, 2021; "Covid: Jab passports possible 'after
all offered vaccine'," BBC News, March 25, 2021

3 Markovitz, Gayle, "What is a 'vaccine passport' and will you need one the next time you travel?"
World Economic Forum, May 5, 2021

4 "Müller bringt Corona-Testpflicht für Arbeitnehmer ins Spiel" ("Berlin mayor Müller puts mandatory Corona tests for employees on the table"), Berliner Zeitung, March 21, 2021

5 "Testpflicht für Flugreisende" ("Mandatory tests for air travelers"), WDR, March 26, 2021

6 "In Potsdam gilt ab Samstag Testpflicht im Einzelhandel" ("Mandatory tests required for retail
business as of Saturday"), RBB, Antenne Brandenburg, March 24, 2021

7 Ganswindt, Till, "Corona-Testpflicht an Schulen - Lehrer in Sachsen werden von Testverweig-
erern angefeindet" ("Compulsory corona testing in schools - Teachers in Saxony are being attacked
by those who refuse to test"), MDR, March 23, 2021

8 Chapell, Bill, "Rutgers To Require Vaccine Proof For 'All Students Planning To Attend This
Fall'," National Public Radio, March 25, 2020

9 Wiedmann, Tom, "COVID Testing Planned for Newark Schools Students, Staff Upon April
Return," Tap IntoNewark, March 24, 2021

eventually) secure in the knowledge that the Unvaccinated have been prevented from entering, or segregated in an "Unvaccinated Only" section.[10] The pass system, designed by IBM, which, if history is any guide, is pretty good at designing such systems (OK, technically, it was *Deutsche Hollerith Maschinen Gesellschaft*, IBM's Nazi-Germany subsidiary[11]), was launched this past weekend to considerable fanfare.

And this is only the very beginning.

Israel's "Green Pass"[12] is the model for the future, which makes sense, in a sick, fascistic kind of way. When you're already an apartheid state, what's a little more apartheid?

OK, I know what the New Normals are thinking. They're thinking I'm "misleading" people again. That I'm exaggerating. That this isn't real segregation, and certainly nothing like "medical apartheid."

After all, as the New Normals will sternly remind us, no one is forcing us to get "vaccinated." If we choose not to, or can't for medical reasons, all we have to do is submit to a "test" (you know, the one where they ram that 9-inch swab up into your sinus cavities) within 24 hours before we want to go out to dinner, or attend the theater or a sports event, or visit a museum, or attend a university, or take our children to school or a playground, and our test results will serve as our "vaccine passports!" We just present them to the appropriate Covid Compliance Officer, and, assuming the results are negative, of course, we will be allowed to take part in New Normal society just as if we'd been "vaccinated."

Either way, "vaccine" or "test," the New Normal officials will be satisfied, because the tests and passes are really just stage props. The point is the display of mindless obedience.

Even if you take the New Normals at their word, if you are under 65 and in relatively good health, getting "vaccinated" is more or less pointless, except as a public display of compliance and belief in the official Covid-19 narrative (i.e., the foundation stone of the New

10 Weintraub, Karen and Elizabeth Weise, "New York launches nation's first 'vaccine passports.'," *USA Today*, March 26, 2021

11 Black, Edwin, "The Nazi Party: IBM & 'Death's Calculator'," *Jewish Virtual Library*, (www. jewishvirtuallibrary.org)

12 Ferguson, Cat and Joshua Mitnick, "Israel's 'green pass' is an early vision of how we leave lockdown," *MIT Technology Review*, March 1, 2021

Normal ideology). Even the high priests of their "Science" confess that it doesn't prevent you spreading the "plague."[13] And the PCR tests are virtually meaningless, as even the WHO finally admitted.[14] You can positive-PCR-test a pawpaw fruit[15] ... but you might want to be careful who you tell if you do that.[16]

In contrast to the "vaccination" and the "test" themselves, the forced choice between them is not at all meaningless. It is not an accident that both alternatives involve the violation of our bodies, literally the penetration of our bodies. It doesn't really matter what is in the "vaccines" or what "results" the "tests" produce. The ritual is a demonstration of power, the power of the New Normals (i.e., global capitalism's new face) to control our bodies, to dominate them, to violate them, psychologically and physically.

Now, don't get excited, my "conspiracy theorist" friends. I haven't gone full-QAnon just yet. Bill Gates and Klaus Schwab are not sitting around together, sipping adrenochrome on George Soros' yacht, dreaming up ways to rape people's noses. This stuff is built into the structure of the system. It is a standard feature of totalitarian societies, cults, churches, self-help groups, and ... well, human society, generally.

Being forced to repeat a physical action which only makes sense within a specific ideology reifies that ideology within us. There is nothing inherently diabolical about this. It is a basic socialization technology. It is how we socialize our children. It is why we conduct weddings, baptisms, and bar mitzvahs. It is how we turn young men and women into soldiers. It is how actors learn their blocking and their lines. It is why the Nazis held all those theatrical rallies. It is why our "democracies" hold elections. It is also basic ceremonial magic ... but that's a topic for a different column.

---

13 Fuller, Deborah, "Can vaccinated people still spread the coronavirus?" *The Conversation*, March 8, 2021 ("Does vaccination completely prevent infection? The short answer is no. You can still get infected after you've been vaccinated. But your chances of getting seriously ill are almost zero.")

14 "WHO (finally) admits PCR test is potentially flawed," *OffGuardian*, January 25, 2021

15 Staff, "President queries Tanzania coronavirus kits after goat test," *Reuters*, May 3, 2020 ("Coronavirus test kits used in Tanzania were dismissed as faulty by President John Magufuli on Sunday, because he said they had returned positive results on samples taken from a goat and a pawpaw.")

16 "John Magufuli: Tanzania's president dies aged 61 after Covid rumours," *BBC*, March 18, 2021

The issue, at the moment, is "the Unvaccinated Question," and the public rituals that are being performed to render the New Normal ideology "reality," and what to do about those of us who refuse to participate in those rituals, who refuse to forswear "old normal" reality and convert to New Normalism (or at least pretend to) so that we can function in society without being segregated, criminalized, or "diagnosed" as "sociopathic" or otherwise psychiatrically disordered.[17]

For us "conspiracy-theorizing reality deniers," there is no getting around this dilemma.

This isn't Europe in the 1930s. There isn't anywhere to emigrate to … or, OK, there is, temporarily, in some of the US states that have been staging rebellions, and other such "old normal" oases, but how long do you think that will last? They're already rolling out the "mutant variants,"[18] and God only knows what will happen when the long-term effects of the "vaccines" kick in.

No, for most of us denizens of the global capitalist empire, it looks like the New Normal is here to stay. So, unless we are prepared to become New Normals, or disguise ourselves as New Normals in public, we are going to have to stand and fight.

It is going to get rather ugly, and personal, but there isn't any way to avoid that. Given that many New Normals are our friends and colleagues, and even members of our families, it is tempting to believe that they will "come to their senses," that "this is all just a hysterical overreaction," and that "everything will go back to normal soon."

This would be a monumental error on our parts … very possibly a fatal error.

Totalitarian movements, when they reach this stage, do not simply stop on their own. They continue to advance toward their full expressions, ultimately transforming entire societies into monstrous mirror-images of themselves … unless they are opposed by serious resistance.

---

17 Dolan, Eric W., "Sociopathic traits linked to non-compliance with mask guidelines and other COVID-19 containment measures," PsyPost, August 22, 2020

18 Goodman, Brenda, MA, "New COVID 'Super Strains' Could Disrupt Life Again," WebMD, January 7, 2021

There is a window at the beginning when such resistance has a chance. That window is still open, but it is closing, fast. I can't tell you how best to resist, but I can tell you it starts with seeing things clearly, and calling things, and people, exactly what they are.

Let's not make the same mistake that other minorities have made throughout history when confronted with a new totalitarian ideology. See the New Normals for what they are, maybe not deep down in their hearts, but what they have collectively become a part of, because it is the movement that is in control now, not the rational individuals they used to be.

Above all, recognize where this is headed, where totalitarian movements are always headed. See, e.g., Milton Mayer's *They Thought They Were Free: The Germans 1933-45*.[19]

No, the Unvaccinated are not the Jews and the New Normals are not flying big swastika flags, but totalitarianism is totalitarianism, regardless of which Goebbelsian Big Lies, and ideology, and official enemies it is selling. The historical context and costumes change, but its ruthless trajectory remains the same.

Today, the New Normals are offering us a "choice" ... conform to their official New Normal ideology or suffer social segregation.

What do you imagine they have planned for us tomorrow?

---

19 *Mayer, Milton, They Thought They Were Free, The Germans, 1933-45, University of Chicago Press, 1955*

The Covidian Cult Part II

April 21, 2021

Back in October of 2020, I wrote an essay called *The Covidian Cult*,[1] in which I described the so-called "New Normal" as a global totalitarian ideological movement. Developments over the last six months have borne out the accuracy of that analogy.

A full year after the initial roll-out of the utterly horrifying and completely fictional photos of people dropping dead in the streets,[2] the projected 3.4% death rate,[3] and all the rest of the official propaganda, notwithstanding the absence of any actual scientific evidence of an apocalyptic plague (and the abundance of evidence to the contrary), millions of people continue to behave like members of an enormous death cult, walking around in public with medical-looking masks, robotically repeating vacuous platitudes, torturing children, the elderly, the disabled, demanding that everyone submit to being injected with dangerous experimental "vaccines," and just generally acting delusional and psychotic.

How did we ever get to this point ... to the point where, as I put it in *The Covidian Cult*, "instead of the cult existing as an island within the dominant culture, the cult has become the dominant culture, and those of us who have not joined the cult have become the isolated islands within it?"

To understand this, one needs to understand how cults control the minds of their members, because totalitarian ideological movements operate more or less the same way, just on a much larger, societal scale. There is a wealth of research and knowledge on this subject (I mentioned Robert J. Lifton in my earlier essay), but, to

1 Hopkins, C. J., "The Covidian Cult," Consent Factory, October 13, 2020

2 Agence France-Presse, "A man lies dead in the street: the image that captures the Wuhan coronavirus crisis," The Guardian, January 31, 2020

3 Lovelace Jr., Berkeley and Noah Higgins-Dunn, "WHO says coronavirus death rate is 3.4% globally, higher than previously thought," CNBC, March 3, 2020

keep things simple, I'll just use Margaret Singer's "Six Conditions of Mind Control" from her 1995 book, *Cults in Our Midst*,[4] as a lens to view the Covidian Cult through. (The italics are Singer. The commentary is mine.)

Six Conditions of Mind Control

1. Keep the person unaware of what is going on and how she or he is being changed a step at a time. Potential new members are led, step by step, through a behavioral-change program without being aware of the final agenda or full content of the group.

Looking back, it is easy to see how people were conditioned, step by step, to accept the "New Normal" ideology. They were bombarded with terrifying propaganda, locked down, stripped of their civil rights, forced to wear medical-looking masks in public, to act out absurd "social-distancing" rituals, submit to constant "testing," and all the rest of it. Anyone not complying with this behavioral-change program or challenging the veracity and rationality of the new ideology was demonized as a "conspiracy theorist," a "Covid denier," an "anti-vaxxer," in essence, an enemy of the cult, like a "suppresive person" in the Church of Scientology.

2. Control the person's social and/or physical environment; especially control the person's time.

For over a year now, the "New Normal" authorities have controlled the social/physical environment, and how New Normals spend their time, with lockdowns, social-distancing rituals, closure of "non-essential" businesses, omnipresent propaganda, isolation of the elderly, travel restrictions, mandatory mask-rules, protest bans, and now the segregation of the "Unvaccinated." Basically, society has been transformed into something resembling an infectious disease ward, or an enormous hospital from which there is no escape. You've seen the photos of the happy New Normals dining out at restaurants, relaxing at the beach, jogging, attending school, and so on, going about their

4 Singer, Margaret and Jania Lalich, "Cults in Our Midst," Jossey-Bass, 1995

"normal" lives with their medical-looking masks and prophylactic face shields. What you're looking at is the pathologization of society, the pathologization of everyday life, the physical (social) manifestation of a morbid obsession with disease and death.

3. Systematically create a sense of powerlessness in the person.

What kind of person could feel more powerless than an obedient New Normal sitting at home, obsessively logging the "Covid death" count, sharing photos of his medical-looking mask and post-"vaccination" bandage on Facebook, as he waits for permission from the authorities to go outdoors, visit his family, kiss his lover, or shake hands with a colleague? The fact that in the Covidian Cult the traditional charismatic cult leader has been replaced by a menagerie of medical experts and government officials does not change the utter dependency and abject powerlessness of its members, who have been reduced to a state approaching infancy. This abject powerlessness is not experienced as a negative; on the contrary, it is proudly celebrated. Thus the mantra-like repetition of the "New Normal" platitude "Trust the Science!" by people who, if you try to show them the science, melt down completely and start jabbering aggressive nonsense at you to shut you up.

4. Manipulate a system of rewards, punishments and experiences in such a way as to inhibit behavior that reflects the person's former social identity.

The point here is the transformation of the formerly basically rational person into an entirely different cult-approved person, in our case, an obedient "New Normal" person. Singer gets into this in greater detail, but her discussion applies mostly to subcultural cults, not to large-scale totalitarian movements. For our purposes, we can fold this into Condition 5.

5. Manipulate a system of rewards, punishments, and experiences in order to promote learning the group's ideology or belief system and group-approved behaviors. Good behavior, demonstrating an un-

derstanding and acceptance of the group's beliefs, and compliance are
rewarded, while questioning, expressing doubts or criticizing are met
with disapproval, redress and possible rejection. If one expresses a ques-
tion, they are made to feel that there is something inherently wrong with
them to be questioning.

OK, I'm going to tell you a little story.

It's a story about a personal experience, which I'm pretty sure
you've also experienced. It's a story about a certain New Normal
who has been harassing me for several months. I'll call him Brian,
because ... well, that's his name, and I no longer feel any compunc-
tion about sharing it.

Brian is a former friend and colleague from the theater world who
has gone full "New Normal" and is absolutely furious that I have
not. So outraged is Brian that I have not joined the cult that he has
been going around on the Internet referring to me as a "conspiracy
theorist" and suggesting that I've had some kind of nervous break-
down and require immediate psychiatric treatment because I do not
believe the official "New Normal" narrative.

Now, this would not be a very big deal, except that Brian is im-
pugning my character and attempting to damage my reputation on
the Facebook pages of other theater colleagues, which Brian feels
entitled to do, given that I'm a "Covid denier," a "conspiracy theorist," and an "anti-vaxxer," or whatever, and given the fact that he has
the power of the state, the media, etc., on his side.

This is how it works in cults, and in larger totalitarian societies. It
isn't usually the *Gestapo* that comes for you. It's usually your friends
and colleagues.

What Brian is doing is working that "system of rewards and punishments" to enforce his ideology, because he knows that most of
my other colleagues in the theater world have also gone full "New
Normal," or at least are looking the other way and staying silent
while it is being implemented.

This tactic, obviously, has backfired on Brian, primarily because
I do not give a fuck what any New Normals think of me, whether
they work in the theater world or anywhere else ... but I am in a
rather privileged position, because I have already accomplished what

I wanted to accomplish in the theater, and I would rather stick my hand in a blender than submit my novels to corporate publishers for review by "sensitivity readers,"[5] so there isn't much to threaten me with. That, and I have no children to support, or administrations to answer to, unlike, for example, Mark Crispin Miller, who is currently being persecuted by the "New Normal" administration at NYU.[6]

The point is, this kind of ideological conditioning is happening everywhere, every day, on the job, among friends, even among families. The pressure to conform is intense, because nothing is more threatening to devoted cultists, or members of totalitarian ideological movements, than those who challenge their fundamental beliefs, confront them with facts, or otherwise demonstrate that their "reality" isn't reality at all, but, rather, a delusional, paranoid fiction.

The key difference between how this works in cults and totalitarian ideological movements is that, usually, a cult is a subcultural group, and thus non-cult-members have the power of the ideology of the dominant society to draw on when resisting the mind-control tactics of the cult, and attempting to deprogram its members.

In our case, this balance of power is inverted. Totalitarian ideological movements have the power of governments, the media, the police, the culture industry, academia, and the compliant masses on their side. Thus, they do not need to persuade anyone. They have the power to dictate "reality." Only cults operating in total isolation, like Jim Jones' People's Temple in Guyana, enjoy this level of control over their members.

This pressure to conform, this ideological conditioning, must be fiercely resisted, regardless of the consequences, both publicly and in our private lives, or the "New Normal" will certainly become our "reality." Despite the fact that we "Covid deniers" are currently outnumbered by the Covidian cultists, we need to behave as if we are not, and hold to reality, facts, and real science, and treat the New Normals as exactly what they are, members of a nascent totalitarian movement, delusional cultists run amok.

If we do not, we will get to Singer's Condition 6 …

5 Flood, Alison, "Vetting for stereotypes: meet publishing's 'sensitivity readers'," The Guardian, April 27, 2018

6 Taibbi, Matt, "Meet the Censored: Mark Crispin Miller," TK News, January 4, 2021

6. Put forth a closed system of logic and an authoritarian structure that permits no feedback and refuses to be modified except by leadership approval or executive order. The group has a top-down, pyramid structure. The leaders must have verbal ways of never losing.

We are not there yet, but that is where we're headed ... global pathologized totalitarianism. So, please, speak up. Call things what they are. Confront the Brians in your life. Despite the fact that they tell themselves that they are trying to help you "come to your senses," "see the truth," or "trust the Science," they are not. They are cultists, desperately trying to get you to conform to their paranoid beliefs, pressuring you, manipulating you, bullying you, threatening you.

Do not engage them on their terms, or let them goad you into accepting their premises. (Once they've sucked you into their narrative, they've won.) Expose them, confront them with their tactics and their motives. You will probably not change their minds in the least, but your example might help other New Normals whose faith is slipping to begin to recognize what has been done to their minds and maybe leave the cult, or at least beging to question it slightly.

The Criminalization of Dissent

May 3, 2021

One of the hallmarks of totalitarian systems is the criminalization of dissent. Not just the stigmatization of dissent or the demonization of dissent, but the formal criminalization of dissent, and any other type of opposition to the official ideology of the totalitarian system. Global capitalism has been inching its way toward this step for quite some time, and now, apparently, it is ready to take it.

Germany has been leading the way. For over a year, anyone questioning or protesting the "Covid emergency measures" or the official Covid-19 narrative has been demonized by the government and the media, and, sadly, but not completely unexpectedly, the majority of the German public. And now such dissent is officially "extremism."

Yes, that's right, in "New Normal" Germany, if you dissent from official state ideology, you are now officially a dangerous "extremist." The German Intelligence agency (the "BfV") has even invented a new category of "extremists" in order to allow themselves to legally monitor anyone suspected of being "anti-democratic and/or delegitimizing the state in a way that endangers security," like … you know, non-violently protesting, or speaking out against, or criticizing, or satirizing, the so-called "New Normal."

Naturally, I'm a little worried, as I have engaged in most of these "extremist" activities. My thoughtcrimes are just sitting there on the Internet waiting to be scrutinized by the BfV. They're probably Google-translating this column right now, compiling a list of all the people reading it, and their Facebook friends and Twitter followers, and professional associates, and family members, and anyone any of the aforementioned people have potentially met with, or casually mentioned, who might have engaged in similar thoughtcrimes.

You probably think I'm joking, don't you? I'm not joking. Not even slightly. The Federal Office for Protection of the Constitution

("*Bundesamt für Verfassungsschutz*") is actively monitoring anyone questioning or challenging the official "New Normal" ideology ... the "Covid Deniers," the "conspiracy theorists," the "anti-vaxxers," the dreaded "Querdenkers" (i.e., people who "think outside the box"), and anyone else they feel like monitoring who has refused to join the Covidian Cult. We're now official enemies of the state, no different than any other "terrorists."

Or ... OK, technically, a little different.

As *The New York Times* reported last week, "the danger from coronavirus deniers and conspiracy theorists does not fit the mold posed by the usual politically driven groups, including those on the far left and right, or by Islamic extremists."[1] Still, according to the German Interior Ministry, we diabolical "Covid deniers," "conspiracy theorists," and "anti-vaxxers" have "targeted the state itself, its leaders, businesses, the press, and globalism," and have "attacked police officers" and "defied civil authorities."

Moreover, in August 2020, in a dress rehearsal for the "Storming of the Capitol," "Covid-denying" insurrectionists "scaled the steps of Parliament" (i.e., the Reichstag). Naturally, *The Times* neglects to mention that this so-called "Storming of the Reichstag" spectacle[2] was performed by a small splinter-group of protesters to whom the German authorities had granted a permit to assemble (*apart from the main demonstration, which was massive and completely peaceful*) on the steps of the Reichstag, which the German police had, for some reason, left completely unguarded. In light of the background of the person the authorities issued this Reichstag-protest permit to — a known former-NPD functionary, in other words, a neo-Nazi — well, the whole thing seemed a bit questionable to me ... but what do I know? I'm just a "conspiracy theorist."

According to *Al Jazeera*, the German Interior Ministry explained that these querdenking "extremists encourage supporters to ignore official orders and challenge the state monopoly on the use of force."[3]

1 Schuetze, Christopher F., "German Intelligence Puts Coronavirus Deniers Under Surveillance," *The New York Times, April 28, 2021*

2 Hopkins, C. J., "The Storming of the Reichstag Building on 29 August, 2020," *Consent Factory, September 2, 2021*

3 "German spy agency to monitor some anti-lockdown protesters," *Al Jazeera, April 28, 2021*

Seriously, can you imagine anything more dangerous? Mindlessly following orders and complying with the state's monopoly on the use of force are the very cornerstones of modern democracy … or some sort of political system, anyway.

But, see, there I go again, "being anti-democratic" and "delegitimizing the state," not to mention "relativizing the Holocaust" (also a criminal offense in Germany) by comparing one totalitarian system to another, as I have done repeatedly on social media, and in a column I published in November 2020,[4] when the parliament revised the "Infection Protection Act" to allow the governemnt to rule by decree, which bears no comparison whatsoever to the "Enabling Act of 1933."[5]

But this isn't just a German story, of course. The "New Normal" War on Domestic Terror is a global war, and it is just getting started. According to a Department of Homeland Security *National Terrorism Advisory System Bulletin*" (and the corporate-media propaganda machine), "democracy" remains under imminent threat from these "ideologically-motivated violent extremists with objections to the exercise of governmental authority" and other such "grievances fueled by false narratives" including "anger over Covid-19 restrictions."[6]

These Covid-denying "violent extremists" have reportedly joined forces with the "white-supremacist, Russia-backed, Trump-loving Putin-Nazis" that terrorized "democracy" for the past four years, and almost overthrew the US government by sauntering around inside the US Capitol Building, scuffling with police, attacking furniture, and generally acting rude and unruly. No, they didn't actually kill anyone, as the corporate media all reported they did,[7] but trespassing in a government building and putting your feet up on politicians' desks is pretty much exactly the same as "terrorism."

---

4 Hopkins, C. J., "*The Germans Are Back!*" Consent Factory, November 22, 2020

5 "*The Enabling Act allowed the Reich government to issue laws without the consent of Germany's parliament, laying the foundation for the complete Nazification of German society. The law was passed on March 23, 1933, and published the following day. Its full name was the 'Law to Remedy the Distress of the People and the Reich.'*" Source: United States Holocaust Memorial Museum

6 Levine, Mike, "*DHS uses federal alert system for 1st time in a year to warn of domestic terrorist threat,*" ABC News, January 27, 2021

7 Greenwald, Glenn, "*The Media Lied Repeatedly About Officer Brian Sicknick's Death. And They Just Got Caught,*" Substack, April 20, 2021

Or whatever. It's not like the truth actually matters, not when you are whipping up mass hysteria over imaginary "Russian assets," "white-supremacist militias," "Covid-denying extremists," "anti-vax terrorists," and "apocalyptic plagues." When you're rolling out a new official ideology — a pathologized-totalitarian ideology — and criminalizing all dissent, the point is not to appear to be factual. The point is just to terrorize the shit out of people.

As Hermann Goering famously explained regarding how to lead a country to war (and the principle holds true for any big transition, like the one we are experiencing currently):

> "[T]he people can always be brought to the bidding of the leaders. That is easy. All you have to do is tell them they are being attacked and denounce the pacifists for lack of patriotism and exposing the country to danger."

Go back and read those quotes from the German Interior Ministry and the DHS again. The message they are sending is unmistakeably clear. It might not seem all that new, but it is. Yes, they have been telling us "we are being attacked" and denouncing critics, protesters, and dissidents for twenty years (i.e., since the War on Terror was launched in 2001, and for the last four years in their War on Populism), but this is a whole new level of it … a fusion of official narratives and their respective official enemies into a singular, aggregate official narrative in which dissent will no longer be permitted.

Instead, it will be criminalized … criminalized and pathologized.

Seriously, go back and read those quotes again. Global-capitalist governments and their corporate media mouthpieces are telling us, in no uncertain terms, that "objection to their authority" will no longer be tolerated, nor will dissent from their official narratives.

Such dissent will be deemed "dangerous" and above all "false." It will not be engaged with or rationally debated. It will be erased from public view. There will be an inviolable, official "reality." Any deviation from that official "reality" or defiance of the "civil authorities" will be labelled "extremism," and dealt with accordingly.

This is textbook totalitarianism, the establishment of an inviolable official ideology and the criminalization of dissent. And that is what is happening, right now. A new official ideology is being established. Not a state ideology. A global ideology.

The "New Normal" is that official ideology. Technically, it's an official *post*-ideology, an official "reality," an unquestionable "fact," which only "criminals" and "psychopaths" would ever deny.

I'll be digging deeper into New Normal ideology and pathologized totalitarianism in my future columns. For now I'll leave you with two more quotes. The emphasis is mine, as ever.

Here's California State Senator Richard Pan, author of an op-ed in the *Washington Post*: "Anti-vax extremism is akin to domestic terrorism," quoted in the *Los Angeles Times*:[8]

> "These extremists have not yet been held accountable, so they continue to escalate violence against the body public ... we must now summon the political will to demand that domestic terrorists face consequences for their words and actions. Our democracy and our lives depend on it ... they've been building alliances with white supremacists, conspiracy theorists and [others] on the far right ..."

And here's Peter Hotez in *Nature* magazine:[9]

> "The United Nations and the highest levels of governments must take direct, even confrontational, approaches with Russia, and move to dismantle anti-vaccine groups in the United States. Efforts must expand into the realm of cyber security, law enforcement, public education and international relations. A high-level inter-agency task force reporting to the UN secretary-general could assess the full impact of anti-vaccine aggression, and propose tough, balanced measures. The task force should include experts who have tackled complex global threats such as terrorism, cyber attacks and nuclear armament, because anti-science is now approaching similar levels of peril."

8 Smith, Erika D., *"Column: He's been a target of anti-vaxxers. Now he has a warning for the rest of us,"* Los Angeles Times, February 5, 2021
9 Hotez, Peter, *"COVID vaccines: time to confront anti-vax aggression,"* Nature, April 27, 2021

We'll be hearing a lot more rhetoric like that as this new, pathologized-totalitarian form of global capitalism gradually develops. It will probably a good idea to assume the New Normals mean exactly what they say.

Greetings from New Normal Germany!

May 24, 2021

On April 1, 1933, shortly after Hitler was appointed chancellor, the Nazis staged a boycott of Jewish businesses in Germany. Members of the Storm Troopers ("*die Sturmabteilung*," or the "Storm Department," as I like to think of them) stood around outside of Jewish-owned stores with Gothic-lettered placards reading, "Germans! Defend yourselves! Do not buy from Jews!"

The boycott itself was a total disaster — most Germans ignored it and just went on with their lives — but it was the beginning of the official persecution of the Jews and totalitarianism in Nazi Germany.

Last week, here in New Normal Germany, the government (which, it goes without saying, bears no resemblance to the Nazi regime, or any other totalitarian regime) implemented a social-segregation system that bans anyone who refuses to publicly conform to official "New Normal" ideology from participating in German society. From now on, only those who have an official "vaccination pass" or proof of a negative PCR test are allowed to sit down and eat at restaurants, shop at "non-essential" stores, or go to bars, or the cinema, or wherever.

Of course, there is absolutely no valid comparison to be made between these two events, or between Nazi Germany and New Normal Germany, nor would I ever imply there was. That would be illegal in New Normal Germany, as that would be considered "relativizing the Holocaust," not to mention being "anti-democratic and/or delegitimizing the state in a way that endangers security"[1] ... or whatever. Plus, it's not like there are SA goons standing outside of shops and restaurants with signs reading, "Germans! Defend yourselves! Don't sell to the Unvaccinated and Untested!" It's just that it's now illegal

---

1 Schuetze, Christopher F., "German Intelligence Puts Coronavirus Deniers Under Surveillance," *The New York Times, April 28, 2021*

to do that, i.e., sell anything to those of us whom the government and the media have systematically stigmatized as "Covid deniers" because we haven't converted to the new official ideology and submitted to being "vaccinated" or "tested."

Protesting the new official ideology is also illegal in New Normal Germany ... OK, I think I should probably rephrase that. I certainly don't want to misinform anyone. Protesting the "New Normal" isn't outlawed per se. You're totally allowed to apply for a permit to protest against the "Covid restrictions" on the condition that everyone taking part in your protest wears a medical-looking N95 mask and maintains a distance of 1.5 meters from every other medical-masked protester ... which is kind of like permitting anti-racism protests as long as all the protesters wear Ku Klux Klan robes and perform a choreographed karaoke of Lynyrd Skynyrd's *Sweet Home Alabama*.

Who says the Germans don't have a sense of humor?

Look, I don't mean to single out the Germans. There is nothing inherently totalitarian, or fascist, or robotically authoritarian and hyper-conformist about the Germans, as a people. The fact that the vast majority of Germans clicked their heels and started unquestioningly following orders (like they did in Nazi Germany) the moment the "New Normal" was introduced last year doesn't mean that all Germans are fascists by nature. Most Americans did the same thing. So did the British, the Australians, the Spanish, the French, the Canadians, and a long list of others. It's just that ... well, I happen to live here, so I've watched as Germany has been transformed into "New Normal Germany" up close and personal, and it has definitely made an impression on me.

The ease with which the German authorities implemented the new official ideology, and how fanatically it has been embraced by the majority of Germans, came as something of a shock. I had naively believed that, in light of their history, the Germans would be among the first to recognize a nascent totalitarian movement predicated on textbook Goebbelsian Big Lies (i.e., manipulated Covid "case" and "death" statistics[2]), and would resist it en masse, or at least

---

2 Knightly, Kit, "How the CDC is manipulating data to prop-up 'vaccine effectiveness'," Off-Guardian, May 18, 2021 ("New policies will artificially deflate 'breakthrough infections' in the vaccinated, while the old rules continue to inflate case numbers in the unvaccinated.")

take a moment to question the lies their leaders were hysterically barking at them. I couldn't have been more wrong.

Here we are, over a year later, and waiters and shop clerks are "checking papers" to enforce compliance with the new official ideology. (And, yes, the "New Normal" is an official ideology. When you strip away the illusion of an apocalyptic plague, there isn't any other description for it). Perfectly healthy, medical-masked people are lining up in the streets to be experimentally "vaccinated." Lockdown-bankrupted shops and restaurants have been converted into walk-in "PCR-test stations." The government is debating mandatory "vaccination" of children in kindergarten.[3] Goon squads are arresting octogenarians for picnicking on the sidewalk without permission.[4] And so on. At this point, I'm just sitting here waiting for the news that mass "disinfection camps" are being set up to solve the "Unvaccinated Question."

Whoops … there I go again, "relativizing the Holocaust." I really need to stop doing that. The Germans take this stuff very seriously, especially with Israel under relentless attack by the desperately impoverished indigenous people it has locked inside an enormous walled ghetto, and is self-defensively ethnically cleansing.[5]

But, seriously, there is no similarity whatsoever between Nazi Germany and "New Normal" Germany. Sure, both systems suspended the constitution, declared a national "state of emergency" enabling the government to rule by decree, inundated the masses with insane propaganda and manipulated "scientific facts," outlawed protests, criminalized dissent, implemented a variety of public rituals, and symbols, and a social segregation system, to enforce compliance with their official ideologies, and demonized anyone who refused to comply … but, other than that, there's no similarity, and anyone who suggests there is is a dangerous social-deviant extremist who probably needs to be quarantined somewhere, or perhaps dealt with in some other "special" way.

---

3 Weiß, Mandy, "Wie sinnvoll ist die Corona-Impfung für Kinder?" ("How sensible is Covid Vaccination for Children?"), MDR, August 3, 2021

4 Rosenbusch, Henning, Video of German police brutally arresting an old man on crutches who was taking part in a "picnic" on the sidewalk with friends on Mother's Day, Twitter, May 14, 2021

5 "Berlin police on alert for antisemitism at pro-Palestinian rallies," Deutsche Welle, May 22, 2021

Plus, the two ideologies are completely different. One was a fanatical totalitarian ideology based on imaginary racial superiority and the other is a fanatical totalitarian ideology based on an imaginary "apocalyptic plague" … so what the hell am I even talking about? On top of which, no swastikas, right? No swastikas, no totalitarianism! And nobody's mass murdering the Jews, that I know of, and that's the critical thing, after all!

So, never mind. Just ignore all that crazy stuff I just told you about "New Normal" Germany. Don't worry about "New Normal" America, either. Or "New Normal" Great Britain. Or "New Normal" wherever. Get experimentally "vaccinated." Experimentally "vaccinate" your kids. Demonstrate your loyalty to the *Reich* … sorry, I meant to global capitalism. Ignore those reports of people dying and suffering horrible adverse effects.[6] Wear your mask. Wear it forever. God knows what other viruses are out there, just waiting to defile your bodily fluids and cause you to experience a flu-like illness, or cut you down in the prime of your seventies or eighties! And, Jesus, I almost forgot "long Covid." That in itself is certainly enough to justify radically restructuring society so that it resembles an upscale hospital theme park staffed by paranoid, smiley-faced fascists in fanciful designer hazmat suits.

Oh, and keep your "vaccination papers" in order. You never know when you're going to have to show them to some official at the airport, or a shop, or restaurant, or to your boss, or your landlord, or the police, or your bank, or your ISP, or your Tinder date … or some other "New Normal" authority figure. I mean, you don't want to be mistaken for a "Covid denier," or an "anti-vaxxer," or a "conspiracy theorist," or some other type of ideological deviant, and be banished from society, do you?

---

6 *"Covid Vaccines: The Tip of the Iceberg," Swiss Policy Research, May 7, 2021*

Manufacturing New Normal "Reality"

June 20, 2021

The goal of every totalitarian system is to establish complete control over society and every individual within it in order to achieve ideological uniformity and eliminate any and all deviation from it. This goal can never be achieved, of course, but it is the *raison d'être* of all totalitarian systems, regardless of what forms they take and ideologies they espouse. You can dress totalitarianism up in Hugo Boss-designed Nazi uniforms, Mao suits, or medical-looking face masks, its core desire remains the same: to remake the world in its paranoid image … to replace reality with its own "reality."

We are right in the middle of this process currently, which is why everything feels so batshit crazy. The global capitalist ruling classes are implementing a new official ideology, or, in other words, a new "reality."

That's what an official ideology is. It's more than just a set of beliefs. Anyone can have any beliefs they want. Your personal beliefs do not constitute "reality." In order to make your beliefs "reality," you need to have the power to impose them on society. You need the power of the police, the military, the media, scientific "experts," academia, the culture industry, the entire ideology-manufacturing machine. There is nothing subtle about this process. Decommissioning one "reality" and replacing it with another is a brutal business. Societies grow accustomed to their "realities." We do not surrender them willingly or easily. Normally, what's required to get us to do so is a crisis, a war, a state of emergency, or … you know, a deadly global pandemic.

During the changeover from the old "reality" to the new "reality," the society is torn apart. The old "reality" is being disassembled and the new one has not yet taken its place. It feels like madness, and, in a way, it is. For a time, the society is split in two, as the two "realities" battle it out for dominance. "Reality" being what it is (i.e., monolithic), this is a fight to the death. In the end, only one "reality" can prevail.

This is the crucial period for the totalitarian movement. It needs to negate the old "reality" in order to implement the new one, and it cannot do that with reason and facts, so it has to do it with fear and brute force. It needs to terrorize the majority of society into a state of mindless mass hysteria that can be turned against those resisting the new "reality."

It is not a matter of persuading or convincing people to accept the new "reality." It's more like how you drive a herd of cattle. You scare them enough to get them moving, then you steer them wherever you want them to go. The cattle do not know or understand where they are going. They are simply reacting to a physical stimulus. Facts and reason have nothing to do with it.

And this is what has been so incredibly frustrating for those of us opposing the roll-out of the "New Normal," whether debunking the official Covid-19 narrative, or "Russiagate," or the "Storming of the US Capitol," or any other element of the new official ideology.

And, yes, it is all one ideology, not "communism," or "fascism," or any other nostalgia, but the ideology of the system that actually rules us, supranational global capitalism. We're living in the first truly global-hegemonic ideological system in human history. We have been for the last 30 years. If you are touchy about the term "global capitalism," go ahead and call it "globalism," or "crony capitalism," or "corporatism," or whatever other name you need to. Whatever you call it, it became the unrivaled globally-hegemonic ideological system when the Soviet Union collapsed in the 1990s. Yes, there are pockets of internal resistance, but it has no external adversaries, so its progression toward a more openly totalitarian structure is logical and entirely predictable.

Anyway, what has been so incredibly frustrating is that many of us have been operating under the illusion that we are engaged in a rational argument over facts (e.g., the facts of Russiagate, Literal-Hitlergate, 9/11, Saddam's WMDs, Douma, the January 6 "insurrection," the official Covid narrative, etc.) This is not at all what is happening. Facts mean absolutely nothing to the adherents of totalitarian systems.

You can show the New Normals the facts all you like. You can show them the fake photos of people dead in the streets in China in March of 2020. You can show them the fake projected death rates. You can explain how the fake PCR tests work, how healthy people are deemed medical "cases." You can show them all the studies on the ineffectiveness of masks. You can explain the fake "hospitalization" and "death" figures, send them articles about the unused "emergency hospitals," the unremarkable age-and-population-adjusted death rates, cite the survival rates for people under 70, the dangers and pointlessness of "vaccinating" children.

None of this will make the slightest difference.

Or, if you've bought the Covid-19 narrative but you haven't completely abandoned your critical faculties, you can do what Glenn Greenwald has been doing recently. You can demonstrate how the corporate media have intentionally lied, again and again, to whip up mass hysteria over "domestic terrorism." You can show people videos of the "violent domestic terrorists" calmly walking into the Capitol Building in single file, like a high-school tour group, having been let in by members of Capitol Security. You can debunk the infamous "fire-extinguisher murder" of Brian Sicknik that never really happened. You can point out that the belief that a few hundred unarmed people running around in the Capitol qualifies as an "insurrection," or an "attempted coup," or "domestic terrorism," is delusional to the point of being literally insane.

This will also not make the slightest difference.

I could go on, and I'm sure I will as the "New Normal" ideology becomes our new "reality" over the course of the next several years. My point at the moment is, this is not an argument. The global-capitalist ruling classes, government leaders, the corporate media, and the New Normal masses they have instrumentalized are not debating with us. They know the facts. They know the facts contradict their narratives. They do not care. They do not have to. Because this isn't about facts. It's about power.

I'm not saying that facts don't matter. Of course they matter. They matter to us. I'm saying, let's recognize what this is. It isn't a debate or a search for the truth. The New Normals are disassembling one "reality" and replacing it with a new "reality."

The pressure to conform to the new "reality" is already intense and it is going to get worse as vaccination passes, public mask-wearing, periodic lockdowns, etc., become normalized. Those who don't conform will be systematically demonized, socially and/or professionally ostracized, segregated, and otherwise punished. Our opinions will be censored. We will be "canceled," deplatformed, demonitized, and otherwise silenced. Our views will be labeled "potentially harmful." We will be accused of spreading "misinformation," of being "far-right extremists," "racists," "anti-Semites," "conspiracy theorists," "anti-vaxxers," "anti-global-capitalist violent domestic terrorists," or just garden variety "sexual harassers," or whatever they believe will damage us the most.

This will happen in both the public and the personal spheres. Not just governments, the media, and corporations, but your colleagues, friends, and family will do this. Strangers in shops and restaurants will do this. Most of them will not do it consciously. They will do it because your non-conformity poses an emotional and existential threat to them, a negation of their new "reality" and a reminder of the reality they surrendered in order to remain a "normal" person and avoid the punishments described above.

This is nothing new, of course. It is how "reality" is manufactured, not only in totalitarian systems, but in every organized social system. Those in power instrumentalize the masses to enforce conformity with their official ideology. Totalitarianism is just the most extreme and most dangerously paranoid and fanatical form of it.

So, sure, keep posting and sharing the facts, assuming you can get them past the censors, but let's not kid ourselves about what we're up against. We're not going to wake the New Normals up with facts. If we could, we would have done so already. This isn't a debate about facts. This is a fight.

Act accordingly.

The Approaching Storm

July 14, 2021

So, it looks like GloboCap isn't going to be happy until they have fomented the widespread social unrest, or de facto global civil war, that they need as a pretext to lock in the new pathologized totalitarianism and remake whatever remains of society into a global pseudo-medicalized police state ... or that appears to be where we're headed currently.

We appear to be heading there at breakneck speed.

I don't have a crystal ball or anything, but I'm expecting things to get rather ugly this Autumn, and probably even uglier in the foreseeable future.

Yes, friends, a storm is coming. It has been coming for the last 16 months. And GloboCap is steering right into it. I, and many others like me, have been tracking its relentless advance like a self-appointed International Pathologized-Totalitarian Hurricane Center ... you know, like the one in Miami, except all the meteorologists are "conspiracy theorists." We have documented the propaganda, the lies, the manipulation of statistics, the abrogation of constitutional rights, the New Normal goon squads, the corporate censorship, and all the rest of the roll-out of the new official ideology and the totalitarian measures deployed to enforce it.

Our efforts have not been in vain, but they haven't been successful enough to change the course that events are now taking ... a course of events that has always been clear, a course that every totalitarian movement needs to take to get where it's going.

You can't remake entire societies into quasi-totalitarian systems without civil unrest, chaos, rioting, war, or some other form of cataclysm. Brainwashing the masses is all fine and good, but, at some point, you need to goad the people who are resisting your new totalitarian "reality" into getting unruly, so you can crack down on them, and transform them into official enemies.

That is clearly what is happening at the moment.

GloboCap is dialing up the totalitarianism and they are rubbing it in people's faces. Here in New Normal Germany, prominent health officials are openly barking out Goebbelsian slogans like "NO FREEDOM FOR THE UNVACCINATED!" and "THE UNVACCINATED ARE A DANGER TO SOCIETY!"[1]

All over Europe, including the UK, where "Freedom Day" is fast approaching,[2] pseudo-medical social-segregation systems are being implemented. In France, Greece, and many other countries, people who refuse to be "vaccinated" are being stripped of their jobs[3] and otherwise punished.

In the USA, where the Unvaccinated are also being segregated, New Normal goon squads are going door-to-door, bullying "vaccine hesitant" families into conforming to the new official ideology.[4]

And so on … I'm tired of citing the facts. They do not make the slightest difference to the vast majority of New Normals anyway. As I've noted in several previous columns, these people have surrendered their rationality, and have been subsumed into a totalitarian movement, which has become their perceptual and social "reality," which their "sanity" now depends upon defending, so the facts mean absolutely nothing to them.

And you already know the facts.

Yes, you. Us. The others. The Unvaccinated. The "Covid deniers." You don't really think any hardcore New Normals have made it this far into this column, do you? They haven't. If they stumbled into it on the Internet and accidentally started to read it, their brains switched off in the opening paragraph … literally, neurologically, switched off. They recognized it as a threat to their "reality" and instantly erased it from their consciousness, or they reported it to the proper authori-

1 "Landes-Kassenärzte-Chef: 'Ungeimpfte sind Gefahr für die Allgemeinheit'" ("Head of state health insurance physicians warns, 'The unvaccinated are a danger to the general public'), Berliner Zeitung, July 11, 2021 ("'Without vaccination there is no freedom … The unvaccinated are a danger to society and should therefore not be given the same freedoms as vaccinated,' said Heinz.")

2 Helm, Toby and Michael Savage, "Public alarm grows at Boris Johnson's plan for Covid 'freedom day'," The Guardian, July 10, 2021

3 "Mandatory vaccination, Covid-19 pass and access to PCR tests: the main points from Macron's address," France24, July 12, 2021 ("France's health minister Olivier Véran said that non-vaccinated health workers won't receive a salary nor be allowed to work after September 15.")

4 Shear, Michael D. and Noah Weiland, "Biden Calls for Door-to-Door Vaccine Push: Experts Say More Is Needed," The New York Times, July 6, 2021

ties, perhaps the FBI,[5] the *Bundesnachrichtendienst*,[6] or Facebook,[7] or some other global corporation.

This is what it has come to, folks ... people are reporting other people's "thoughtcrimes" to global Internet corporations and the law enforcement agencies of "democratic" governments in the hopes of destroying or damaging their lives, or, at the very least, getting them censored or otherwise erased from public view.

As I noted in my previous column, our societies have been torn apart. We are living in two mutually hostile "realities," a state which cannot continue indefinitely.

The problem for us (i.e., "the Unvaccinated") is that we probably constitute somewhere around 20 to 25 percent of the population, so we are massively outnumbered by New Normals. The problem for the New Normals is that we probably constitute somewhere around 20 to 25 percent of the population, which is way too many people to imprison or otherwise remove from society.

Thus, their plan is to make our lives as miserable as humanly possible, to segregate us, stigmatize us, demonize us, bully us, harass us, and otherwise pressure us to conform at every turn. They are not going to put us on the trains to the camps. GloboCap is not the Nazis. They need to maintain the simulation of democracy. So they need to transform us into an underclass of "anti-social conspiracy theorists," "anti-vaxxer disinformationists," "white-supremacist election-result deniers," "potentially violent domestic extremists," and whatever other epithets they come up with, so that we can be painted as dangerously unhinged freaks and cast out of society in a way that makes it appear that we have cast out ourselves.

This process is already well underway, and it's only going to get more intense, which will inevitably lead to social unrest. The hardcore "Unvaccinated" are not going to go quietly. Again, this isn't Nazi Germany. There are too many of us who are already resisting. They

---

5 *"Family members and peers are often best positioned to witness signs of mobilization to violence. Help prevent homegrown violent extremism. Visit https://go.usa.gov/x6mjf to learn how to spot suspicious behaviors and report them to the #FBI. #NatSec,"* FBI, *Twitter, July 11, 2021*

6 Schuetze, Christopher F., *"German Intelligence Puts Coronavirus Deniers Under Surveillance,"* The New York Times, April 28, 2021

7 Taibbi, Matt, *"Meet the Censored: C.J. Hopkins, Critic of the 'New Normal',"* TK News, May 13, 2021

can segregate us, ban us from travelling, blackout our protests, censor us, deplatform us, cancel our bank accounts, and otherwise harass us, but they cannot forcibly disappear us. So, they are going to keep goading us until we lose it. We have demonstrated incredible discipline so far, but eventually, we're going to run out patience. It's going to get messy. People will get hurt.

Which, of course, is exactly what GloboCap wants. Nothing will make them happier than if we turn ourselves into the "violent extremists" they've been conjuring into existence for the last five years. They desperately need us to become those "extremists" before we "embolden" too many others with our "disinformation," "vaccine hesitancy," "election result denial," and general distaste for the whole global-capitalist ideological program.

Unfortunately, they are probably going to get their wish.

What we need is an organized, global campaign of classic, non-violent civil disobedience, but they are not going to give us time to organize that. They are going to keep the pressure on, and crank up the pace, and the official propaganda, and the absurdity, and confusion, and the ever-changing rules, and the mass hysteria, and the blatant lies, until we start flipping out in restaurants and pubs, and schools, and on public transportation, and segregated New Normal establishments start getting nocturnally vandalized, or worse, and other forms of "direct action" are taken.

At which point, game over, because they will have won. We will be the "extremists" they warned themselves about, and they'll be able to do whatever they want with us, and our former (now New Normal) friends will applaud, or just look away in silence.

Or, I don't know, maybe I'm wrong. Maybe some New Normals are still reading this essay, and can still, at this late stage, regain their senses. Maybe we can still avoid the storm, and the full implementation of "New Normal Reality."

I know, you think I'm a hopeless idealist, but let me tell you a quick anecdote before I let you go.

I've been kind of nudging, or politely badgering, Glenn Greenwald, who I respect and have always respected, to grow a pair and at least speak out against the totalitarian features of the New Normal. Glenn is totally on board with the official Covid narrative, and has made it clear that he has no interest in using his investigative-journalism skills to investigate that official narrative. Despite that, I have continued to nudge him, and politely prod him, and otherwise urge him, to maybe post a few critical words, or raise a few investigative-journalist-type questions, about the most flagrant official propaganda campaign in the history of official propaganda campaigns and the blatantly totalitarian actions of governments all across the world.

For example, I posted this on Twitter recently (along with a photo of Joseph Goebbels giving one of his bug-eyed speeches), and tagged Glenn to try to get his attention.

> "15 months into the New Normal, as government officials openly bark out spittle-flecked, Goebbelsian slogans like "THERE IS NO FREEDOM FOR THE UNVACCINATED!" and "THE UNVACCINATED ARE A DANGER TO SOCIETY!", the silence from certain quarters is deafening."

Shortly thereafter — and I'm sure this was just a coincidence, because Glenn doesn't follow the Consent Factory on Twitter — he tweeted this bit of New Normal blasphemy:

> "The UK is one of the most vaccinated countries on earth. 70% have at least one dose. More than half have both. The CDC says vaccinated people need not wear masks. Why do experts who keep insisting the vaccine works demand people act as if it doesn't? Why ignore CDC advice?"

So, apparently, it is in fact still possible for people who believe the official Covid narrative as if it were the Word of God to speak out against some aspect of it, or just politely question the logic of it, or otherwise stop behaving like "Good Germans" as a new iteration of totalitarianism is rolled out right in front of their eyes.

That's it. That's my anecdote.

Yes, I know. I'm clutching at straws, but I have this crazy faith in people. On top of which, I'm getting old, so I'm not looking forward to the street-fighting part of this as much as I would have 30 or 40 years ago.

Oh, yeah, and, I almost forgot, to all my friends in the New Normal UK … have a lovely Freedom Day!

The Covidian Cult Part III

September 2, 2021

In *The Covidian Cult (Part I)* and *(Part II)*, I characterized the so-called "New Normal" as a "global totalitarian ideological movement." Since I published those essays, more and more people have come to see it for what it is, not "insanity" or "an overreaction," but, in fact, a new form of totalitarianism, a globalized, pathologized, depoliticized form, which is being systematically implemented under the guise of "protecting the public health."

In order to oppose this new form of totalitarianism, we need to understand how it both resembles and differs from earlier totalitarian systems. The similarities are fairly obvious — the suspension of constitutional rights, governments ruling by decree, official propaganda, public loyalty rituals, the outlawing of political opposition, censorship, social segregation, goon squads terrorizing the public, and so on — but the differences are not as obvious.

Whereas 20th-Century totalitarianism (i.e., the form most people are generally familiar with) was more or less national and overtly political, New Normal totalitarianism is supranational, and its ideology is much more subtle. The New Normal is not Nazism or Stalinism. It is global-capitalist totalitarianism, and global capitalism doesn't have an ideology, technically, or, rather, its ideology is "reality." When you are an unrivaled global ideological hegemon, as global capitalism has been for the last 30 years or so, your ideology automatically becomes "reality," because there are no competing ideologies. Actually, there is no ideology at all. There is only "reality" and "unreality," "normality" and "deviations from the norm."

Yes, I know, reality is reality … that's why I'm putting all these terms in scare quotes, so, please, spare me the lengthy emails conclusively proving the reality of reality and try to understand how this works.

There is reality (whatever you believe it is), and there is "reality," which dictates how our societies function. "Reality" is constructed (i.e., simulated), collectively, according to the ideology of whatever system controls society. In the past, "reality" was openly ideological, regardless of which "reality" you lived in, because there were other competing "realities" out there. There aren't anymore. There is only the one "reality," because the entire planet — yes, including China, Russia, North Korea, and wherever — is controlled by one globally hegemonic system.

A globally hegemonic system has no need for ideology, because it doesn't have to compete with rival ideologies. So it erases ideology and replaces it with "reality." Reality (whatever you personally believe it is, which of course is what it really is) is not actually erased. It just doesn't matter, because you do not get to dictate "reality." Global capitalism gets to dictate "reality," or, more accurately, it simulates "reality," and in doing so it simulates the opposite of "reality," which is equally if not more important.

This global-capitalist-manufactured "reality" is a depoliticized, ahistorical "reality," which forms an invisible ideological boundary establishing the limits of what is "real." In this way, global capitalism (a) conceals its ideological nature, and (b) renders any and all ideological opposition automatically illegitimate, or, more accurately, non-existent. Ideology as we knew it disappears. Political, ethical, and moral arguments are reduced to the question of what is "real" or "factual," which the GloboCap "experts" and "fact checkers" dictate.

Also, because this "reality" is not a cohesive ideological system with fundamental values, core principles, and so on, it can be drastically revised or completely replaced more or less at a moment's notice. Global capitalism has no fundamental values — other than exchange value, of course — and thus it is free to manufacture any kind of "reality" it wants, and replace one "reality" with a new "reality" any time that serves its purposes, like stagehands changing a theatrical set.

For example, the "Global War on Terror," which was the official "reality" from 2001 until it was canceled in the Summer of 2016, when the "War on Populism" was officially launched. Or, now, the "New Normal," which replaced the "War on Populism" in the Spring of 2020. Each of which new simulations of "reality" was rolled out abruptly, clumsily even, like that scene in 1984 where the Party switches official enemies right in the middle of a Hate Week speech.

Seriously, think about where we are currently, 18 months into our new "reality," then go back and review how GloboCap blatantly rolled out the New Normal in the Spring of 2020 … and the majority of the masses didn't even blink. They seamlessly transitioned to the new "reality" in which a virus, rather than "white supremacists," or "Russian agents," or "Islamic terrorists," had become the new official enemy. They put away the scripts they had been reciting verbatim from for the previous four years, and the scripts they had been reciting from for the previous 15 years before that, and started frantically jabbering Covid cult-speak like they were auditioning for an over-the-top Orwell parody.

*

Which brings us to the problem of the Covidian cult … how to get through to them, which, make no mistake, we have to do, one way or another, or the New Normal will become our permanent "reality."

I called the New Normals a "Covidian Cult," not to gratuitously insult or mock them, but because that is what totalitarianism is … a cult writ large, on a societal scale. Anyone who has tried to get through to them can confirm the accuracy of that analogy. You can show them the facts until you're blue in the face. It will not make the slightest difference. You think you are having a debate over facts, but you are not. You are threatening their new "reality." You think you are struggling to get them to think rationally. You are not. What you are is a heretic, an agent of demonic forces, an enemy of all that is "real" and "true."

The Scientologists would label you a "suppressive person." The New Normals call you a "conspiracy theorist," an "anti-vaxxer," or a "virus denier." The specific epithets don't really matter. They are just labels that cult members and totalitarians use to demonize those they perceive as "enemies" … anyone challenging the "reality" of the cult, or the "reality" of the totalitarian system.

The simple fact of the matter is, you can't talk people out of a cult, and you can't talk them out of totalitarianism. Usually, what you do, in the case of a cult, is, you remove the person from the cult. You kidnap them, take them to a safehouse or wherever, surround them with a lot of non-cult members, and deprogram them gradually over the course of several days. You do this because, while they are still inside the cult, you cannot get through to them. They cannot hear you. A cult is a collective, self-contained "reality." Its power flows from the social organism composed of the cult leaders and the other cult members. You cannot "talk" this power away. You have to physically remove the person from it before you can begin to reason with them.

Unfortunately, we do not have this option. The New Normal is a global totalitarian system. There is no "outside" of the system to retreat to. We can't kidnap everyone and take them to Sweden. As I noted in Part I of this series, the cult/society paradigm has been inverted. The cult has become the dominant society, and those of us who have not been converted have become a collection of isolated islands existing, not outside, but within the cult.

So we need to adopt a different strategy. We need to make the monster show itself, not to those of us who can already see it, but to the New Normal masses, the Covidian Cultists. We need to make Jim Jones drop the "peace-and-love" crap, move into the jungle, and break out the Kool-Aid. We need to make Charles Manson put down his guitar, cancel orgy-time, and go homicidal hippie.

This is how you take down a cult from within. You do not try to thwart its progress; you push it toward its logical conclusion. You make it manifest its full expression, because that is when it implodes, and dies. You do not do that by being polite, conciliatory, or avoiding conflict. You do that by generating as much internal conflict within the cult as you can.

In other words, we need to make GloboCap (and its minions) go openly totalitarian … because it can't. If it could, it would have done so already. Global capitalism cannot function that way. Going openly totalitarian will cause it to implode … no, not global capitalism itself, but this totalitarian version of it. In fact, this is starting to happen already. It needs the simulation of "reality," and "democracy," and "normality," to keep the masses docile. So we need to attack that simulation. We need to hammer on it until it cracks, and the monster hiding within it appears.

That is the weakness of the system … the New Normal totalitarianism will not work if the masses perceive it as totalitarianism, as a political/ideological program, rather than as "a response to a deadly pandemic." So we need to make it visible as totalitarianism. We need to force the New Normals to see it as what it is. I do not mean that we need to explain it to them. They are beyond the reach of explanations. I mean that we need to make them see it, feel it, tangibly, inescapably, until they recognize what they are collaborating with.

Stop arguing with them on their terms, and instead directly attack their "reality." When they start jabbering about the virus, the variants, the "vaccines," and all the other Covid cult-speak, do not get sucked into their narrative. Do not respond as if they were rational. Respond as if they were talking about "Xenu," "body thetans," "Helter Skelter," or any other cultoid nonsense, because that is exactly what it is. Same goes for their rules and restrictions, the "face coverings," the "social distancing," and so on. Stop arguing against them on the grounds that they don't work. Of course they don't work, but that is not the point (and arguing that way sucks you into their "reality"). Oppose them because of what they are, a collection of bizarre compliance rituals performed to cement allegiance to the cult and simulate an atmosphere of "deadly pandemic."

There are many ways to go about doing this, i.e., generating internal conflict. I have been doing it my way, others are doing it theirs. If you're one of them, thank you. If you're not, start. Do it however and wherever you can. Make the New Normals face the monster, the monster they are feeding … the monster they have become.

The Great New Normal Purge

October 12, 2021

So, the Great New Normal Purge has begun ... right on cue, right by the numbers.

As we "paranoid conspiracy theorists" have been warning would happen for the past 18 months, people who refuse to convert to the new official ideology are now being segregated,[1] stripped of their jobs,[2] banned from attending schools,[3] denied medical treatment,[4] and otherwise persecuted.

Relentless official propaganda demonizing "the Unvaccinated" is being pumped out by the corporate and state media, government leaders, health officials, and shrieking fanatics on social media. "The Unvaccinated" are the new official "Untermenschen," an underclass of subhuman "others" the New Normal masses are being conditioned to hate.

You can see the hatred in the New Normals' eyes.[5]

But it isn't just a purge of "the Unvaccinated." Anyone deviating from the official ideology is being systematically demonized and persecuted. In Germany, Australia, and other New Normal countries, protesting the New Normal is officially outlawed.[6] The New Normal Gestapo is going around to people's homes to interrogate

---

1 Calvana, Bobby Caina, "No shot, no proof, no service: NYC businesses begin checks," Associated Press News, August 17, 2021

2 "New York's largest healthcare provider fires 1,400 unvaccinated workers," Reuters, October 4, 2021

3 Nietzel, Michael T., "The State University Of New York Is The Latest College To Give Unvaccinated Students The Boot," Forbes, October 1, 2021

4 Colton, Emma, "UCHealth denies kidney transplant to unvaccinated woman in stage 5 renal failure," FOX News, October 6, 2021

5 For example, the eyes of Keith Olbermann as he delivers a vein-bulging, spittle-flecked tirade worthy of Joseph Goebbels from the balcony of his apartment overlooking Central Park. YouTube, October 2, 2021

6 Schuetze, Christopher F., "German Intelligence Puts Coronavirus Deniers Under Surveillance," The New York Times, April 28, 2021

them about their anti-New Normal Facebook posts.[7] Corporations are openly censoring content that contradicts the official narrative.[8] New Normal goon squads roam the streets, checking people's "vaccination" papers.[9]

And it's not just governments and corporations carrying out the New Normal Purge. Friends are purging friends. Wives are purging husbands. Fathers are purging children. Children are purging parents. New Normals are purging old normal thoughts. Public health authorities are revising definitions to make them conform to New Normal "Science."[10]

And so on. A new official "reality" is being manufactured, right before our eyes. Anything and anyone that doesn't conform to it is being purged, unpersoned, memory-holed, erased.

None of which should come as a surprise.

Every nascent totalitarian system, at some stage of its takeover of society, launches a purge of political opponents, ideological dissidents, and other "anti-social deviants." Such purges can be brief or open-ended, and they can take any number of outward forms, depending on the type of totalitarian system, but you cannot have totalitarianism without them.

The essence of totalitarianism (regardless of which costumes and ideology it wears) is a desire to completely control society, every aspect of society, every individual behavior and thought. Every totalitarian system, whether an entire nation, a tiny cult, or any other form of social body, evolves toward this unachievable goal, the total ideological transformation and control of every element of society

---

7 Libs of Tik Tok, "Australian police show up at someone's doorstep to question him about his social media posts" (Video), Twitter, October 10, 2021

8 Pruitt-Young, Sharon, "YouTube Is Banning All Content That Spreads Vaccine Misinformation," National Public Radio, September 29, 2021

9 Taylor, Chloe, "Austrian police conduct random checks to enforce Covid lockdowns for the unvaccinated, CNBC, November 17, 2021

10 Camero, Katie, "Why did CDC change its definition for 'vaccine'? Agency explains move as skeptics lurk," Miami Herald, September 27, 2021 ("Social media is calling bluff on the Centers for Disease Control and Prevention for modifying its definition of the words 'vaccine' and 'vaccination' on its website. Before the change, the definition for 'vaccination' read, 'the act of introducing a vaccine into the body to produce immunity to a specific disease.' Now, the word 'immunity' has been switched to 'protection.' The term 'vaccine' also got a makeover. The CDC's definition changed from 'a product that stimulates a person's immune system to produce immunity to a specific disease' to the current 'a preparation that is used to stimulate the body's immune response against diseases.'")

(or whatever type of social body it comprises). This fanatical pursuit of total control, absolute ideological uniformity, and the elimination of all dissent is what makes totalitarianism totalitarianism.

Thus, each new totalitarian system, at some point in its evolution, needs to launch a purge of those who refuse to conform to its official ideology. It needs to do this for two basic reasons: (1) to segregate or otherwise eliminate actual political opponents and dissidents who pose a threat to the new regime; and (2) and more importantly, to establish the ideological territory within which the masses must now confine themselves in order to avoid being segregated, or eliminated.

The purge must be conducted openly, brutally, so that the masses understand that the rules of society have changed, forever, that their former rights and freedoms are gone, and that from now on any type of resistance or deviation from official ideology will not be tolerated, and will be ruthlessly punished.

The purge is usually launched during a "state of emergency," under imminent threat from some official "enemy" (e.g., "communist in-filtrators," "counter-revolutionaries," or ... you know, a "devastating pandemic"), such that the normal rules of society can be indefinitely suspended "for the sake of survival." The more terrified the masses can be made, the more willing they will be to surrender their free-dom and follow orders, no matter how insane.

The lifeblood of totalitarianism is fear ... fear of both the system's official enemy (which is constantly stoked with propaganda) and of the totalitarian system itself. That the brutality of the system is ra-tionalized by the threat posed by the official enemy doesn't make it any less brutal or terrifying. Under totalitarian systems (of any type or scale) fear is a constant and there is no escape from it.

The masses' fear is then channeled into hatred ... hatred of the official "Untermenschen," whom the system encourages the masses to scapegoat. Thus, the purge is also a means of allowing the masses to purge themselves of their fear, to transform it into self-righteous hatred and unleash it on the "Untermenschen" instead of the totali-tarian system, which, obviously, would be suicidal.

Every totalitarian system — both the individuals running it and the system, structurally — instinctively understands how this works.

New Normal totalitarianism is no exception.

Just reflect on what has happened over the last 18 months ... day after day, month after month, the masses have been subjected to the most destructive psychological-terror campaign in the history of psychological-terror campaigns. Sadly, many of them have been reduced to paranoid, anus-puckering invalids, afraid of the outdoors, afraid of human contact, afraid of their own children, afraid of the air, morbidly obsessed with disease and death ... and consumed with hatred of "the Unvaccinated."

Their hatred, of course, is utterly irrational, the product of fear and propaganda, as hatred of "the Untermenschen" always is. It has absolutely nothing to do with a virus, which even the New Normal authorities admit. "The Unvaccinated" are no more of a threat to anyone than any other human being, except insofar as they threaten the New Normals' belief in their delusional ideology.

No, we are way past rationality at this point. We are witnessing the birth of a new form of totalitarianism. Not "communism." Not "fascism." Global-capitalist totalitarianism. Pseudo-medical totalitarianism. Pathologized totalitarianism. A form of totalitarianism without a dictator, without a definable ideology. A totalitarianism based on "science," on "fact," on "reality," which it creates itself.

I don't know about you, but, so far, it has certainly made quite an impression on me. So much so that I have mostly set aside my usual satirical schtick to try to understand it, what it actually is, why it is happening, why it is happening now, where it is going, and how to oppose it.

The way I see it, the next six months will determine how successful the initial stages of the roll-out of the new totalitarianism will be. By April of 2022, either we'll all be showing our "papers" to the New Normal Gestapo to be able to earn a living, attend a school, dine at a restaurant, travel, and otherwise live what's left of our everyday lives, or we will have thrown a monkey wrench into the machinery.

I don't expect GloboCap to abandon the roll-out of New Normal totalitarianism over the longer term, as they are clearly committed to implementing it, but we have the power to ruin their opening act (which they have apparently been planning and rehearsing for some time).[11]

---

11 "The WEF and the Pandemic," Swiss Policy Research, October 2021

So, let's go ahead and do that, shall we? Before we get purged, or unpersoned, or whatever. I'm not sure, as I haven't seen a "fact-check," but I believe there are some commercial airline pilots in the USA who are showing us the way.[12]

---

12 *Ungar-Sargon, Batya, "Working-Class Americans Are Standing Up for Themselves—and the Left Is Denouncing Them," Newsweek, October 11, 2021 ("Southwest Airlines canceled over 1,000 flights this weekend. Thousands of passengers were left stranded in airports across the country on Sunday, after a quarter of all flights never took off. Southwest blamed air traffic control issues for the cancelations, but to many, they seemed connected to Southwest's new COVID-19 vaccine mandate, which its pilots asked a court to block. Were the canceled flights the result of a "sick out" on the part of pilots refusing to get vaccinated?")*

Winter is Coming

October 31, 2021

Winter is coming … and you know what that means. That's right, it's nearly time once again for the global-capitalist ruling classes to whip the New Normal masses into a state of mindless mass hysteria over an imaginary apocalyptic virus. the same imaginary apocalyptic virus that they have whipped the New Normal masses into a state of mass hysteria over throughout the Winter for the last two years.

They've got their work cut out for them this time. Seriously, how much more mass hysterical could the New Normals possibly get at this point?

The vast majority of the Western world has been transformed into a pseudo-medical dystopia in which you have to show your "health-purity papers" to enter a café and get a cup of coffee. People who refuse to get experimentally "vaccinated" against a virus that causes mild-to-moderate symptoms (or, often, no symptoms at all) in about 95% of the infected, and the overall infection fatality rate of which is approximately 0.1% to 0.5%,[1] are being systematically segregated, stripped of their jobs, denied medical treatment, demonized as "a danger to society," censored, fined, and otherwise persecuted.

If you think I'm overstating the case … well, I refer you to the *Courier Mail* in Australia, a recent page-one headline of which reads: "PUBLIC ENEMY NO.1 UNVAXED BORDER JUMPER PUTS STATE ON ALERT!"[2] There's a circled QR code affixed to the picture of the "unvaxed border jumper" with a message reading, "Don't be like Duran. Scan code to get vaxed."

Yes, the Great New Normal Purge is on. "The Unvaccinated" and other infidels and heretics are being hunted by fanatical, hate-drunk mobs, dragged before the New Normal Inquisition, and made examples of all over the world.

---

1 *"Studies on Covid-19 Lethality,"* Swiss Policy Research, May 2020 (a large collection of studies by a wide variety of recognized international experts and organizations, updated through 2022)

2 Stoltz, Greg and Emily Toxward, *"PUBLIC ENEMY NO.1! Unvaxed border jumper puts state on alert,"* Courier Mail, October 22, 2021

In New Normal Germany, popular footballer Joshua Kimmich is being publicly drawn and quartered for refusing to submit to being "vaccinated" and profess his faith in the New Normal World Order.[3] In the USA, "the Unvaccinated" stand accused of murdering Colin Powell, an 84-year-old, cancer-ridden war criminal.[4] Australia is planning to imprison people and fine them $90,000[5] for the "crime" of not wearing a medical-looking mask, or attempted worship at a synagogue,[6] or whatever. In Florida (of all places), fanatical school staff tied a medical-looking mask to the face of a non-verbal Down-syndrome girl with nylon cord, day after day, for over six weeks, until her father discovered what they were doing.[7]

I could go on, but I don't think I have to. The Internet is brimming with examples of such mass-hysterical and sadistic behavior.

And that's not to mention the mass hysteria rampant among the New Normals themselves … for example, the parents who are lining up to get their children needlessly "vaccinated" and then rushed into the emergency room with "totally manageable myocarditis."[8]

Still, as mass hysterical as things are, count on GloboCap to go balls out on the mass hysteria for the next five months. The coming Winter is crunch time, folks. They need to cement the New Normal in place, so they can dial down the "apocalyptic pandemic." If they're forced to extend it another year … well, not even the most brainwashed New Normals would buy that.

Or … OK, sure, the most brainwashed would, but they represent a small minority. Most New Normals are not fanatical totalitarians. They're just people looking out for themselves, people who will go

---

3 Nevett, Joshua, "Joshua Kimmich: German footballer's vaccine hesitancy dismays experts," BBC News, October 26, 2021

4 Saletan, William, "Who Killed Colin Powell? How vaccine refusers endanger everyone else," Slate, October 21, 2021

5 Ilanbey, Sumeyya, "Two-year jail terms loom for health order breaches under pandemic laws," The Age, October 26, 2021

6 Seyfort, Serena and Chanel Zagon, "Police hand out fines after surrounding Melbourne synagogue over COVID-19 lockdown breach," 9News, September 8, 2021

7 Reilly, Patrick, "Father accuses school of tying mask to head of disabled daughter," New York Post, October 24, 2021; Mates, Thomas, "Brevard school acknowledges putting mask on girl with Down syndrome, police find no crime committed. Mask was secured with a nylon shoelace, police found no evidence the mask caused the girl any distress," ClickOrlando.com, November 29, 2021

8 Johnson, Carolyn Y. and Laurie McGinley, "FDA review appears to pave the way for Pfizer-BioNTech vaccine for children 5 to 11," The Washington Post, October 22, 2021

along with almost anything to avoid being ostracized and punished. But, believe it or not, there is a limit to the level of absurdity they're prepared to accept, and the level and duration of relentless stress and cognitive dissonance they are prepared to accept.

Most of them have reached that limit. They have done their part, followed orders, worn the masks, got the "vaccinations," and are happy to present their "obedience papers" to government officials, restaurant hostesses, or anyone who demands to see them. Now, they want to go back to "normal." But they can't because ... well, because of us.

See, GloboCap can't let them return to "normal" (i.e., the new totalitarian version of "normal") until everyone (i.e., everyone who matters) has submitted to being "vaccinated" and is walking around with a scanable certificate of ideological conformity in their smartphones. They would probably even waive the "vaccination" requirement if we would just bend the knee and pledge allegiance to the WEF, or BlackRock, or Vanguard, or whoever, and carry around a QR code confirming that we believe in "Science," the "Covidian Creed," and whatever other ecumenical corporatist dogma.

Seriously, the point of this entire exercise (or at least this phase of this entire exercise) is to radically, irrevocably, transform society into a monolithic corporate campus where everyone has to scan their IDs at every turn of an endless maze of perpetually monitored, eco-friendly, gender-fluid, ideologically uniform, non-smoking, totally meat-free "safe spaces" owned and operated by GloboCap, or one of its agents, subsidiaries, and assigns.

The global-capitalist ruling classes are determined to transform the entire planet into this fascistic Woke Utopia and enforce unwavering conformity to its valueless values, no matter the cost, and we, "the Unvaccinated," are standing in their way.

They can't just round us up and shoot us — this is global capitalism, not Nazism or Stalinism. So they need to break us, to break our spirits, to coerce, gaslight, harass, and persecute us until we surrender our autonomy willingly. And they need to do this during the next five months.

Preparations therefor are now in progress.

In the UK, despite a drop in "cases,"[9] and the fact (which the "authorities" have been forced to acknowledge) that the "Vaccinated" can spread the virus just like "the Unvaccinated,"[10] the government is preparing to go to "Plan B"[11] and roll out the social-segregation system that most of Europe has already adopted. In Germany, the "Epidemic Emergency of National Importance" (i.e., the legal pretense for enforcement of the "Corona restrictions") is due to expire in mid-November (unless they can seriously jack up the "cases," which seems unlikely at this point), so the authorities are working to revise the "*Infektionsschutzgesetz*" (the "Infection Protection Act") to justify maintaining the restrictions indefinitely, despite the absence of an "epidemic emergency."[12]

And so on. I think you get the picture. This Winter is probably going to get a little nutty, or ... OK, more than just a little nutty. In terms of manufactured mass hysteria, it is probably going to make Russiagate, the War on Populism, the Global War on Terror, the Red Scare, and every other manufactured mass-hysteria campaign you can possibly think of look like a high-school production of Richard Wagner's *Götterdammerung*.

In other words, kiss reality (or whatever is left of reality at this point) goodbye. The clock is ticking, and GloboCap knows it. If they expect to pull this Great Reset off, they're going to need to terrorize the New-Normal masses into a state of protracted pants-shitting panic and uncontrollable mindless hatred of "the Unvaccinated," and anyone else challenging their new official ideology.

A repeat of the Winters of 2020 and 2021 is not going to cut it. It is going to take more than the now standard repertoire of fake and manipulated statistics, dire projections, photos of "death trucks," non-overflowing "overflowing hospitals," and all the other familiar

9 *"Britain's COVID-19 cases down nearly 10% over past week," Reuters, October 28, 2021*

10 *Roberts, Michelle, "Covid: Double vaccinated can still spread virus at home," BBC, 28 October 2021*

11 *Savage, Michael, Robin McKie, and James Tapper, "UK government paves way to bring in tough 'plan B' Covid rules," The Guardian, October 23, 2021*

12 *"COVID: Germany set to end national state of emergency," Deutsche Welle, October 27, 2021 ("Representatives of Germany's likely next government spoke out Wednesday in favor of letting current COVID regulations expire on November 25 ... but they suggested an amendment of the Infection Protection Act to allow individual restrictive measures such as mandatory face masks in public places to continue being implemented.")*

features of the neo-Goebbelsian propaganda juggernaut we have been subjected to for over 18 months.

They are facing a growing working-class rebellion.[13] Millions of people in countries all over the world are protesting in the streets, organizing strikes, walk-outs, "sick-outs," and other forms of opposition. Despite the corporate media's Orwellian attempts to blackout any coverage of it, or demonize us all as "far-right extremists," the New Normals are very aware that this is happening. And the official narrative is finally falling apart. The actual facts are undeniable by anyone with an ounce of integrity,[14] so much so that even major GloboCap propaganda outlets like *The Guardian* are being forced to grudgingly admit the truth.[15]

No, GloboCap has no choice at this point but to let loose with every weapon in its arsenal — short of full-blown despotism, which it cannot deploy without destroying itself — and hope that we will finally break down, bend the knee, and beg for mercy.

I don't know exactly what they've got in mind, but I am definitely not looking forward to it. I'm already pretty worn out as it is. From what I gather, so are a lot of you. If it helps, maybe look at it this way. We don't have to take the battle to them. All we have to do is not surrender, withstand the coming siege, and make it to April.

Or, if the strikes,[16] sick-outs,[17] and "bad weather"[18] continue, it might not even take that long.

13 Gutentag, Alex, "Revolt of the Essential Workers," Tablet, October 26, 2021

14 Knightly, Kit, "30 facts you NEED to know: Your Covid Cribsheet," OffGuardian, September 22, 2021

15 Davis, Nicola, "Jabs do not reduce risk of passing Covid within household, study suggests," The Guardian, October 28, 2021

16 "Wave of Italian protests against mandatory work pass," BBC, October 15, 2021

17 Edelman, Susan, Rich Calder, Dean Balsamini, Melissa Klein and Steven Vago, "26 FDNY firehouse companies out of service over vaccine mandate staff shortage," New York Post, October 30, 2021

18 Muntean, Pete and Ramishah Maruf, "American Airlines cancels more than 600 flights on Sunday," CNN, October 31, 2021

Pathologized Totalitarianism 101

November 22, 2021

So, GloboCap has crossed the Rubicon. The final phase of its transformation of society into a pathologized-totalitarian dystopia where mandatory genetic-therapy injections and digital compliance papers are commonplace is now officially underway.

On November 19, 2021, the government of New Normal Austria decreed that, as of February 1, 2022, experimental mRNA injections will be mandatory for the entire population.[1]

This decree comes in the midst of Austria's official persecution of "the Unvaccinated,"[2] i.e., political dissidents and other persons of conscience who refuse to convert to the new official ideology and submit to a series of mRNA injections, purportedly to combat a virus that causes mild-to-moderate flu-like symptoms (or, more typically, no symptoms at all) in about 95% of the infected and the overall infection fatality rate of which is approximately 0.1% to 0.5%.[3]

Austria is just the tip of the New Normal spear. Prominent New-Normal fascists in Germany, like *Der Führer* of Bavaria, Markus Söder,[4] and Minister of Propaganda Karl Lauterbach,[5] are already calling for an *allgemeine Impfpflicht* (i.e., "compulsory vaccination

---

1 Hirsch, Cornelius and Lukas Kotkamp, "Austria becomes first Western country to resort to mandatory coronavirus vaccination," Politico, November 19, 2021

2 "Covid: Austria introduces lockdown for unvaccinated," BBC, November 15, 2021 ("About two million people who have not been fully vaccinated against Covid-19 have been placed in lockdown in Austria as the country faces a surge in cases.")

3 "Studies on Covid-19 Lethality," Swiss Policy Research, May 2020 (a large collection of studies by a wide variety of recognized international experts and organizations, updated through 2022)

4 "Söder: Werden um Impfpflicht nicht herumkommen" ("Söder: We will not be able to avoid vaccination"), NTV, November 19, 2021 ("Bavaria's Prime Minister Söder calls for compulsory vaccination for everyone and calls for a debate on this next spring.")

5 "Lauterbach: Ohne Impfpflicht erreichen wir Impfquote nicht" ("Without mandatory vaccinations we will not achieve the vaccination quota"), Berliner Zeitung, November 22, 2021 (N.B. Lauterbach is actually Federal Minister of Health. Joseph Goebbels was Germany's last Minister of Propaganda)

requirement"), which should not come as a surprise to anyone. The Germans are not going sit idly by and let the Austrians publicly out-fascist them, are they? They have a reputation to uphold, after all! Italy will probably be next to join in, unless Lithuania[6] or Australia[7] beats them to the punch.

But, seriously, this is just the beginning of the Winter siege I wrote about recently. The plan seems to be to New-Normalize Europe first — generally speaking, Europeans are more docile, respectful of all authority, and not very well armed — and then use it as leverage to force the new pathologized totalitarianism on the USA, the UK, and the rest of the world.

I do not believe this plan will succeed. Despite the most intensive propaganda campaign in the history of propaganda campaigns, there remain enough of us who steadfastly refuse to accept the "New Normal" as our new reality ... and a lot of us are angry, extremely angry, militantly, explosively angry.[8]

We're not "vaccine hesitant" or "anti-vaxxers" or "Covid-denying conspiracy theorists." We are millions of regular working-class people, people with principles, who value freedom, who are not prepared to go gently into the globalized, pathologized-totalitarian night. We no longer give the slightest shit whether our former friends and family members who have gone New Normal understand what this is. We do. We understand exactly what this is. It is a nascent form of totalitarianism, and we intend to kill it — or at least critically wound it — before it matures into a full-grown behemoth.

---

6 *Lietuva, Gluboco, "In just 6 weeks, the Covid Pass has transformed my country into a regime of control and segregation. This is the new society created in Lithuania, the nation furthest along the path to the authoritarianism inevitably facing all countries which impose a Covid Pass regime. The Covid Pass in Lithuania is called the "Opportunity Pass". The Opportunity Pass allows you the opportunity to participate in society. Without the Opportunity Pass, you don't have opportunity: your rights are restricted. My wife and I don't have the Covid Pass. We refuse to accept the authoritarianism and control of the new regime. So we've lost our jobs and been banished from most of society. It's been 6 weeks so far. There is currently no end date planned for the new regime," Twitter, October 23, 2021*

7 *Seyfort, Serena and Chanel Zagon, "Police hand out fines after surrounding Melbourne synagogue over COVID-19 lockdown breach," 9News, September 8, 2021 ("Six people have so far been slapped with $5,452 fines each for illegally gathering at a Melbourne synagogue where some rule-breakers climbed roofs to dodge police. The ultra-Orthodox group is believed to have gathered to mark Jewish New Year, entering the Ripponlea synagogue about 5am yesterday and refusing to leave until nightfall in a 14-hour standoff.")*

8 *"Rotterdam police clash with rioters as Covid protest turns violent," BBC, November 20, 2021*

Now, I want to be absolutely clear. I am not advocating or condoning violence. But it is going to happen. It is happening already.

Totalitarianism (even this "pathologized" version of it) is imposed on society and maintained with violence. Fighting totalitarianism inevitably entails violence. It is not my preferred tactic in the current circumstances, but it is unavoidable now that we have reached this stage, so it is important that those of us fighting this fight recognize that violence is a natural response to the violence (and the implicit threat of violence) that is being deployed against us by the New Normal authorities and the masses they have whipped into a fanatical frenzy.

It is also important (essential, I would argue) to make the violence of the New Normal visible, i.e., to frame this fight in political terms, and not in the pseudo-medical terms propagated by the official Covid narrative. This isn't an academic argument over the existence, severity, or the response to a virus. This is a fight to determine the future of our societies.

This fact, above all, is what the global-capitalist ruling classes are determined to conceal. The roll-out of the New Normal will fail if it is perceived as political (i.e., a form of totalitarianism). It relies on our inability to see it as what it is. So it hides itself and the violence it perpetrates within a pseudo-medical official narrative, rendering itself immune to political opposition.

We need to deny it this perceptual redoubt, this hermeneutic hiding place. We need to make it show itself as what it is, a "pathologized" form of totalitarianism. In order to do that, we need to understand it … its internal logic, and its strengths, and weaknesses.

Pathologized Totalitarianism

I have been describing the New Normal as "pathologized totalitarianism" and predicting that compulsory "vaccination" was coming since at least as early as May 2020.[9] I use the term "totalitarianism" intentionally, not for effect, but for the sake of accuracy. The New Normal is still a nascent totalitarianism, but its essence is unmistakably evident.

---

9 Hopkins, C. J., "The New Pathologized Totalitarianism," Consent Factory, June 29, 2020

I described that essence in a recent column:

> "The essence of totalitarianism (regardless of which costumes and ideology it wears) is a desire to completely control society, every aspect of society, every individual behavior and thought. Every totalitarian system, whether an entire nation, a tiny cult, or any other form of social body, evolves toward this unachievable goal ... the total ideological transformation and control of every single element of society ... this fanatical pursuit of total control, absolute ideological uniformity, and the elimination of all dissent, is what makes totalitarianism totalitarianism."

In October 2020, I published *The Covidian Cult*, which has since grown into a series of essays examining New-Normal (i.e., pathologized totalitarianism) as "a cult writ large, on a societal scale." This analogy holds true for all forms of totalitarianism, but especially for New Normal totalitarianism, as it is the first global form of totalitarianism in history, and thus:

> "The cult/culture paradigm has been inverted. Instead of the cult existing as an island within the dominant culture, the cult has become the dominant culture, and those of us who have not joined the cult have become the isolated islands within it."

In *The Covidian Cult (Part III)*, I noted:

> "In order to oppose this new form of totalitarianism, we need to understand how it both resembles and differs from earlier totalitarian systems. The similarities are fairly obvious — i.e., the suspension of constitutional rights, governments ruling by decree, official propaganda, public loyalty rituals, the outlawing of political opposition, censorship, social segregation, goon squads terrorizing the public, and so on — but the differences are not as obvious."

And I described how New Normal totalitarianism fundamentally differs from 20th-Century totalitarianism in terms of its ideology, or seeming lack thereof:

> "Whereas 20th-Century totalitarianism was more or less national and overtly political, New Normal totalitarianism is supranational, and its ideology is much more subtle. The New Normal is not Nazism or Stalinism. It's global-capitalist totalitarianism, and global capitalism doesn't have an ideology, technically, or, rather, its ideology is 'reality'."

But the most significant difference between 20th-Century totalitarianism and this nascent, global totalitarianism is how New Normal totalitarianism "pathologizes" its political nature, effectively rendering itself invisible, and thus immune to political opposition. Whereas 20th-Century totalitarianism wore its politics on its sleeve, New Normal totalitarianism presents itself as a non-ideological (i.e., supra-political) reaction to a global public health emergency.

And, thus, its classic totalitarian features — e.g., the revocation of basic rights and freedoms, centralization of power, rule by decree, oppressive policing of the population, demonization and persecution of a scapegoated underclass, censorship, propaganda, etc. — are not hidden, because they are impossible to hide, but are recontextualized in a pathologized official narrative.

The "Untermenschen" become "the Unvaccinated." Swastika lapel pins become medical-looking masks. Aryan ID papers become "vaccination passes." Irrefutably senseless social restrictions and mandatory public-obedience rituals become "lockdowns," "social distancing," and so on. The world is united in a Goebbelsian total war, not against an external enemy (i.e., a racial or political enemy), but against an internal, pathological enemy.

This pathologized official narrative is more powerful and insidious than any ideology, as it functions, not as a belief system or ethos, but rather, as objective "reality." You cannot challenge or refute "reality." "Reality" has no political opponents. Those who challenge "reality" are "insane," i.e., "conspiracy theorists," "anti-vaxxers," "Covid deniers," "extremists," etc. And, thus, the pathologized New Normal narrative also pathologizes its political opponents, simultaneously stripping us of political legitimacy and projecting its own violence onto us.

20th-Century totalitarianism also blamed its violence on its scapegoats (i.e., Jews, socialists, counter-revolutionaries, etc.) but it did not attempt to erase its violence. On the contrary, it displayed it openly, in order to terrorize the masses. New Normal totalitarianism cannot do this. It can't go openly totalitarian, because capitalism and totalitarianism are ideologically contradictory.

Global-capitalist ideology will not function as an official ideology in an openly totalitarian society. It requires the simulation of "democracy," or at least a simulation of market-based "freedom." A society can be intensely authoritarian, but, to function in the global-capitalist system, it must allow its people the basic "freedom" that capitalism offers to all consumers, the right/obligation to participate in the market, to own and exchange commodities, etc.

This "freedom" can be conditional or extremely restricted, but it must exist to some degree. Saudi Arabia and China are two examples of openly authoritarian GloboCap societies that are nevertheless not entirely totalitarian, because they can't be and remain a part of the system. Their advertised official ideologies (i.e., Islamic fundamentalism and communism) basically function as superficial overlays on the fundamental global-capitalist ideology which dictates the "reality" in which everyone lives. These "overlay" ideologies are not fake, but when they come into conflict with global-capitalist ideology, guess which ideology wins.

The point is, New Normal totalitarianism (and any global-capitalist form of totalitarianism) cannot display itself as totalitarianism, or even authoritarianism. It cannot acknowledge its political nature. In order to exist, it must not exist.

Above all, it must erase its own violence (i.e., the violence that all politics ultimately comes down to) and appear to us as an essentially beneficent response to a legitimate "global health crisis" (and a "climate change crisis," and a "racism crisis," and whatever other "global crises" GloboCap thinks will terrorize the masses into a mindless, order-following hysteria).

This pathologization of totalitarianism — and of the political/ideological conflict we have been engaged in for the past 20 months — is the most significant difference between New Normal totalitarianism and 20th-Century totalitarianism. The entire global-capitalist apparatus (i.e., corporations, governments, supranational organizations, the corporate and state media, academia, etc.) has been put into service to achieve this objective.

We need to come to terms with this fact.

We do. Not the New Normals. *Us.*

GloboCap is on the verge of remaking society into a smiley-happy pathologized-totalitarian dystopia where they can mandate experimental genetic "therapies," and any other type of "therapies" they want, and force us to show our "compliance papers" to go about the most basic aspects of life. This remaking of society is *violent*. It is being carried out by force, with violence and the ever-present threat of violence.

We need to face that, and act accordingly.

Here in New Normal Germany, if you try to go shopping without a medical-looking mask on your face, armed police will arrive and remove you from the premises (I'm saying this from personal experience). In New Normal Australia, if you go to synagogue,[10] the media will be alerted and the police will surround you. In Germany, Australia, France, Italy, The Netherlands, Belgium, and many other countries, if you exercise your right to assemble and protest, the police will hose you down with water cannons,[11] shoot you with rubber bullets[12] (and sometimes real bullets[13]), spray toxic agents into your eyes,[14] and just generally beat the crap out of you.

---

10 *Ibid., Note 7.*

11 *"Polizei beendet Demo mit Wasserwerfern - 365 Festnahmen" ("Police Shut Down Demo with Water Cannons - 365 Arrests"), Radio Berlin Brandenburg, November 18, 2020*

12 *Osbourne, Samuel, "COVID-19: Australian riot police fire rubber bullets at anti-lockdown protesters in Melbourne," Sky News, September 22, 2021*

13 *Associated Press, "Dutch police open fire on rioters in demonstration against COVID restrictions," National Public Radio, November 20, 2021 ("Police opened fire on protesters in rioting that erupted in downtown Rotterdam around a demonstration against COVID-19 restrictions late Friday night.")*

14 *Pearson, Erin and Ashleigh McMillan, "Police investigating shoving, spraying of woman at anti-lockdown protest," The Age, September 20, 2021 ("Footage of police knocking a female protester to the ground before dousing her with OC spray during Saturday's anti-lockdown protest is being investigated by professional standards officers.")*

And so on. Those of us fighting for our rights and opposing this pathologized totalitarianism are all-too familiar with the reality of its violence, and the hatred it has fomented in the New Normal masses. We experience it on a daily basis. We feel it every time we're forced to wear a mask, when some official (or waiter) demands to see our "papers." We feel it when when we are insulted and threatened by our governments, when we are gaslighted and demonized by the corporate and state media, by doctors, celebrities, random strangers, and by our colleagues, friends, and family members.

We recognize the look in their eyes. We remember where it comes from, and what it leads to.

It isn't just ignorance, mass hysteria, confusion, or an overreaction, or fear ... or, OK, yes, it is all of those things, but it is also textbook totalitarianism (notwithstanding the new pathologized twist).

Totalitarianism 101.

The Year of the New Normal Fascist

December 16, 2021

And so, as 2021 goose-steps toward its fanatical finish, it is time for my traditional year-end wrap-up. It's "The Year of the Ox" in the Chinese zodiac, but I'm christening it "The Year of the New Normal Fascist." And what a phenomenally fascist year it has been!

I'm not talking amateur fascism. I am talking professional Class-A fascism. Government and corporate sanctified fascism. Bug-eyed, spittle-flecked, hate-drunk fascism. I'm talking mobs of New Normal fascists shrieking hatred and threats at "the Unvaccinated" as they are dragged off "Vaccinated Only" trains,[1] painting Nazi-era ✍

---

1 1. Matissek, Daniel, "Polizeiliche Hetzjagd auf Ungeimpften im Zug Unter Applaus der Fahrgäste ("Police Hunt Down Unvaccinated on a Train to the Applause of Passengers"), Reitschuster.de, December 15, 2021 ("The feeling of total powerlessness was terrible ... I was on an InterCity Express train from Munich to Berlin. Shortly after Nuremberg there was tumult on the train, a man in a suit hastily rushed to the back, pursued by the conductor and some passengers. At the train station in Erlangen the police stormed in. The man recognized the inevitability of the situation and stood by the nearest toilet door, hands up. Nevertheless, he was thrown to the ground, the plastic handcuffs were put on him and he was dragged off the train with a great deal of screaming. Then a group photo of the officers with their target was taken. It is now clear what happened. The man got on quickly, didn't have a ticket, and wanted to buy it from the conductor but couldn't provide proof of vaccination. He probably hoped to be able to get off in Erlangen. The staff and self-appointed police prevented that. The brutal episode, the hunt through the train, the mutual backslapping of those involved, all of it would have been somehow bearable if it hadn't been for the 80 to 90 passengers in my car, who all praised the behavior of those involved, applauded, laughed, and raged about the danger to public health posed by this one man, who of course wore a mask. In complete contrast to these admirers of power and order. Most of them didn't fully put their masks back on until the conductor appeared. All the way to Bamberg they ranted about what should happen to "unvaccinated vermin": Locking them up, work camps, even castration was suggested. I walked through the car to see who was making these loud proposals. It was a mixed bag of society. The green hipsters, recognizable by their Greta stickers on their laptops. The self-satisfied pensioners, the shift workers with the after-work beer, the eco-moms with the bawling toddlers, the married couple on the way to the coast. And in the middle, me. I was unable to speak up, I was too cowardly, and the shame of that cowardice froze me. I don't remember what happened between Bamberg and Berlin-Südkreuz. I fell into a kind of trance, I could still feel tears streaming down my face, but I was unable to utter a word or move. I just sat there. A shell of myself ... what I had experienced on this train journey I only knew from history books. It wasn't just 'joining in', it was the desire to be at the forefront, to get involved in the spiral of destruction, which my fellow travelers proudly expressed.")

messages on their windows of their stores,[2] leaders of government fomenting mass hatred,[3] TV commentators literally quoting sadistic Nazi SS doctors,[4] "leftists" going full-fascist on Facebook,[5] concentration camps, Goebbelsian propaganda, censorship of dissent ... the whole nine yards.

Here in Europe, things are particularly fascist. One by one, New Normal countries are rolling out social-segregation systems, ordering "lockdowns" of "the Unvaccinated," and otherwise persecuting those who refuse to conform to official New Normal ideology.

Austria has made "vaccinations" compulsory.[6] Germany is about to follow suit.[7] "Covid passes" have been approved in the UK.[8] Greece is fining "Unvaccinated" pensioners by reducing the amount of their pension payments.[9] Swedes are voluntarily "chipping" themselves.

In New Normal Germany, "the Unvaccinated" are under de facto house arrest. We are banned from society. We are banned from traveling. We are banned from protesting. Our writings are censored. We're demonized and dehumanized by the New Normal government, the state and corporate media, and the New Normal masses on a daily basis.

---

2 "'Kauft nicht bei Ungeimpften' – das sagt der Heringsdorfer Ladenbesitzer zur Schmiererei" ("Don't buy from the Unvaccinated' – graffiti painted on a Heringsdorf shopkeeper's window"), Ostsee-Zeitung, December 8, 2021 ("The graffiti painted on a shop window in Heringsdorf on Usedom is causing a stir. The shop owner, Uwe Marschall, is a critic of the Corona measures, who has called for 'tormenting the state' at a demonstration in Wolgast.")

3 Hoffmann, Christina, "Scholz will klotzen, nicht kleckern" ("Scholz wants to think big, not take half measures"), ZDF, December 15, 2021 ("Society is not divided. Most are in solidarity. The vaccination deniers, lateral thinkers, and extremists are not. We will not put up with a tiny minority of uninhibited extremists trying to impose their will on our entire society," announced Olaf Scholz in his state of the union address.)

4 Bosetti, Sarah, "Would the division of society really be such a bad thing? It wouldn't break apart in the middle, but rather far to the bottom right. And such an appendix is not, strictly speaking, essential for the survival of the entire organism," Twitter, December 3, 2021 (N.B. "The Jew is the suppurating appendix in the body of humanity," Nazi SS-doctor Fritz Klein)

5 Street, Paul, "So I am not kidding here. When is someone going to draft legislation for internment camps and separate quarantined regions for Amerikaners who simply refuse vaccinations and masks?" Facebook, July 2021

6 Hirsch, Cornelius and Lukas Kotkamp, "Austria becomes first Western country to resort to mandatory coronavirus vaccination," Politico, November 19, 2021

7 Olterman, Philip, "Germany's chancellor-to-be Olaf Scholz 'backs mandatory Covid jabs'," The Guardian, November 30, 2021

8 "Covid pass starts in England despite biggest rebellion of Johnson era," BBC, December 15, 2021

9 Salo, Jackie, "Greece to impose monthly fine on unvaccinated adults over 60," New York Post, November 30, 2021

New Normal goon squads roam the streets, brutalizing pensioners,[10] raiding mom-and-pop shops, checking "papers,"[11] measuring social distances, literally, as in with measuring sticks.[12] The Gestapo even arrested Santa Claus for not wearing a mask at a Christmas market.[13]

In the schools, fascist New Normal teachers ritually humiliate the "Unvaccinated" children, forcing them to stand in front of the class and justify their "Unvaccinated" status, while the "Vaccinated" children and their parents are applauded,[14] like some New Normal version of the Hitler Youth.

When New Normal Germany's new Chancellor, Olaf Scholz, announced that, "for my government there are no more red lines as far as doing what needs to be done," apparently he wasn't joking. It's only a matter of time until he orders New Normal Propaganda Minister Karl Lauterbach to make his big *Sportpalast* speech, where he will ask the New Normals if they want "total war" … and I think you know the rest of this story.

But this isn't just a story about New Normal Germany, or New Normal Europe, or New Normal Australia. And it isn't just a story about mass hysteria, or an "overreaction" to a corona virus. The "New Normal" is a global GloboCap co-production, a multi-trillion-dollar co-production, which has been in development for quite some time, and this year has gone exactly to script.

Given all the drama over the past 12 months, it's easy to forget that the year began with the occupation of Washington DC by thousands of US (i.e., GloboCap) forces in the wake of the "Terrorist Assault on the Capitol" (a/k/a the "January 6 Insurrection," or the

---

10 Haintz, Markus, "Germany #CovidRegime Policeman attacks elderly man without any warning, grabs him from behind by the neck and brings him to the ground for no apparent reason. I will now send another criminal complaint to the prosecutor," Twitter (video), December 14, 2021

11 Schuetze, Christopher F., "German public transportation controllers start checking vaccine papers," The New York Times, November 24, 2021 ("Passengers will have to show proof of vaccination, recovery from Covid, or a negatve daily test under a system of random checks.")

12 Kika, Thomas, "Video of German Police Using Rulers to Measure Distance Between People Viewed 700K Times," Newsweek, December 12, 2021

13 Kaonga, Gerrard, "Santa Claus Detained by Police at Christmas Market in Viral Video," Newsweek, December 14, 2021

14 Knipp-Selke, Andrea and Heike Riedmann, "Die Spaltung der Gesellschaft ist längst in den Schulen angekommen" ("The division of society has long since arrived in the schools"), Welt, December 1, 2021

"Attempted Coup," or some such nonsense) carried out by a few hundred totally unarmed Donald Trump supporters, who were allegedly intent on "overthrowing the government" and "destroying Democracy" with … well, their bare hands.

This was the long-awaited "Return to Normal" spectacle that had been in the pipeline for the previous four years … the public humiliation of The Unauthorized President (and of the "populists" who put him in office) and the GloboCap show of force that followed.

Here's how I described it back in January:

> "In other words, GloboCap is teaching us a lesson. I don't know how much clearer they could make it. They just installed a new puppet president, who can't even simulate mental acuity, in a locked-down, military-guarded ceremony which no one was allowed to attend, except for a few members of the ruling classes. They got some epigone of Albert Speer to convert the Mall (where the public normally gathers) into a 'field of flags,' symbolizing 'unity.' They even did the Nazi Lichtdom thing. To hammer the point home, they got Lady Gaga to dress up as a Hunger Games character with a 'Mockingjay' brooch and sing the National Anthem. They broadcast this spectacle to the entire world."

As I assume is obvious to everyone by now, the "Return to Normal" was a "Return to the New Normal" … which the global-capitalist ruling establishment was already imposing on the entire world.

The message couldn't possibly be clearer.

As Arnold Schwarzenegger succinctly put it, the message is "screw your freedom."[15] The message is "shut up and toe the fucking line." The message is "show me your fucking papers." "Use the fucking pronouns." "Eat the fucking bugs." "Get the fucking 'vaccinations.' Do not fucking ask us 'how many.' The answer is 'as many as we fucking tell you.'" The message is, there will be no more unauthorized pres-

---

15 Kato, Brooke, "Arnold Schwarzenegger rips anti-maskers: 'Screw your freedom'," New York Post, August 12, 2021

idents, no more leaving the European Union, no more "populist" rebellions against the global hegemony of global-capitalism and its soul-crushing, valueless, "woke" ideology.

GloboCap is done playing grab-ass. They announced that back in March of 2020. They informed us in unmistakable terms that our lives were about to change, *forever*. They branded and advertised this change as "the New Normal," in case we were … you know, cognitively challenged. They did not hide it. They wanted us to understand exactly what was coming, a global-capitalist version of totalitarianism, in which we will all be happy little fascist "consumers" showing each other our "compliance certificates" in order to be allowed to live our lives.

I don't need to review the entire year in detail. I'm pretty sure you remember the highlights … the roll-out of the "safe and effective" "vaccines" that don't keep you from catching or spreading the virus, and which have killed and injured thousands of people, but which you now have to get every three or four months to be allowed to work or go to a restaurant; the roll-out of the global social-segregation/digital compliance-certificate system that makes absolutely no medical sense, but which the "vaccines" were designed to force us into; *The Criminalization of Dissent*; *The Manufacturing of "Reality"*; *The Propaganda War*; *The Covidian Cult*; the launch of *The Great New Normal Purge*; the whole *Pathologized Totalitarianism* package.

I'd like to end on an optimistic note, because, Jesus, this fascism business is depressing. So I'll just mention that, as you have probably noticed, more and more people are now "waking up," or relocating their intestinal fortitude, and finally speaking out against "vaccine" mandates, and "vaccination passes," and social segregation, and the rest of the fascist New Normal program. I intend to encourage this "awakening" vociferously. I hope that those — and you know who you are — who have been reporting the facts and opposing the New Normal, and have been ridiculed, demonized, gaslighted, censored, slandered, threatened, and otherwise abused, on a daily basis for 21 months, as our more "prominent" colleagues — and you know who you are — sat by in silence, or took part in the Hate Fest, will join me in applauding and welcoming these "prominent" colleagues to the fight … finally.

Oh, and, if you're one of those "prominent" colleagues and you start beating your chest and sounding off like you've just rediscovered investigative journalism and are now leading the charge against the New Normal for your YouTube viewers or your Substack readers, please understand if we get a little cranky. Speaking for myself, yes, it's been a bit stressful, doing your job and taking the shit for you out here in the trenches for the past 21 months. Not to mention how it has virtually killed my comedy … and I'm supposed to be a political satirist.

But there I go, getting all "angry" again … whatever. As the good doctor said, "buy the ticket, take the ride." And it's the season of joy, love, and forgiveness, and publicly crucifying ideological dissidents, and paranoia, and mass hysteria, and persecuting "Unvaccinated" relatives, and … OK, I might have had one too many.

Happy holidays to one and all, except, of course, the New Normal fascists, especially the ones that are torturing the children.

God, forgive me, but I hope they fucking choke.

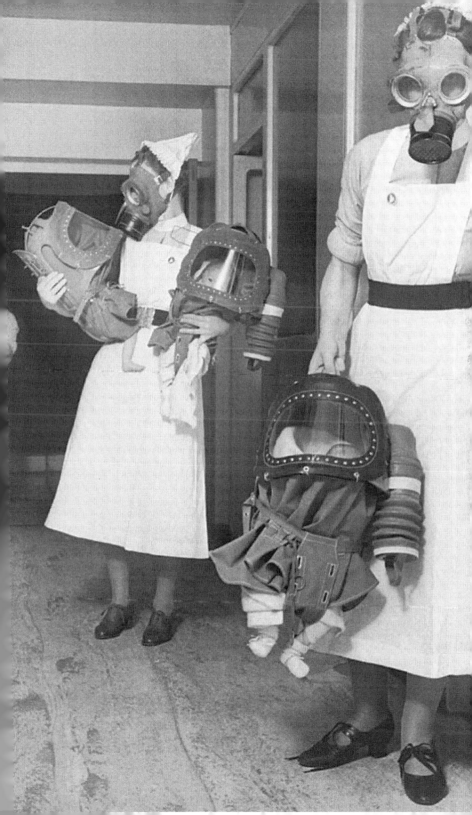

Epilogue

"It never happened. Nothing ever happened. Even while it was happening it wasn't happening. It didn't matter. It was of no interest." — Harold Pinter

The Last Days of the Covidian Cult

January 18, 2022

This isn't going to be pretty, folks. The downfall of a death cult rarely is. There is going to be wailing and gnashing of teeth, incoherent fanatical jabbering, mass deleting of embarrassing tweets. There is going to be a veritable tsunami of desperate rationalizing, strenuous denying, shameless blame-shifting and other forms of ass-covering, as suddenly former Covidian Cult members make a last-minute break for the jungle before the fully-vaxxed-and-boosted "Safe and Effective Kool-Aid" servers get to them.

Yes, that's right, as I'm sure you've noticed, the official Covid narrative is finally falling apart, or is being hastily disassembled, or historically revised, right before our eyes.

The "experts" and "authorities" are finally acknowledging that the "Covid deaths" and "hospitalization" statistics are artificially inflated and totally unreliable[1] (which they have been from the very beginning[2]), and they are admitting that their miracle "vaccines" don't work[3] (unless you change the definition of the word "vaccine"[4]), and

---

1 Cole, Brendan, "Jake Tapper Rails Against 'Misleading' CDC COVID Hospitalization Numbers," *Newsweek*, January 11, 2022 ("CNN anchor Jake Tapper has criticized as "misleading" the admission by the head of the Centers for Disease Control and Prevention that it counted COVID patients who had been admitted to hospital for something else. Tapper was reacting to comments CDC director Rochelle Walensky made on Fox News on Sunday that "up to 40 percent" of patients had been admitted to hospitals with another medical emergency but had been later detected as having COVID.")

2 Knightly, Kit, "Covid19 Death Figures 'A Substantial Over-Estimate'," *OffGuardian*, April 5, 2020

3 Nolan, Stephanie, "Most of the World's Vaccines Likely Won't Prevent Infection From Omicron," *The New York Times*, December 17, 2021

4 Camero, Katie, "Why did CDC change its definition for 'vaccine'? Agency explains move as skeptics lurk," September 27, 2021 ("Social media is calling bluff on the Centers for Disease Control and Prevention for modifying its definition of the words 'vaccine' and 'vaccination' on its website. Before the change, the definition for 'vaccination' read, 'the act of introducing a vaccine into the body to produce immunity to a specific disease.' Now, the word 'immunity' has been switched to 'protection.' The term 'vaccine' also got a makeover. The CDC's definition changed from 'a product

that they have killed a few people,[5] or maybe more than a few people,[6] and that lockdowns were probably "a serious mistake."[7]

I am not going to bother with further citations. You can surf the Internet as well as I can. The point is, the "Apocalyptic Pandemic" PSYOP has reached its expiration date.

After almost two years of mass hysteria over a virus that causes mild-to-moderate common-cold or flu-like symptoms (or absolutely no symptoms whatsoever) in about 95% of the infected and the overall infection fatality rate of which is approximately 0.1% to 0.5%,[8] people's nerves are shot. We are all exhausted. Even the Covidian cultists are exhausted. And they are starting to abandon the cult en masse.

It was always mostly just a matter of time. As Klaus Schwab put it back in June of 2020:[9]

"[T]he pandemic represents a rare but narrow window of opportunity to reflect, reimagine, and reset our world."

It isn't over, but that window is closing, and our world has not been "reimagined" and "reset," not irrevocably, not just yet. Clearly, GloboCap underestimated the potential resistance to the Great Reset, and the time it would take to crush that resistance. And now the clock is running down, and the resistance isn't crushed. On the contrary, it is growing. And there is nothing GloboCap can do to stop it, other than go openly totalitarian, which it can't, as that would be suicidal.

---

that stimulates a person's immune system to produce immunity to a specific disease' to the current 'a preparation that is used to stimulate the body's immune response against diseases.'")

5 *"Lisa Shaw: Presenter's death due to complications of Covid vaccine," BBC, August 26, 2021 ("Lisa Shaw, who worked for BBC Radio Newcastle, died at the age of 44 in May after developing headaches a week after getting her first dose of the vaccine. Newcastle coroner Karen Dilks heard Ms Shaw suffered blood clots in the brain which ultimately led to her death.")*

6 *"The March 11, 2022 release of VAERS data found 25,641 cases where Vaccine is COVID19 and Patient Died," [US] National Vaccine Information Center, March 11, 2022*

7 *Merrick, Rob, "David Frost brands Covid lockdowns a 'serious mistake' and says No 10 failed to 'challenge' scientists," Independent, January 13, 2022*

8 *"Studies on Covid-19 Lethality," Swiss Policy Research, May 2020 (a large collection of studies by a wide variety of recognized international experts and organizations, updated through 2022)*

9 *Schwab, Klaus, "Now is the time for a 'great reset'," World Economic Forum, June 3, 2020*

As I noted in a recent column:[10]

> "New Normal totalitarianism — and any global-capitalist form of totalitarianism — cannot display itself as totalitarianism, or even authoritarianism. It cannot acknowledge its political nature. In order to exist, it must not exist. Above all, it must erase its violence (the violence that all politics ultimately comes down to) and appear to us as an essentially beneficent response to a legitimate 'global health crisis' …"

The simulated "global health crisis" is, for all intents and purposes, over. Which means that GloboCap has screwed the pooch. The thing is, if you intend to keep the masses whipped up into a mindless frenzy of anus-puckering paranoia over an "apocalyptic global pandemic," at some point, you have to produce an actual apocalyptic global pandemic. Faked statistics and propaganda will carry you for a while, but eventually people are going to need to experience something at least resembling an actual devastating worldwide plague, in reality, not just on their phones and TVs.

Also, GloboCap seriously overplayed their hand with the miracle "vaccines." Covidian cultists really believed that the "vaccines" would protect them from infection. Epidemiology experts like Rachel Maddow assured them that they would:

> "Now we know that the vaccines work well enough that the virus stops with every vaccinated person," Maddow said on her show the evening of March 29, 2021. "A vaccinated person gets exposed to the virus, the virus does not infect them, the virus cannot then use that person to go anywhere else," she added with a shrug. "It cannot use a vaccinated person as a host to go get more people."[11]

And now they are all sick with … well, a cold, basically, or are

10 Hopkins, C. J., "Pathologized Totalitarianism 101," November 22, 2021

11 O'Brien, Courtney, "Viewers demand apology from MSNBC, Rachel Maddow for previous COVID vaccine comments," Fox News, December 28, 2021

"asymptomatically infected," or whatever. And they are looking at a future in which they will have to submit to "vaccinations" and "boosters" every three or four months to keep their "compliance certificates" current, in order to be allowed to hold a job, attend a school, or eat at a restaurant, which ... OK, hardcore cultists are fine with, but there are millions of people who have been complying, not because they are delusional fanatics who would wrap their children's heads in cellophane if Anthony Fauci ordered them to, but purely out of "solidarity," or convenience, or herd instinct, or ... you know, cowardice.

Many of these people (i.e., the non-fanatics) are starting to suspect that maybe what we "tin-foil-hat-wearing, Covid-denying, anti-vax, conspiracy-theorist extremists" have been telling them for the past 22 months might not be as crazy as they originally thought. They are back-pedaling, rationalizing, revising history, and just making up all kinds of self-serving bullshit, like how we are now in "a post-vaccine world,"[12] or how "the Science has changed,"[13] or how "Omicron is different,"[14] in order to avoid being forced to admit that they're the victims of a GloboCap PSYOP and the worldwide mass hysteria it has generated.

Which ... fine, let them tell themselves whatever they need to for the sake of their vanity, or their reputations as investigative journalists, celebrity leftists, or Twitter revolutionaries. If you think these "recovering" Covidian Cult members are ever going to publicly acknowledge the damage they have done to society, and to people and their families, since March 2020, much less apologize for all the abuse they heaped onto those of us who have been reporting the facts ... well, they're not. They are going to spin, equivocate, rationalize, and lie through their teeth, whatever it takes to convince themselves and their audience that, when the shit hit the fan, they didn't click heels and go full "Good German."

---

12 Greenwald, Glenn, "There is no relationship any longer between restrictive policies imposed in the name of COVID in a post-vaccine world and science -- none whatsoever. None of it makes rational sense and hasn't for awhile. And, as usual, academia leads the way in incoherence, neurosis, and panic," Twitter, December 16, 2021

13 Cohen, Ben, "Eight ways Omicron changes what you thought you knew about COVID-19," Toronto Star, December 21, 2021

14 "How is Omicron different? Here's what you need to know," CNN, January 4, 2022

Give these people hell if you need to. I feel just as angry and betrayed as you do. But let's not lose sight of the ultimate stakes here.

Yes, the official narrative is finally crumbling, and the Covidian Cult is starting to implode, but that does not mean that this fight is over. GloboCap and their puppets in government are not going to cancel the whole "New Normal" program, pretend that the last two years never happened, and gracefully retreat to their lavish bunkers in New Zealand and their mega-yachts.

Totalitarian movements and death cults do not typically go down gracefully. They usually go down in a gratuitous orgy of wanton, nihilistic violence as the cult or movement desperately attempts to maintain its hold over its wavering members and defend itself from encroaching reality. And that is where we are at the moment … or where we are going to be very shortly.

Cities, states, and countries around the world are pushing ahead with implementing the New Normal biosecurity society, despite the fact that there is no longer any plausible justification for it. Austria is going ahead with forced "vaccination."[15] Germany is preparing to do the same.[16] France is rolling out a national segregation system to punish "the Unvaccinated."[17] Greece is fining "unvaccinated" pensioners.[18] Australia is operating "quarantine camps."[19] Scotland. Italy. Spain. The Netherlands. New York City. San Francisco. Toronto.

The list goes on, and on, and on.

I don't know what is going to happen. I'm not an oracle. I'm just a political satirist. But we are getting dangerously close to the point where GloboCap will need to go full-blown fascist if they want to finish what they started.

If that happens, things are going to get very ugly.

---

15 *Weise, Zia, "Austria's vaccine mandate to apply from February 1," Politico, January 16, 2022*

16 *"Germany's SPD expects vote on general vaccine mandate in March," Reuters, January 12, 2022*

17 *Reuters, "French parliament approves vaccine pass law to tackle Covid," The Guardian, January 16, 2022 ("The new law will require people to have a certificate of vaccination to enter public places such as restaurants, cafes, cinemas and long-distance trains.")*

18 *"Greece punishes unvaccinated elderly with monthly fines," Al Jazeera, January 17, 2022*

19 *"Howard Springs: Australia police arrest quarantine escapees," BBC, December 1, 2021 ("Australian police have arrested three people who broke out of a Covid quarantine compound in the middle of the night … Police said the trio scaled a fence to break out of the facility. Officers found them after a manhunt on Wednesday. All had tested negative to Covid the day before.")*

I know, things are already ugly, but I'm talking a whole different kind of ugly. Think Jonestown, or Hitler's final days in the bunker, or the last few months of the Manson Family.

That is what happens to totalitarian movements and death cults once the spell is broken and their official narratives fall apart. When they go down, they try to take the whole world with them. I don't know about you, but I'm hoping we can avoid that. From what I have heard, it isn't much fun.

Acknowledgements

Heartfelt thanks to Julie Blumenthal, Robert F. Kennedy, Jr., Matt Taibbi, Catherine Austin Fitts, Max Blumenthal, Anthony Freda, Catte Black, Kit Knightly, Mathias Bröckers, John Siman, Gunnar Kaiser, Max Stadler, Sabine Amann, Trish Wood, Robert Cibis, James Patrick, Jens Lehrich, Anselm Lenz, Gunther Sosna, Fritz the Cat, Teny Sahakian, Jeremy Nell, Clifton Duncan, James Dellingpole, Hans de Vries, Robert Dupper, Sietske Bergsma, Gwendolin Kirchhoff, Charles Eisenstein, Dr. Jospeh Mercola, Daniel Miller, Vanessa Beeley, Lew Rockwell, Daniel McAdams, Patrick Henningsen, Hugo Fernandez, Meghan Murphy, Hrvoje Morić, Brian McWilliams, Steve Denning, Ben Ritchey, Steven J. Stein, John W. Reed, Niklaus Pfatschbacher, Alfred Elias, Lorraine Potter, Erin Crosland, Kenzen Cruz, Jean Palmer, Chris Livadas, John R. Baker, Jr., Claire Bell, Lucilightning, Michael Fleischer, Daniel Hardaker, David Gosselin, J.M. Cauley, Dennis D. Duffy, Patrick Bruen, Jay Trout, Samantha Lily Clarke, Scott Wardinsky, Ingrid Buckner, Tina M. Brewer, James Costa, Tom Horn Band, Ryland Dooley, Marcel Jahnke, Michael Kokoletsos, David Coburn, Mark Jago, Patrick McAndrew, Dave Franko, John Harris Dean, Thomas E. Meads, Pete Kulenek, Isis Essential Oils, Jeffrey Lyons, Ben Reid, Denise Curran, Melanie Hudnall, Montfort Proust, Leah Whalen, Aaron F. Weiss, John Stone, Ileana Bumbulici, Tomek McGrath, Tim Padgett, Luis Karam, Rob L. Skaggs, Mario Martin, Warren La Duke, Richard Cartwright, Chris Voisard, Bette Holtman, Ludwig Graßl, John Reilly, Angelo Pandolfo, Margaret Anna Alice, Lisa Schwartz, Lara Hamilton, Karen M. Black, Spiritual Entertainment Ltd, Margaret Shapiro, Bonnie Davis, Carla Venezia, Christine MacPherson, Martin Bassani, Helen Kingman, Beatrice Gordis, Robley Browne, Jack Reilly, Jackson E. Snider, Andrew No, Cathy Christian, Tom Harrington, Wanda Sanders, Jeffrey Campbell, Klaus Wenk, Millard J. Melnyk, Susan Causley, Riff Mondo, Nikolai Razouvaev, Marjorie St. Clair Lynch, Chris McAlister, Todd Brock, Anais Starr, Bonnie Long, A. K. Cutler, J. C. Wetzel, Matthew Dahlitz, Stella Morabito, Keith Heller, Jody Wells, Marsha Karen Anderson, Mal Conklin, Kathie Vitanza, Howard Stone, Eugeen Ggysels, Michael Brennan, John Mansfield, Juan Penhos, Daniel Sieber, Lee Jones, Gary Slabaugh,

Jean Palmer, Julia Lane, Catherine Currie, Brett McSweeney, Eric Anderson, Carolyn Kean, Greg Pharo, Yani Mitchell, Ava Delorenzo, Elizabeth Hatleli, Michael Riches, R. J. Benish, Joseph Morovich, Dave Brewer, Jessica Wolf, Catherine Homan, Parker Tringas, Casey McMahon, Tom Daquanni, K. B. Lowrey, Mike Dimpfl, Amelia Goodyear, David Ames, Jason McVetta, Karen Kael, Sylvia Fogel, Penny Hutchison, Leah Whalen, Wolf Dieter Aichberger, Jan Eisfelder, Tracey Shaw, Cristobal Richter, Joanne Sims Dinsmore, Petra Bueskens, Amy Kane, Solari, Inc., Wallace Stevens, Petra Bueskens, C. M. Palmer, Lois Land, Nils Koll, Alex Robinedith, R. L. Skaggs, Patrick Landuyt, Mark Cantwell, S. Zendel, Hugh Nowlan, Robert Havers, Scott Newton, Ruth Elkin, Beverly Elliott, Sebastian Tigges, Jesse Welty, Scott Coubrough, Nicholas Franco, Jerry Grasso, Angus Phillips, Ed Bernal, Cate Caldwell, Mark Leslie, Amy Keeper, Susanna Phillips, Jesse Welty, Georg Roßburger, Denise Wilson, Julie Piantedosi, Frank L. Berry, Cynthia Bates, Christian Sauer, Johnny Gomore, Paul Collits, Bri Waters, Frederick Hink, Moira Krum, Vasko Kohlmayer, Mark Robinson, Gerald Verdon, Keith Heller, Jeff Barefoot, Patrick Albin, Lauren Veta, Grant Palmer, Boris Negrarosa, Peggy Sheehan, Ed Pauhana, Walden Mathews, Kelley Judd, Grainne O'Dwyer, Mark Schiffer, Tristan Spillmann, Molly Empow, Ron Rey, W.S. Redden, Michael Bär, Mario Martin, Karl Curtis, Bertram Rensch, Klaudusz Thomas, Tess Hottenroth, Anna Nicolai, Captain Pat Jukes, L. D. Price, Alasdair Maclean, Michael Kahn, Jim Meeks, Jennifer Stock, Doug G. Glaass, Karina Cotler, E. A. Martignoni, Marla Mullen, John E. Beaulieumd, Susie Kneedler, Wolfgang Ruber, Rose McEreg, Michael Kokoletsos, Jeannie Skelly, John Wright, Frank Lay, Ryan Chapman, Alice Pennels, Jim Meeks, Laurie Hartig, John Brunner, Rand Bleimeister, Rob Long, T. R. Kahler, Heather Peacock, Peter Houlding, Christine Lindewald, Diana Schieke, Jennifer Zilm, Rand Bradley, Darlene Falcon, Abby Rockefeller, Mark Savage, Mark Jago, Zachary Adam Cohen, Kelly's Fitness, S.K. Kessenich, Zachary Adam Cohen, and everyone else who republished, translated, and financially and otherwise supported the publication of these essays.

C. J. Hopkins is an award-winning playwright, novelist and political satirist. His plays and experimental stage-texts have been produced internationally at theatres and festivals including Riverside Studios (London), 59E59 Theaters (New York), Belvoir St. Theatre (Sydney), Traverse Theatre (Edinburgh), the Du Maurier World Stage Festival (Toronto), Needtheater (Los Angeles), 7 Stages (Atlanta), English Theater Berlin, Edinburgh Festival Fringe, Adelaide Fringe, Brighton Festival, and Noorderzon Festival (the Netherlands). His playwriting awards include the 2002 Best of the Scotsman Fringe Firsts (*Horse Country*), the 2004 Best of the Adelaide Fringe (*Horse Country*), and a 2005 Scotsman Fringe First (*screwmachine/eyecandy*). His plays are published by Bloomsbury Publishing/Methuen Drama and Broadway Play Publishing, Inc. His political satire and commentary appears in many online publications, and has been widely translated. His debut novel, *Zone 23*, is published by Snoggsworthy, Swaine & Cormorant.

Anthony Freda, cover designer of this book and the two previous volumes of *Consent Factory Essays*, is an illustrator, painter, visual political activist, and adjunct professor at the Fashion Institute of Technology in New York City. His artwork has appeared in *Time*, *The New Yorker*, *Rolling Stone*, *The New York Times*, *Village Voice*, and many other publications, and is part of the permanent collection of the US National September 11th Museum in New York. More information at his official website: anthonyfreda.com

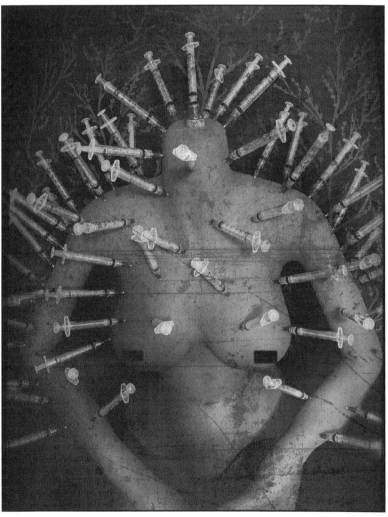

Untitled, 2021

Also by C. J. Hopkins ...

"C. J. Hopkins is the rare writer who's so good at identifying uncomfortable truths that he essentially has to be removed from consideration for mass circulation. He's brave, original, enlightening, and hilarious, and his writing has an element of the forbidden that makes it even more fun."
— Matt Taibbi

C. J. Hopkins clearly figured out the global capitalist game a while ago ... If you are ready to leave the matrix, Hopkins can help guide you out, laughing all the way, yet appreciating the real risks and many of the important issues before us."
— Catherine Austin Fitts

"C. J. Hopkins imagines a future far more worrying and far more woke, and with far sleeker corporate boosterism, than any mere Huxlean or Orwellian or Bradburian dystopia ... in this New World of Total Corporate Domination of Everything, you will stand up and cheer for a muscle-bound cishet deplorable who smokes cigarettes." — John Siman, Naked Capitalism

Made in the USA
Las Vegas, NV
09 May 2022

48656173R00131